Mojave Lands

PUBLISHING FOR THE WORLD
125 Years

THE JOHNS HOPKINS UNIVERSITY PRESS

Center Books on Contemporary Landscape Design

Frederick R. Steiner
Consulting Editor

George F. Thompson
Series Founder and Director

Published in cooperation with
the Center for American Places,
Santa Fe, New Mexico,
and Harrisonburg, Virginia

Mojave Lands

Interpretive Planning and the
National Preserve

Elisabeth M. Hamin

The Johns Hopkins University Press
Baltimore and London

© 2003 The Johns Hopkins University Press
All rights reserved. Published 2003
Printed in the United States of America on acid-free paper
9 8 7 6 5 4 3 2 1

The Johns Hopkins University Press
2715 North Charles Street
Baltimore, Maryland 21218-4363
www.press.jhu.edu

Library of Congress Cataloging-in-Publication Data

Hamin, Elisabeth M., 1961–
    Mojave lands : interpretive planning and the national pre-
serve / by Elisabeth M. Hamin.
        p.   cm. — (Center books on contemporary landscape
design)
Includes bibliographical references and index.
ISBN 0-8018-7121-2 (acid-free paper)
1. Mojave National Preserve (Calif.)—Management.
2. Mojave National Preserve (Calif.)—Environmental conditions.
3. Deserts—Law and legislation—California—History—20th
century.   4. Wilderness areas—Law and legislation—California—History—20th century.   5. Environmental law—United
States—History—20th century.   6. Public lands—California—
Management—History—20th century.   7. United States. National Park Service—History—20th century.   I. Title.   II. Series.
    F868.M65 H36 2003
    333.78′3′0979495—dc21   2002003576

A catalog record for this book is available from the British
Library.

In memory of my father, Dwight H. Infield Jr., who taught me a love of wild places, and in gratitude to Mark T. Hamin, who makes it all worthwhile.

Contents

Illustrations and Tables

Acknowledgments

This work benefited greatly from the advice and guidance of Ann Louise Strong, Seymour Mandelbaum, and Roger Raufer in the original conception and performance of the research. Comments and suggestions from Jim Throgmorton, Fritz Steiner, Dan Marcucci, one anonymous reviewer, and Mark Hamin greatly improved the quality of the writing and the thought in this version of the manuscript. The support of George F. Thompson and Randall B. Jones at the Center for American Places brought this text to fruition. I am indebted to all of them for the gift of their time and wisdom.

Many other people contributed to this work. First and foremost are the residents of the Mojave area, whose willingness to speak frankly with me made the research possible. Many people in Washington and Sacramento gave of their time, energy, and patience in describing the mysteries of political and administrative life. I am especially indebted to those who also took time to review parts of this work, and to Rob Fulton in particular, for the careful corrections that assured an accurate portrayal of the Mojave. Those who took time from their weekend to talk with me about the results of this work deserve particular thanks, as does Superintendent Mary Martin.

Colleagues and friends at the University of Massachusetts, Iowa State University, and the University of Pennsylvania made helpful comments, provided useful sources, and generally were supportive of the work. Kiran Darapureddy provided able research assistance, and Dave James assisted with the graphics. Stacey Ross and Claudia Buttery provided essential administrative support. My students in undergraduate and graduate theory sharpened and challenged my thinking by making me explain all of this. Marie Blanchard provided careful copy editing, much improving the text of the book. Parts of this work have been presented at the Associated Collegiate Schools of Planning (1995, 1996, 1997), and at the University of Iowa's Project on the Rhetoric of Inquiry (1996). Comments received from participants in each of these sessions were helpful. John Forester provided helpful comments on parts of the manuscript, as did Charles Hoch.

Iowa State University's College of Design provided partial funding for this research. The California Desert Studies Consortium, managers of the Desert Studies Center, provided subsidized housing and the facilities for the public meeting, hospitality, and a beautiful location for watching the desert night settle over the mountains.

To all of these people go my thanks. Errors and omissions, of course, remain my own.

Abbreviations

ACEC	Area of Critical Environmental Concern
AMP	Allotment Management Plan, for grazing
AUM	Animal Unit Month, for grazing
BLM	Bureau of Land Management
BOM	Bureau of Mines
CDCA	California Desert Conservation Area
CDFW	California Department of Fish and Wildlife
CDPA	California Desert Protection Act
DMG	Desert Manager's Group
DOD	Department of Defense
DOI	Department of Interior
EMNSA	East Mojave National Scenic Area
FLPMA	Federal Lands Policy and Management Act of 1976
GAO	General Accounting Office
GMP	General Management Plan
IAFWA	International Association of Fish and Wildlife Agencies
MNP	Mojave National Preserve
MPA	Mining in the Parks Act of 1976
NCA	National Cattlemen's Association
NMA	National Mining Association
NPCA	National Parks and Conservation Association
NPS	National Park Service
NRA	National Rifle Association
NSA	National Scenic Area
ORV	Off-Road Vehicle (e.g., Jeep)
USFWS	United States Fish and Wildlife Service
USGS	United States Geological Survey
WLF	Wildlife Legislative Fund

Mojave Lands

Introduction

The human struggle, the successes and failures, the use and abuse, both noble and foolish, are readily apparent in the desert. Symbols and relationships seem to arise that stand for the human condition itself. It is a simple, if almost incomprehensible, equation: The world is as terrible as it is beautiful, but when you look more closely, it is as beautiful as it is terrible. We must maintain constant vigilance, to protect the world from ourselves, and to embrace the world as it exists.
— RICHARD MISRACH AND REYNER BANHAM, *Desert Cantos*

We are preoccupied with time. If we could learn to love space as deeply as we are now obsessed with time, we might discover a new meaning in the phrase to live like men. —EDWARD ABBEY, *Desert Solitaire*

Preserving land, and particularly land that is also home to human residents, brings out the best and worst of political and planning processes. Designating a new unit of the national park system involves economics, bureaucracies, ideologies, and passions. The process creates shifting identities of us and them, good guys and bad guys, the pushed around and the powerful. It also creates opportunities to reconsider how we as a society, as local communities, and as individuals want these processes to work, how we want to be identified by ourselves and by others. In determining these identities we reevaluate humans' place in nature and the balance between individual and common goods. The process creates possibilities.

This book is about one of these possibilities—the designation of the Mojave National Preserve. In 1994 President William J. Clinton signed the California Desert Protection Act, which increased the size of Death Valley National Park, upgraded Joshua Tree from a national monument to a national park, and created the Mojave National Preserve (MNP). This was a bitterly contested bill, and within the bill, the most contested part was the Mojave designation. The preserve was so contested, in fact, that whether or not to fund the MNP in the 1995 budget was one of the major reasons that the federal government actually shut down, not once but a series of times.[1]

By designating the Mojave National Preserve, Clinton increased the protection on almost three million acres of southern California desert, creating the third largest unit of the national park system in the lower forty-eight states. The preserve stands between the first casinos at the Nevada state line and the desert junction of Barstow, and is the dry, spare landscape travelers speed past on the main highway connecting Los Angeles and Las Vegas. It is probably the landscape most often seen in car advertisements, so many Americans know its looks, if not its name. The preserve's land has been federal since it was taken from Mexico in 1846, and has long been managed by the Bureau of Land Management (BLM). BLM management means multiple-use management, with hunting, mining, and ranching being not just tolerated but viewed as central goals for the land. The 1994 bill transferred the MNP to the National Park Service, with its dual mission of environmental preservation and provision of recreation.

Up to this part of the story, the designation of the MNP sounds like a classic land protection fight, which in many ways it was. The main political force pushing for the designation was the big environmental organizations—the Sierra Club, the Wilderness Society, and the like—and the main opponents to the designation were industry groups for mining, ranching, and hunting, along with local residents. The success of the designation shows the ascendance of the New West—urbanites, information and service workers, and their elected officials—over the Old West—the miners and ranchers who have long had sole access to the benefits of this land and their local representatives who fought this tooth and nail. This is an important story, but no longer a particularly new one; other writers have already told a similar tale.[2]

Where the story becomes particularly interesting is with the outcome of the designation. With the passage of the 1994 bill, Congress required that most of the previous uses of the Mojave continue. Hunting and ranching will go on indefinitely, mining will continue although with more limitations, and current landowners can build on their land. In effect, Congress mandated that the National Park Service must become a multiple-use manager, balancing their official mission of environmental protection and recreation with other traditional uses of the land, including hunting and ranching. This inherent conflict in the NPS's mandate is where part of the potential for wider reverberations begins.

Several decades ago, Joseph Sax called on the National Park Service to become a laboratory for new ideas.[3] The MNP offers just the occasion for that. In the Mojave, the National Park Service has the opportunity to develop the idea of sustainable rural landscapes, showing what these might look like in this particular place by encouraging human uses of the land that support ecological protection. The environmental community has an opportunity to think about new ways to protect land, ways that build on the stewardship of existing residents rather than assuming that protected landscapes are peopleless landscapes.

Even more broadly, this funny term "preserve" could come to mean areas designated for the best in balancing natural and human needs. There has been much written recently about sustainable places—cities, towns, communities, landscapes. The unfortunate reality is that we will not really know what they are and how to make them until we begin making them, and each one will necessarily look different, because sustainability is defined by the direct relationship of people with each other in the particular place. The country could use this idea of "preserve" to be a testing ground for sustainable landscapes in a variety of ecosystems and human communities. The park service, as one of our most trusted government agencies and also one with a solid base of ecological values, is in an enviable position for providing leadership on this. In the same sort of way that the National Park Service has been a leader in defining the appropriate conditions of "nature," it can become a leader in helping find ways to live well, but live within the limits of that nature.

There is another unexpected outcome from the MNP designation. The national parks are serving a new purpose—large-scale growth management. Located as it is between the sprawling metropolitan areas of Los Angeles and Las Vegas, the MNP ensures that these cities can never grow together into one vast, sprawling urban region. This was clearly a motive of some, although not all, of the park promoters, but not one they readily discussed with the public or legislators—and not surprisingly. Not only is growth management always problematic in the United States, but this is an example of very-long-range planning, which is particularly distrusted. Using the park system this way redefines the meaning and purposes of the national park system itself.

This book, then, is the story of how these outcomes came to be, not so much through the conscious intent of legislators, lobbyists, and planners, but rather through the unintended outcomes of compromises made in the give-and-take of legislation. The process had both a brute and subtle character. It is, perhaps, most appropriate that these things happened in that most extreme and yet intimate of American landscapes—the desert.

One of the central questions of the designation fight became whether the land was beautiful enough to be in the national park system, or whether it was "plain desert." My sense is that it is both. In the morning and evening, the light covers the ground with color and the sky has no boundaries. Mountains loom and dry lakes shimmer. At dusk in some desert areas there are so many mice and rabbits crossing the road that driving is like bobbing and weaving through a video game. During the day, bright snakes and earth-toned salamanders are easily found. Much of the preserve, however, is regularly spaced creosote bushes, flat lands, and the occasional Joshua tree. Temperatures regularly top 110 degrees, and in the summer the afternoon sun strikes like a physical blow to one's shoulders, while the winds blow incessantly. Hiking long distances is not for the novice, since every hiker must carry a minimum of one gallon of water for each day's hiking. This is a landscape for those who appreciate solitude, those comfortable with enduring rather than conquering, people looking for eternity more than scenery—at least now. One possible future for the Mojave was, and perhaps still is, to become like Death Valley. The boundaries of that longstanding unit of the park system sport golf courses, swimming pools, fine restaurants, and shopping areas—all of the accoutrements that let humans forget the essential nature of the desert.

This is a landscape that has been used by humans for centuries, and by postcolonial settlers for about one hundred years. Native American petroglyphs remind us of whole peoples no longer there. General George Patton's tank troops used the dry lake beds for practice, and the tracks are still visible. It is hard to find a hike that doesn't require stepping around cow pods; without rain to wash them away, these reminders of the area's extensive ranching tend to just desiccate. Hopeful miners drove their vehicles just about everywhere within the area, creating an intensively roaded area—assuming you count washboards as roads. Trophy hunters come here to shoot big horn sheep, a threatened species. Each year the state holds a lottery, where perhaps five lucky hunters get to shoot a sheep for a nominal ticket purchase; meanwhile one very rich hunter outbids other trophy hunters for the sole auctioned-off ticket.

The ways the various desert users argued about the preserve designation form the heart of this book. Lobbying arms for the mining industry, the National Rifle Association, the Cattleman's Association, and hunters' groups all strongly opposed the Mojave designation, arguing that there was no reason to reduce access to these federal lands. Most residents of the preserve (in-holders) chose their homes because they wanted a great deal of privacy and sky. Many struggled bitterly to prevent the designation and what they saw as the unnecessary imposition of a Big Brother government structure. The BLM had been managing the area reasonably well, thank you, and urbanites and tree huggers should just butt out and worry about their own lands.

Environmentalists, by contrast, looked at what they saw as a poorly managed landscape and begged to differ. They saw the growth of Los Angeles and Las Vegas looming on the horizon; they lived amidst the sprawl of the L.A. metro area or the desert town of Barstow, and they knew what happened to good desert left unprotected. Maybe not today, maybe not tomorrow, but soon enough the bulldozers would come, either for mining or for second homes. The cattle would have eaten all the grass that the endangered desert tortoise and the other desert species need, leaving nothing growing but inedible weeds. Then it would be too late, so the time to act was now—and never mind the shortsighted and greedy local residents. Certainly people's property interests informed their position in the debate, but more subtly and more interestingly, individuals' relationships with the desert itself and their values more generally shaded their interests, and their arguments.

Somewhere between all this was the desert, vulnerable or resilient, tough or fragile, depending on one's view. In this fight, one's view seemed to matter a lot, which brings me to the theoretical argument of this book; that is, an argument about how planning and policy analysis, particularly in situations of great conflict, can be improved. This approach, which I call "interpretive planning," draws on recent insights developed by writers working on communicative and narrative theory and practice in planning, policy analysis, and conflict resolution. For ease of reading, I will often shorten planning and policy analysis to just "planning," but I believe the insights will be relevant to both fields, while of course requiring adjustment to particular situations.

My basic premise seems so obvious as to be a given—that when we do planning and policy analysis, particularly in situations of complexity and conflict, we need to take careful consideration of the *stories* people tell about what has and should happen and why. These stories are how people talk about their particular values and beliefs or worldviews, and unless we understand those values and beliefs and include them in our analysis, we will not fully understand the situation. The methods of narrative and qualitative research provide guidance on ways to analyze these stories in a rigorous and concentrated fashion, as befits an important data source in the planning process. Stories also play a role in a process of consensus building to achieve acceptable and desirable outcomes. The result is the ability to explicitly bring values and worldviews into the process of planning, allowing for better solutions—more creative approaches, more feasible plans.

What is difficult about this is how to do it—how can we actually change our regular planning and policy analysis processes, based as they are on quantitative data and a presumption of available unbiased facts, to accommodate stories or narratives, and implied worldviews and values? My answer is largely the body of this text—the structure and content of this book is an example of the process I suggest. In the next section of this chapter, I give what I hope will be a fairly straightforward account of interpretive planning, both why and how. In the last chapter I provide a more detailed account of interpretive planning, including sources for these ideas.

Interpretive Paradigm

Recently, social science theorists have begun turning away from a strongly science-based, detached, and dispassionately logical style of thinking. Instead, many scholars and practitioners are much more attuned to approaches that are more holistic in terms of moral and aesthetic reason, those that claim that the relationship between inquirer and topic of inquiry is to be explored rather than hidden and that generally bring a more humanist sense to their endeavors. This suggests a focus on stories and storytelling as the natural way for people to communicate, and an awareness of the significance of layers of interpretation. While authors differ over various important aspects of this, generally we can determine the outlines of an emerging interpretive view of the world as follows:

1. Humans are storytellers. We all use stories all of the time to make sense of the world, to frame and highlight experience and place an experience within what we judge to be an appropriate perspective. Stories are, in essence, how we think about the world and our place within it. The way we tell those stories helps define both who we are and our relationships to those with whom we talk.

2. Values are not peripheral or suspect; instead, they are integral to the way we judge our lives and the way we construct our stories. What counts as a fact often depends on the views and position of the individual. Values give shape and perspective to our stories, and facts, values, interests, and theories are all implicated in how we construct a problem and tell a story.

3. Rather than a goal of pure rationality, the narrative paradigm suggests a goal of reasonableness. Reasonable conclusions are reached through a process of shared conversation and debate, as opposed to the goal of a rationality reached through isolated individual logical deduction. Moral deliberation, aesthetic responses, passions, and webs of relationships are explicitly considered rather than assumed to be irrelevant. The result is understood to be both historically and spatially located, and up for continual reconsideration. This suggests that there can be multiple rationalities at work in any situation, and that difficulties in communication between individuals or groups, while sometimes caused by errors or ignorance, are more often the result of clashes in worldviews.

4. We are not solely individual actors, but also actors within communities. We tell stories to communicate to others, not just to explain things to ourselves. Our stories are rarely accepted verbatim by our listeners; instead, the listeners interpret our stories, judging them, selecting relevant bits, often ignoring the author's intention. These interpreted stories are often retold to others, or replies are made to the originating author, involving us then in interpretive communities.

5. Within those interpretive communities, rhetoric also serves to create group identity and solidify the social bonds of the individuals who share particular story lines. Stories are told not just to persuade but also to clarify "them" and "us." Small groups interact with other groups and share stories, and these individual stories become affiliated with stories from like-minded groups to form a network of narratives. Adhering to this general network creates and identifies coalitions; failing to adhere peripheralizes the individual or group.

6. Our individual as well as group narratives are embedded in larger narratives, and are specific to a place and a time. The story of my own life is a part of the story of the transition from the twentieth to the twenty-first century; the story of the Mojave National Preserve is specific to that desert and those people in the 1990s. Our stories are also constrained by the narratives of others—we do not create ourselves from a blank slate—so we are only co-authors of our life stories.

Traditionally, planning and policy analysis has dealt primarily with gathering facts, modeling them, and making recommendations based on the outcomes of those models. Under interpretive planning, gathering the stories of those for and with whom we plan becomes as important as gathering numerical data about the situation, and those stories are included in the process of developing recommendations. This poses challenges for those who must take action in the world. Storytelling is selective, individualistic, geographically and historically specific, and in general an awkward data source. As a result, while planners readily acknowledge that politics, relationships, history, and values are central to the planning process, our day-to-day techniques for explicitly managing analysis of these has remained fairly ad hoc even as theory about the roles of stories and storytelling has become quite developed. This book suggests one way to bring rigor and nuance to analyzing the stories people tell about policies and conflicts, the process I call interpretive planning. Interpretive planning uses the following steps.

INTERPRETIVE PLANNING PROCESS MODEL

1. Gather background data, including appropriate quantitative data as well as a political and administrative history and documents expressing the positions held by various participants to the debate or conflict.
2. Interview participants to the debate to determine how the situation came about, their positions, and the reasons they feel that way (understood as their stories of what ought or ought not happen, and why).
3. Construct the narratives (or stories) of the debate, based on both the textual and interview data acquired in the prior steps.
4. Analyze the frames of reference at work in the debate, which include the values, ethics, and worldviews of the participants.
5. Reframe the debate, providing a different, more widely acceptable perspective on the issue at hand based on points of concurrence determined through the prior framing, but adding the planner's vision, expertise, and knowledge of the situation resulting from prior qualitative and quantitative analysis.
6. Institutionalize dialogue, including public discussion of the narratives, frames, and reframing developed in the above steps. This step allows participants to critique (correct, support, deny, revise, reinterpret) the planner's findings, if this opportunity has not been created before. The result should be consensus on desirable results of the planning or policy, as well as steps to take to achieve those results.
7. Implement the policies resulting from this public dialogue.

Interpretive planning suggests a role for the planner that is something other than the technical analyst of rational planning or the empowerer/public-participation facilitator of communicative planning theory. The interpretive planner retains both of these roles, but also brings his or her own knowledge, vision, and creativity to bear on the issue at hand.

At the most fundamental level, interpretive planning argues that the basic data source for planners and policy analysts is the people with and for whom they plan. Planning and policy analysis is not about demographics, or about zoning, or about management options. It is about creating equitable, desirable, and just futures for the people with whom we plan, for the land and its creatures upon which we depend, and for all the generations that follow. This is something planners have long understood, but is easily lost in current planning processes. Understanding why the people with whom we plan feel the way they do, listening to their stories and according them the same seriousness and the same rigor that we accord our quantitative data is an important step in planning a desirable, mutually acceptable, and achievable future.

One limitation of my research is that I am not the planner for the Mojave National Preserve; hence, I did not use the outcomes of the interpretive planning analysis in an ongoing collaborative process. Consequently, I focused on developing the analytic techniques that form the foundations of interpretive planning. Future research should document how and where inclusion of interpretive analysis techniques has occurred, its results, and ways it has been adapted to meet particular situational needs.

In the final chapters of this text, I discuss some of the drawbacks of the approach as I suggest it. One, however, I wish to mention now. Full-scale interpretive planning tends to be expensive. It is undoubtedly very time- and resource-consuming to do all the interviews, pay for transcriptions, analyze the material, construct the frames, formalize the reframing, and then engage in public dialogue about it. The rigorousness of analysis that I present here is likely to be appropriate only in cases where there has been a great deal of conflict over a complex issue. In more common situations, such as creating a new comprehensive plan or designing policy for a less fraught issue, the interpretive planner might not do a full-scale interpretive analysis. Instead, she or he might do a limited set of interviews and just take notes, then use those notes to quickly identify the main narratives of the issues, and proceed with the analysis and dialogue. There is, then, a good deal of flexibility in how this approach can be implemented.

CHAPTER 1

A Solitary—but Not Lonely—Place

Most Americans who talk about the problems of "the desert" are talking about the Mojave. It is the best known, most visited, and most studied of American deserts; but it is also, in an important historical sense, the most reliably typical of American deserts, the national standard . . . No wonder it is the desert of definition for so many Americans—studied, loved, quarreled over.   —P. REYNER BANHAM, *Scenes in America Deserta*

First-time explorers beware: the desert doesn't coddle. It is harsh and uncompromising to the unprepared. Yet it does give quarter to patient and inquiring minds.   —JERRY SCHAD, *California Deserts*

The Mojave landscape in midday light is harsh, barren, unpromising; but as the night falls and the light softens, colors creep over the bare soils and distant mountains, and the solitude of the place becomes bountiful, a blessing rather than a curse. It is a wild place, and yet there is hardly a mile of it that does not have some sign of human occupation. Like the land, the people who call this place home are complicated. They have chosen to live on land obviously unsuited to human life, land so empty that calling it rural seems an exaggeration. There is a layered quality here that resists easy understanding. But the layers must be revealed to make sense of the place, and to that we turn.

Land and History

Geography and Biology

The Mojave desert is named after some of its precolonial inhabitants, the Mohave Native American tribe.[1] The defining characteristic of the Mojave is that it is true desert—it receives on average about six inches of rainfall a year, and the land has the ability to evaporate more rainfall than it receives.[2] That rainfall, however, is unevenly distributed across the desert. In Bagdad, Cali-

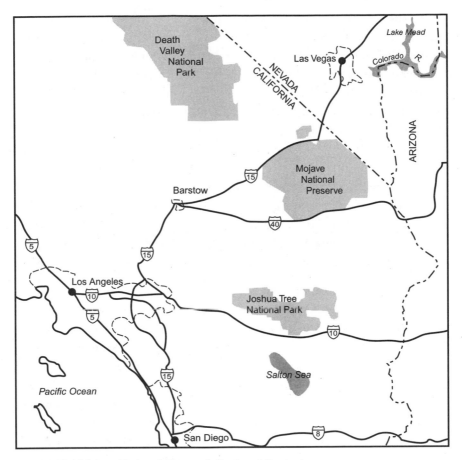

Map 1.1: The Mojave National Preserve's Regional Context.
Map by David James.

fornia, just outside the preserve on Route 66, "not a drop of rain fell on the earth for 767 days, from September 3, 1912 to November 8, 1914," according to Gregory McNammee.[3] The administrative boundaries of the Mojave National Preserve (MNP) include the confluence of the Mojave, Great Basin, and Sonoran deserts,[4] the boundaries of which are, like most biotic boundaries, porous and gradual. Most of the preserve land is Mojave desert, but the confluence of the three creates an area of great biotic diversity.[5]

The Mojave is often called the high desert, because its elevations range generally between two and four thousand feet, with some mountain peaks higher and dry lakes (remnant lake beds which very rarely fill with water) much lower. The mountain ranges to the west and south of the Mojave create a rain-shadow effect such that almost all of the local cloud-born humidity is dumped on the other side of the mountain slopes before reaching the Mojave. Much of the meager precipitation the desert receives comes as snowfall in the winter. In summer, it is not uncommon for the temperature to fluctuate fifty degrees in twenty-four hours. These large fluctuations occur because the radiation stored up by day in the unvegetated soil is rapidly reflected back out across an unclouded night sky. Temperatures on hot days in the summer easily reach above 115 degrees in low spots of the Mojave, whereas winter temperatures are well below freezing at higher elevations. Afternoons often bring strong, incessant winds, created by temperature differentials between the relatively cooler mountains and the hot desert floor.[6]

Mary Austin, writing in 1926, described the Mojave desert this way:

This is the nature of that country. There are hills, rounded, blunt, burned, squeezed up out of chaos, chrome and vermilion painted, aspiring to the snow-line. Between the hills lie high level-looking plains full of intolerable sun glare, or narrow valleys drowned in a blue haze. The hill surface is streaked with ash drift and black, unweathered lava flows. After rains, water accumulates in the hollows of the small closed valleys, and, evaporating, leaves hard dry levels of pure desertness that get the local name of dry lakes . . . Here are the long heavy winds and breathless calms on the tilted mesas where dust devils dance, whirling into a wide, pale sky. Here you have no rain when all the earth cries for it, or quick downpours called cloud-bursts for violence. A land of lost rivers with little in it to love; yet a land that once visited must be come back to inevitably. If it were not so there would be little told of it.[7]

Visitors to the region seek a place where nature governs and humans are little seen. To many of the people I spoke with in the desert, solitude is the point of a visit; with perhaps 250,000 annual visitors spread over the preserve's 1.6 million acres, seeing another visitor is rare.[8] Most of these visitors stay near the campgrounds, the roads, and a few better-known attractions, so that as one travels into any fairly remote part of the area—in other words, most of it—the chance of seeing another human becomes slight indeed.

The Mojave has much to offer ecology-minded visitors, and many consider it the most interesting and varied of North American deserts. Because the area has large changes in altitude as one moves from valley floors to mountain tops, there is great diversity in biotic communities.[9] Visitors are likely to see jackrabbits, lizards, mice, bats, and a variety of birds. If they are lucky and observa , visitors may see coyotes, mule deer, desert tortoises, burros, snakes (including the regal ring-necked snake), great horned owls, and hummingbirds. Fauna that exist in the preserve but are difficult to see include big horn sheep, Gila monsters, mountain lions, bobcats, roadrunners, and golden eagles.[10]

One advantage for visitors is the lack of undergrowth, making animals relatively easy to see. The fauna are surprisingly plentiful. As Mary Austin writes:

> Go as far as you dare in the heart of a lonely land, you cannot go so far that life and death are not before you. Painted lizards slip in and out of rock crevices, and pant on the white hot sands. Birds, hummingbirds even, nest in the cactus scrub; woodpeckers befriend the demoniac yuccas, out of the stark, treeless waste rings the music of the night-singing mockingbird. If it be summer and the sun well down, there will be a burrowing owl to call. Strange, furry, tricksy things dart across the open places, or sit motionless in the conning towers of the creosote.[11]

In the desert, the earth is stripped bare; its geologic and human history is there for anyone to read. The MNP is reported to contain 12,000 archeological sites and 1,500 prehistoric sites, including petroglyphs, pictographs, rock shelters, milling sites, roasting pits, camp sites, and prehistoric trails. More recent sites include several Army outposts dating back to the European settling of the west, mining ruins and ghost towns, and early railroad remains.[12]

The most notable features of the area include these:[13]

Cima Dome: The most symmetrical natural dome in the United States, created by volcanic action and erosion, it now covers 75 square miles and rises nearly 1,500 feet above its 4,000-foot desert floor. Because it is so large and rises gradually, it is actually hard to see the dome when one is on it. Cima Dome boasts the world's largest, tallest, and densest Joshua tree forest, with related plant and animal life.

Cinder Cones: Covering 25,600 acres and containing thirty-two large volcanic formations, the area is dominated by the cones that rise high to create red-black anomalies on the landscape. One of the cones was mined until the NPS closed it down.[14]

Providence Mountains and Mitchell Caverns: Located within the MNP boundaries and managed as a California state park, the Providence Mountain area has excellent hiking. Mitchell Caverns is a deep limestone cavern system

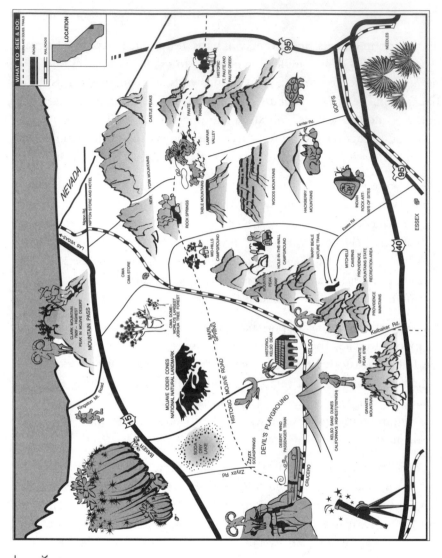

Map 1.2: Visitor Sites in the Mojave National Preserve. Map adapted from Peter Burk (1994b).

boasting stalactites and stalagmites, flowstone, cave shields, and cave ribbons. Mitchell Caverns were home to the Chemeheuvi for nearly five hundred years prior to European settlement.

Kelso Dunes: In this forty-five-square-mile formation of several sculpted sand dunes, some dunes tower over seven hundred feet high. Kelso Dunes are particularly interesting because they are "booming dunes," where the vibrations from visitors' footsteps can set off a series of low rumblings.

Hole-in-the-Wall and Mid Hills Campgrounds: Constructed by the Bureau of Land Management, these primitive campgrounds provide the only organized camping in the area. A good hiking trail connects the two, and Hole-in-the-Wall has wonderful volcanic formations which form a maze for hikers, including descent to the valley below via iron rings the BLM set in the rocks.

Fort Piute: Established in 1860s as part of a chain of outposts stretching from Nevada to western California, this lonely fort housed U.S. Army troops. This military presence provided pioneer travelers with protection from Native American raids. All that remains today are the stone foundations of the fort, with Native American petroglyphs on the rocks above, and soldiers' graffiti versions of petroglyphs as well.

Old Mojave Road: This was a major trade and transportation route between Arizona and the Coast, and originated from Native American travels. Thanks to the efforts of local enthusiasts, this route is still open for four-wheel recreation.[15]

Cow Cove: An important and highly scenic petroglyph site, with enigmatic carvings on hundreds of rocks on the hill above the cove. Access to this site was a relatively easy jeep drive under BLM management, but under the California Desert Protection Act (CDPA) the area has been designated a wilderness area and cars and jeeps must stop several miles from the cove.

Soda Dry Lake (Zzyzx): This desert oasis rises like a green mirage out of the shimmering heat of the gray-white, incredibly flat Soda Dry Lake. A radio evangelist founded Zzyzx, creating an outstanding health resort without ever gaining ownership of the BLM land. It is now run as the Desert Studies Center by a consortium of California state universities. Soda Dry Lake has a riparian area that hosts the Mojave chub, a fish that has become extinct in all other locations; the lake provides important perennial water for many species.

Kelso Depot: This town has one of the few permanent water sources in the desert, and became a stopover point where railroad crews traveling between Salt Lake City and Los Angeles could rest and obtain supplies. The depot itself, built in 1924, is a good example of Spanish style architecture. Kelso ceased to be a railroad stop in the mid-1980s. A citizen coalition including both Sierra Club members and BLM staff saved the depot from being razed in 1985 and stabilized the structure. It will be the park service's information center for the MNP.

The most common way to enjoy visiting in the Mojave is to drive to particular sites, then hike around them. This makes particular sense given the reality of carrying water in the desert. The heat and the extreme dryness of the air mean that one needs to drink about a gallon of water per day. That is a lot of weight to carry, and suggests that long hikes, even full day hikes, are beyond the capacity of most visitors. Fortunately for visitors, the Mojave has an extensive, though far from smooth, road system. About 50 percent of the area is within one mile of a road and more than 95 percent is within three miles of a road.[16] This is a legacy of the mining days, when prospectors drove over most of the area searching for metals and gold. It is also a result of the ease of creating a new road in the desert, where having just a few vehicles pass over the same path can break the desert crust and leave a visible trail.

Early History of the Mojave

The Mojave, according to some specialists, may be the site of the oldest human habitation in the Americas. It is clear that by ten thousand years ago groups of aboriginal peoples ranged across present-day California. That was the close of the Pleistocene epoch, when glaciers were still receding, the area's climate was wetter and milder, and today's dry lakes were full of water and life. Over the next thousand years, the climate became drier and hotter, and a more nomadic, plant-and-seed-gathering culture predominated. Pueblo Indians visited the area to mine turquoise and trade with other tribes, and trails laid out by these early inhabitants became the major transportation routes across the desert. Three Native American tribes, the Piutes, the Mohave, and the Chemehuevi, lived in the area by the time the Spanish arrived in 1776. These inhabitants were well adapted to desert conditions, gathering local plants and hunting indigenous animals for food and raw materials, using caves for shelter, and migrating from lower to higher elevations with the seasons. They engaged in ceremonial activities, of which the petroglyphs at Cow Cove and others across the area are a lasting reminder.[17]

European exploration of the Mojave began with the Spanish. In 1776, on his journey from the coast to Arizona, Father Francisco Garcés traveled through the desert, following the Old Mojave Trail. Not too long after Garcés's visit came the Spanish missions and the Spanish Trail, part of which is now known as the Mojave Trail. In the 1820s, trappers and explorers began traversing the area, including such notable figures as Jedediah Strong Smith, Kit Carson, and John C. Fremont. In the 1840s, these same men guided settlers' wagon trains across the desert as the Mojave Trail became an important, but perilous, route to the Californian promised lands.[18] As described by Patricia Limerick: "Overland travelers did not tame, transform, or punish the desert. They simply endured it. On the overland trail, in the desert, humans exerted their will to live, against the overwhelming force of inanimate matter. Triumph consisted not in mastery, but in escape."[19] The desert stretch of that overland road remained the "jornada del muerto" (journey of death) until modern transportation—trains and automobiles—arrived around the turn of the nineteenth century.[20]

The gold rush of 1849 created a population boom for western California, but as yields on the western slopes diminished, hard-rock miners began turning east toward the Mojave and Death Valley. The increasing white population and land values the minerals brought were not good news for the Native American tribes. In 1859 the Mohave Nation, weakened by war, disease, and alcohol, was defeated by the U.S. Army, and in 1867 under similar circumstances the Chemehuevis surrendered. The Mojave Trail became the Government Road as the army improved it and set up a series of military posts at the area's few natural springs, such as Fort Piute and Camp Rock Spring. With this security in place, European-American settlement of the area accelerated.[21]

In the east Mojave, silver and gold mining began in 1863 and halted in the 1890s (then resumed with leach-heap technologies in the 1980s).[22] By the 1880s, industrialists were harvesting Joshua trees for paper pulp, cattle were grazing the desert grasses, and settlers were attempting to dry farm marginal desert lands.[23] Meanwhile, patients with tuberculosis and other respiratory illnesses were discovering the healthy desert air. In 1883 the Southern Pacific Railroad completed a connection between Needles and Barstow, the first of many lines crossing the area. Small communities formed at water sources along the tracks to serve travelers and railroad workers.[24]

As early as 1886, most of the current uses of the land—livestock grazing, mining, military bases, transportation arteries, and Anglo residences—had become "entrenched in some form," as noted by the BLM.[25] Dennis Casebier reports a homesteader boom between 1910 and the 1920s. While many of these settlers were white, there was also a project for a black community in Lanfair Valley. Seventeen black families lasted long enough to get patents to their homestead land, an achievement indeed in the desert's harsh conditions.[26] By 1930, the desert, which had been equated with death by its first European travelers, became a thing to preserve. Death Valley was designated a national monument in 1933, and Joshua Tree was designated a national monument in 1936.[27]

Preserve-Area Residents

The land is more lightly settled now than it was by the 1930s, as the unusually wet early-settlement years have returned to dry. Determining just how many people currently live in the preserve area is difficult. Estimates range from 71 residents within the preserve area to 500 in the preserve and surrounding towns. In all cases, these counts include denizens of Lanfair Valley, a relatively more populous area in the southeast of the preserve in which, according to the final terms of the California Desert Protection Act, all private land is excluded. This means that people who live there are not technically residents of the preserve. As a result, a generous estimate of residents at the time of the preserve designation in the mid-1990s including those in the Lanfair exclusion might be 250, and excluding those in the Lanfair exclusion might make it fifty people.[28]

There are no towns within the preserve boundaries, only scattered settlement areas. Population within the MNP appears to be stable or declining, at rates that vary across settlement areas from no change to an 8 percent decline during the 1980s.[29] The two towns nearest the preserve that are large enough to be counted in the census are Barstow (55 miles from the preserve's western boundary) and Needles (several miles from the southern boundary). For these larger towns, the population trends are more positive, with growth in the 1990s ranging from 1 percent for Barstow to 3 percent for Needles.[30]

A Socioeconomic Picture of MNP Residents

So who lives in the preserve area? We can derive a sense of this from census data for the four zip codes that include some parts of the preserve, but also include areas outside it.[31] For this area, which is broader than just the preserve, the total 1990 population according to the census is 1,179, with 387 house-

Table 1.1 Land Tenure in the EMNSA

Owner	Acres	Percent
BLM/NPS	1,296,000	86%
State of California	58,000	4%
Catellus (Santa Fe Railroad)[a]	87,000	6%
Other private	59,000	4%
Total	1,500,000	100%

Source: U.S. Bureau of Land Management, *East Mojave National Scenic Area Management Plan*, 1988, p. 106.

[a] Ownership of the railroad lands goes back to the 1870s, when Congress deeded alternating sections of land to railroads to encourage the development of the lines. At that time, Southern Pacific Railroad acquired the 87,000 acres of federal land; Southern Pacific was later purchased by the Santa Fe Railroad, which received the deeded land. In 1990, Santa Fe spun off its real estate holdings into a subsidiary, the Catellus Development Company, which now owns these lands. Most of the parcels lie in the southern part of the MNP, and typically have the pattern of two or three adjoining sections interspersed with federal lands. Stephen R. Mark, *Wilderness Review in the East Mojave National Scenic Area*, master's thesis, University of California, 1984, p. 111.

holds. Baker, which is a gateway community for Joshua Tree National Park, has a state prison for 250 males that employs a large percentage of the community. Exclusive of this estimated prison population, total population is 929. Most of the population is white, with almost 19 percent of the population claiming Hispanic origin. The gender breakdown after adjusting for prisoners is 52 percent male. People are fairly mobile; only 35 percent of the population lives in the same house as in 1985, but most people moved from within the same county. Education levels are generally low, with almost 43 percent of the population not having a high school degree, and only over 5 percent having a post-secondary degree. A great many of the housing units in the area were vacant—almost 30 percent. There are more renters than homeowners; visual inspection indicates there are a large number of house trailers, many of which are probably rental units.

While many local residents believe that ranching and mining are cornerstones of the local economy, in fact the largest single occupation in the area is retail work, performed by almost 29 percent of employed persons. Information and service workers (those in public administration, which includes the positions at the prison, finance and real estate, education, and service workers) account for almost 37 percent of the local employment. Construction, manufacturing, and utilities employ almost 17 percent of the population. The area's traditional economic bases—agriculture (ranching), mining, and transportation—combined provide only 18 percent of the total employment.[32] On the whole, average per capita income ($26,888) and median household income ($27,059) for the area are comfortable, but these are influenced by the twenty-eight households reporting incomes of over $100,000.

Land Tenure in the MNP

Land ownership in the East Mojave National Scenic Area (EMNSA), which became the Mojave National Preserve, is primarily federal, and the percent of land under private ownership is very small. Under the terms of the CDPA the department of the interior can exchange the Catellus lands for surplus federal lands outside the area of the CDPA. As of June 2000, the NPS and a nonprofit partner had purchased almost all the Catellus acres.[33] Some of the state lands, held to provide for state teachers' retirement funds, can also be exchanged for surplus federal lands outside the preserve.[34]

Peter Burk, a park supporter, analyzed the private lands for size and ownership in 1993 and found that there were approximately seven hundred landowners within the EMNSA area who own approximately 2,044 parcels.[35] Sixty-nine landholders, or about 10 percent of all owners, own more than one parcel and these multiple parcel owners account for 34 percent of the total private lands. A review of those sixty-nine names of multiple-parcel holders indicates that all but one are individuals, as compared to corporations or syndicates, and the one corporate holding is a mining company.[36] Most of the landholdings range in value between $5,000 and $60,000, with one notable outlier—a local ranching family that owns almost four thousand acres with an assessed value of $424,870. Of the landowners, only eight were determined to be residents of the area, but that may be an incomplete count.[37] Land in the Mojave under private sales was valued at an average of between $266 per acre and $305 per acre in the early 1990s.[38] By 2000, the NPS reported that total private lands were 86,708 acres exclusive of Catellus lands largely concentrated in Lanfair Valley.[39]

The area's private landholdings are centered in the Lanfair Valley and several of the settlement areas. Mark describes them this way: "Isolated private holdings can take the form of less than a quarter section with maybe one often abandoned dwelling on it to those comprising a square mile or more. These latter properties contain most of the area's fewer than a dozen ranches."[40] The Lanfair exclusion in the 1994 bill eliminating all private property parcels within the settlement area from preserve boundaries has positive and negative outcomes for those residents. By removing the land from NPS management, lawmakers exempted those owners from the extra regulation that comes from being a park service in-holder; otherwise the exemption has little effect.[41]

Development Pressure in and near the MNP Area

Development pressures in the area are increasing. Generally, these pressures come in two varieties. The first is development of homes for either retirement/second home purchasers or, in the longer term, as part of the L.A./Las Vegas conurbation. In 1998 Las Vegas-based developers announced intentions to develop over four hundred acres of land just beyond the northern edge of the preserve near the gateway town of Baker, with plans to build a whole new community including several hundred homes, some commercial properties, a recreational vehicle park, and a lighted golf course.[42]

Much of Los Angeles's current growth is occurring in San Bernardino County, which includes the Mojave preserve and suburban areas of the Los Angeles metropolitan area. While Los Angeles's population grew at an annual rate of 3 percent over the last ten years, San Bernardino County grew at over 10 percent. Clark County, Nevada, located northeast of the preserve, includes the Las Vegas metropolitan area. This metro area grew at an astonishing 15.7 percent each year over the decade 1985–1995. Both counties are building housing in a low-density pattern. The result is that the San Bernardino residential area is increasing in size by approximately 102 square miles each year and Clark County is increasing at 91 square miles each year—and a significant amount of land consumption is in the direction of the Mojave National Preserve. This growth is still quite a distance from the preserve's borders—between sixty and a hundred miles in the direction of Los Angeles and thirty miles in the direction of Las Vegas.[43] Significant residential development would impact the empty character of the landscape, as well as the brilliance of the night sky—two of the essential characteristics of this desert.

A second category of risk comes from the traditional role of desert as dumping ground, worthless land that can be well used to take up the messiness of urban life. Clark County, Nevada, will build a major new airport in Ivanpah Valley, on Bureau of Land Management land just ten miles northeast of the preserve borders. The BLM transferred the land to Clark County in 2000, as allowed in the BLM's originating legislation if such a transfer fulfills a public purpose.[44] This airport will serve Las Vegas and the desert area, and "could eventually become one of the nation's busiest air transportation facilities"; the result would make the sky over the northern portion of the preserve "a flyway for 747s."[45] The potential for light and noise pollution is great, and an airport would encourage private development of lands in and near the preserve.[46]

A rail-cycle dump, which involves putting Los Angeles's trash on trains and bringing it to a dump site located between Barstow and the preserve's western border, was also being considered. Another desert rail-cycle dump, farther from the preserve in El Centro, is in operation. By encouraging raven populations, these facilities harm the endangered desert tortoises, since ravens think baby tortoise is a particularly delicious meal.[47] Ward Valley, located twenty-six miles west of Needles near I-40 and very near the preserve, was under consideration by U.S. Ecology as the site for a western-states low-level nuclear waste repository.[48] In a different sort of land use category, but still one of enormous impact, was the proposal by the Fort Mohave Native American tribe to put nine major casinos along the Colorado River. These would be located near their current casino, which is twenty miles east of the preserve. The clash between these sorts of developments, housing designed to take advantage of the beauty of the landscape, and classic unwanted land uses designed to take advantage of the lack of neighbors is obvious. The potential cost to a functioning national preserve is obvious as well.

New West / Old West

Even in the sorts of developments proposed for the desert, one sees the juncture of what can be called the Old West and the New West. Carl Abbott, Sy Adler, and Margery Post Abbott capture this intersection particularly well and are worth quoting at length:

> In the closing decades of the twentieth century, the seeds of tourism have grown into a powerful and diversified force for social and economic change. From New Mexico to Alaska, strong and articulate interests are shaping a New West on the foundations of the Old West. The New West is an archipelago of thriving cities reaching out to "resettle" old and often fading resource regions for recreation and retirement, ex-urban commuting and telecommuting, and locations for service industries . . .
>
> Inside or outside the traditional West, the differences between old and new societies are many: attitudes toward natural resources, orientation to local communities or national networks, sources of livelihood, levels of comfort with large-scale organizations and bureaucratic processes. The Old West depends directly on

the production and processing of natural resources. New Westerners tend to value preservation or conservation of those same resources (except, perhaps, for their development into golf courses and ski runs). They also know how to wield credentialed expertise. New Westerners tend to look out their windows and see scenery, not resources, thus modifying the meanings of place. In the most fundamental contrast, the New West is a set of bases for networked lives; the Old West is a set of narrowly focused but deeply embedded communities.[49]

Historian Richard White understands the difference as one of a metropolitan West and a rural West, with the rural West believing that they provide rearguard protection of the old western values in the face of increasing change coming from the urban areas.[50] When Old West members decry the meddling of environmentalists in what to them should be local issues of land management, they recognize that western urbanites share more values with easterners than with them. And, given increasingly urban demographics, the city dwellers carry more and more elected weight.

Tourism in the Desert

Visitation Patterns and Value of Tourism

Despite the intensity with which the Mojave designation was debated, or perhaps because of it, during the designation process there was never very good information on how many people come to the desert and why. In 1976 the BLM determined that the East Mojave experienced about 44,000 visitor-days (one individual staying one day equals one visitor day) that year, or about 2 percent of all visitor-days to the entire Southern California desert area.[51] In 1990 the BLM did a traffic count that estimated 250,000 annual visits to the area, but this included local traffic and pass-through traffic.[52] Kelbaker Road, which runs through the middle of the preserve, provides the only paved connection between I-15 to the north and I-40 to the south for many, many miles, so pass-through traffic may be significant. The NPS estimates that the preserve received just under 400,000 visitors in 1999.[53]

A different BLM-commissioned study of 1990 provides some information on visitor characteristics, although none on total numbers.[54] Oddly, this study does not provide a quantitative summary of the primary activities of visitors. Numbers can be ascribed, however, based on reported sample size (n = 470) for surveying visitor satisfaction by primary activity as follows:

- Auto-touring / Sightseeing: 41 percent
- Nature Study: 18 percent
- Hiking / Developed Camping: 14 percent
- Off-Road Vehicle Use: 14 percent
- Hunting: 3 percent.[55]

This suggests that 73 percent of all visitors were interested in low-impact activities, for whom the National Park Service management style would probably be beneficial. Only 14 percent of visitors would be negatively impacted by increased regulation of off-road use under NPS management, and only 3 percent of visitors would have been harmed by preventing hunting in the preserve. If we use the very rough annual visitation estimate of 250,000 visitor days, 3 percent of visitors hunting would bring 7,500 hunter days annually in the preserve. Given multiple days per hunting visit, with the typical hunter making three visits per year, perhaps 500 people hunt in the preserve on a given year.[56] The NPS estimated that under the BLM, the area was penetrating only about 3.2 percent of its potential regional market.[57] This certainly suggests that visitation could increase a great deal.

Another way of evaluating potential visitation for the Mojave is to compare it to the other desert units of the national park system. Joshua Tree drew 1,150,000 visitors in 1991, with each spending an average of $31 per day. Non-local visitors were estimated to have contributed about $26 million in direct revenues to the local economy, which were estimated to have produced almost $53 million in direct and indirect tourism-induced sales. Death Valley's estimated annual visitation was around 900,000, with $42 million in direct revenues generated and over $51 million in direct and indirect tourism-related sales.[58] Death Valley has more developed activities, including golf courses and fine hotels, than Joshua Tree, which probably accounts for its higher per-person spending.

Joshua Tree, with its fairly minimal development, would be more comparable to the Mojave, and a Mojave national park might have expected visitation and revenues in amounts similar to Joshua Tree. The Mojave National Preserve is unlikely to have the same tourism draw, as the NPS's report suggests: "The term 'preserve' is probably not associated with a travel destination in the minds of most tourists. In fact, it may have a negative connotation. They may believe a 'preserve' to be a place set aside for wildlife or something else that needs protection . . . but not for people."[59]

Visitation at all preserves is fairly low. The park service reports that Big Cypress Preserve in Florida had the most visitation of any preserve, at 212,700 visits in 1992; Big Thicket Preserve in Texas had only 72,300. Visitation at Alaska's preserves is significantly lower than Alaska's national parks. And, according to the NPS, "economic revenue generated from these [preserve] areas is not high."[60]

If we assume, for the sake of argument, that the Mojave in five years achieves half the current level of visitation at Joshua Tree and experiences similar per-visitor-day retail and related sales, this suggests 575,000 visitor days in the preserve, spending $13 million in direct sales and $26.5 million in direct and indirect revenues, excluding inflation. Retail sales in 1992 for Barstow, which is likely to benefit substantially from increased tourism, were $301 million.[61] An additional $13 million in direct sales would increase Barstow's receipts by 4 percent, and the indirect revenues by almost 9 percent. Some significant percentage of the increase would no doubt be spread across all of the settlements in the area—Baker, Nipton, Needles, and the one retail store in Cima.

There is some anecdotal indication that visits have already increased. In Baker, retail sales and new business development are reported by local sources to already have increased in response to the bill. A January 1997 *New York Times* article reported on how the designation of Joshua Tree National Park has impacted the gateway community of Twentynine Palms. That municipality experienced an increase in tax receipts on hotel and motels guests from $155,000 in fiscal year 1995 (July 1, 1995 through June 30, 1996) to $171,000 in fiscal year 1996, which is an increase of more than 10 percent. As the article notes, the increase came in spite of the three-week federal closure of national parks resulting from the budget impasse of 1996—closures which came during the winter, which is high season for desert visitation.[62] The tourism prognosis for the MNP gateway communities appears to be one of moderate economic growth.

Commentary

The image of the area that emerges from this analysis is of a lightly populated preserve becoming less populated each year, while the nearby metropolitan areas grow extravagantly. Employment in the vicinity of the preserve has already made the transition from resource-based to service and retail work, with a moderate income. Low educational achievements may hinder technological or industrial economic development in the area. Many tourism-related retail and service positions as well as smaller entrepreneurial positions do not require advanced education, so the education attainment in the area matches tourist employment characteristics fairly well. Clearly, the Mojave area is part of the Old West, but is becoming part of what Abbott, Adler, and Abbott (1997) characterize as the "urban shadow" of the metropolitan New West.

Most local properties, other than ranches and some scattered settlement areas, are not included in the preserve because of the Lanfair exclusion. While this may assuage fears of the NPS's taking over private lands, it creates a potential management nightmare for the park service with two thousand-plus private parcel "holes" within the exterior boundaries of the preserve. The federal government owns the vast majority of land both within and outside the preserve. While this provides some limits on the development potential of the area, BLM land can be converted to large public-purpose developments such as airports or dumps, or traded to developers for higher-ecological quality lands elsewhere. In 1993, most of the private land not held by Catellus appeared to be owned by absentee landholders, the great majority of whom seemed to be individuals as compared to corporations or syndicates. This tends to suggest that at that time, development speculation had not yet set in, but recently development pressure has increased. Some of this increase was no doubt due to the designation itself, as the area gained visibility among the many people wanting to buy land near or inside of national park units.

Development could come in two different forms. The first is regular suburban-type sprawl that has affected so much of the southwestern desert. Both Los Angeles and Las Vegas, with their low-density building styles, can be characterized as desert-eating machines. The Mojave area before the designation may have been headed toward becoming part of a vast southwestern desert conurbation stretching from Las Vegas to Los Angeles. Space in this area, however, is remarkably large; all of Las Vegas's urbanized area could comfortably fit inside the boundaries of the preserve. Suburban growth has not yet significantly impacted the neighboring towns of Barstow or Needles, and growth at the Nevada state line consists of one casino and two mines—albeit large ones —so this suburban horizon is still far in the distance, both in time and space.

Closer in time and space, and more likely given the preserve designation, is resort and second home development. Across the nation, gateway communities are experiencing extremely rapid growth. The quality of life and scenic beauty they can offer provides, as noted by Howe, McMahon, and Propst (3), "a magnet for millions of Americans looking to escape the congestion, b[   ]ity, and faster tempo of life in suburbs and cities." Many of these new residents are likely to be "equity exiles," retiring baby boomers who sell their city homes and use the profit to relocate to more desirable scenic rural locations. Across the nation, baby boomers are expected to double the demand for second homes and resort lodging in gateway communities over the next twenty years.[63]

Imagine someone selling a home in the Los Angeles area and purchasing an $80,000 home in Baker—that would still leave a lot of cash to live on. In a later chapter, we will meet a preserve couple who exactly match this profile. Sadly, of course, these in-migrants often end up bringing with them the same problems they hoped to escape—witness the likely light pollution resulting from a golf course lit for evening play. Nevertheless, as population growth continues in the surrounding metropolises, the Mojave is likely to become an attractive area for second homes and retirement homes, just the sort of development the NPS is unable to prevent under the terms of the California Desert Protection Act.

Additionally, the traditional role of desert as dumping ground is visible in proposals for the area. The airport, rail-cycle dump, and Ward Valley proposals are all on BLM lands. There is little evidence that if the preserve had stayed in BLM management, the BLM would have been able to shield it any better than it has been able to shield other parts of their desert.

While current levels of visitation are quite light, the enormous population of the Los Angeles and Las Vegas metropolitan areas suggests a huge number of potential tourists. Given the profile of visitors' activities in the area, the low-impact uses favored by the NPS appear appropriate for the great majority of visitors. One outcome of the decision to make the Mojave a preserve rather than national park is ironic, in that this designation is likely to limit the visibility of the area as a tourist destination, thus preventing the sort of economic development that often occurs in national park gateway communities. Still, there are indications that the designation has already increased tourism business in the gateway communities.

From these trends we can glean a possible future for the preserve. Already, within and around the preserve relatively few residents are employed in traditional economic uses such as ranching and mining. We can anticipate that as NPS management increases restrictions on traditional economic uses, fewer current residents may find that sort of employment. Instead, there is likely to be an increase in moderately wealthy second-home purchasers as well as people with footloose sorts of work (high technology types, artists, telecommuters) living on the many scattered private parcels in the preserve as well as in the gateway communities.[64] The results suggest that significant change is likely to come to the area. Without careful management and planning, this sort of development has the potential to impair the exact charms the desert has to offer—solitude, nature, silence, stars—an outcome beneficial neither to the current residents of the area nor to the preserve itself.

CHAPTER 2

Parks, Preserves, and Land Management Bureaus

The weird solitude, the great silence, the grim desolation, are the very things with which every desert wanderer eventually falls in love. You think that very strange perhaps? Well, the beauty of the ugly was sometime a paradox, but to-day people admit its truth; and the grandeur of the desolate is just as paradoxical, yet the desert gives it proof.

— JOHN VAN DYKE, *The Desert*

The finest quality of this stone, these plants and animals, this desert landscape is the indifference manifest to our presence, our absence, our coming, our staying or our going. Whether we live or die is a matter of absolutely no concern whatsoever to the desert.

— EDWARD ABBEY, *Desert Solitaire*

In the desert, you see, there is everything and nothing . . . it is God without mankind.   — HONORÉ DE BALZAC, *A Passion in the Desert*

Perhaps the most hotly debated question throughout the designation controversy was whether or not the Mojave belonged in the national park system. When it became clear that this part of the desert would become some kind of national park unit, the next question was its designation—would it be a national park or a national preserve? I explore the differences between the two below, and describe a third option that was never considered—creating a greenline park. Key issues in the designation debate centered on the quality of protection and administration the area received under the Bureau of Land Management. To provide perspective on this, we will examine the plans under which the BLM managed the area, and the planning process the NPS has undertaken for the area.

What Makes a National Park?

Official Criteria for National Park Units

Understanding the criteria for national parks requires a bit of knowledge of the history of the park service and its changing mission. Americans, after the founding of the country and prior to the 1900s, faced a curious problem. They were citizens in a huge, increasingly important country whose economic might was beginning to be clear but which lacked its own postcolonization culture or history. How were they to evidence pride in their country when an English clergyman could, with all good conscience, ask in 1820, "In the four quarters of the globe, who reads an American book? or goes to an American play? or looks at an American picture or statue?"[1] This cultural anxiety was a key factor in the origin of the national park idea. Americans could not compete with the human-made wonders of old Europe; they could, however, compete with the natural wonders of anywhere.[2]

The United States had landscapes of unquestionable uniqueness, and so long as preserving them did not interfere with the important tasks of economic development, these natural areas would become the country's unique contribution to world culture. In choosing the national parks, the first criterion established judged the sublime quality of the landscape. Park areas needed to be monumental so that they confirmed the nation's singular natural beauty. Parklands also had to be economically worthless; from the beginning, Congress bowed to arguments that commercial resources should either be excluded from park boundaries or should be opened to exploitation regardless of their location. So, it was rugged, marginal, surplus public land that would be chosen for preservation.[3]

By the 1930s, many of the "crown jewels," the grandly sublime large natural areas of the country such as Yellowstone and Yosemite, had been protected in the national park system. The park service then broadened park selection criteria to include areas less pristine, more urban, and of recreational and historical significance, rather than only those with landscape beauty.[4] The new emphasis reflected the changing needs of an urbanizing country, in which finding natural areas for rest and relaxation was becoming difficult for much of the population. In more recent years, the park service once again broadened selection criteria by adding explicitly ecological considerations. As noted by Robert Foresta: "With increasing environmental awareness in the

1960s and 1970s, and a shift in ecological thought among environmentalists and the public at large, the major national parks came to be valued both as important parts of the global ecosystem and as unique, distinct areas where nature-altering human activities must not be allowed to take place."[5]

The 1972 *National Parks for the Future Report* encouraged the NPS to implement its new role in the designation of new parks.[6] The report recommended that "new natural-resource parks should be established and land should be acquired to provide a system representative of all principal physiographic regions in the nation . . . [P]reservation of biotic assemblages or representation of physiographic regions rather than popular appeal or aesthetics are to be the most important criterion for selection."[7]

The NPS implemented these recommendations with the 1972 National Park System Plan, which adopted physiographic and ecological representativeness as the primary criteria in evaluating natural areas. This plan, however, indicated wide gaps in representative coverage, thereby laying the groundwork for continued growth in the national park system.[8] A 1978 NPS management document outlined a complex new set of criteria for accepting new areas into the system: proposals were to be examined for their national significance, suitability and feasibility, and management alternatives.[9] Historian Thomas Wikle describes these criteria: "The degree to which areas exhibited national significance was determined by a professional's evaluation, the National Park Service Advisory Board, and the secretary of the interior. Furthermore, areas had to represent themes missing from the system. The suitability and feasibility criterion meant that administration, protection, and preservation had to be possible—areas had to be large enough and of a shape that would accommodate administrative needs while not infringing on the rights of private landowners. In addition, areas had to need to be protected by the park service and to be made available for public appreciation."[10] It is under these revised criteria that the park service evaluates new areas for inclusion in the national park system.

The Unofficial Criterion—Politics

Whether or not a proposed unit matches the explicit criteria often ends up being much less important than the wishes of the elected representatives for that area or that state. The process of designating a new park unit is described in some detail in the next chapter. Here it suffices to say that in recent years, it is not the park service that typically proposes new units; rather, it is congressional representatives or senators. Additionally, it is up to Congress to allocate funds for the park service, and fund allocation is of course a primary way of directing agency priorities. After undertaking an extensive analysis of park system expansions, William Lowry concluded that "the expansion of the American system is individualized and entrepreneurial, determined on a case-by-case basis of political calculations rather than according to any systematic plan focused on natural resources."[11] As we will see in the next chapter, this political focus is apparent in the California Desert Protection Act and the designation of the Mojave.

Parks vs. Preserves

Not only does the Congress control which units will be added to the park system, it also determines the management goals for individual units. The legislative guidelines set up within each unit's authorizing bill determine how the park service will manage any particular unit. In these bills, Congress indicates what the need for the particular unit is, its goals, and the uses that are to be prevented or allowed. Congress also selects a particular unit type for that area —national recreation area? national preserve? national park? something else? These unit categories are important for communicating the purposes of units to the public and for their rhetorical power, but the actual management guidelines come from the criteria written into each individual unit's authorizing bill. Within the park system there are a great variety of designations, but two are of particular interest for this discussion—national park and national preserve.

Within national parks as well as most other types of park system units, uses other than tourism and preservation are usually disallowed. Public hunting in particular is never allowed in national parks, and grazing is rare. The designation of preserve indicates more variety in use, and is of very recent vintage. The National Park Service describes "national preserve" as a category "established primarily for the protection of certain resources. Activities such as hunting and fishing or the extraction of minerals and fuels may be permitted if they do not jeopardize the natural values."[12] The first national preserves were established in 1974—Big Cypress National Preserve in south Florida and Big Thicket National Preserve in east Texas. While both represent important ecological areas, as parks historian E. Glenn Carls reports, neither qualified for national park status because of previous alterations to the environment and pre-existing land uses, including extensive logging and oil production.[13] Under national preserve designation, many uses of the land that would not be per-

Table 2.1 Land Use under the BLM Plans

Use Class	Acres in CDCA (in millions) (*1980 Plan*)	Acres in East Mojave (*1988 Plan*)	Description of Management Goals and Acceptable Uses
C (Controlled)	1.9 (13%)	271,000 (21%)	Suitable for wilderness; closed to mineral entry and vehicles; grazing allowed
L (Limited)	5.9 (52%)	884,000 (69%)	Managed to protect resources; mining allowed but regulated; vehicles limited to approved routes
M (Moderate)	3.3 (28%)	120,000 (10%)	Balance between use and protection; off-highway racing, power plants, chemical control of vegetation all allowed
I (Intensive)	0.5 (4%)	none	Managed to meet human needs; large-scale mining, off-highway vehicles, etc. allowed
U (Unclassified)	0.3 (3%)	4,400 (1%)	Scattered or isolated parcels, usually surrounded by private lands

Source: U.S. Bureau of Land Management, *East Mojave National Scenic Area Management Plan,* 1988, pp. 27–29.

missible in a national park are allowed to continue, including hunting, trapping, grazing, agriculture, and oil and gas extraction. Neither, however, has a significant in-holding resident population. Several preserves were also included in the Alaskan park designations, but the purposes of these are slightly different. Many of them are buffer areas surrounding national parks or monuments with a primary goal of continuing traditional subsistence hunting for indigenous peoples. For our purposes, we will focus on the way *preserve* has been used in the lower forty-eight states.[14]

Susan Bratton notes that preserves "are continuations of the biological trend, but emphasize representative ecosystems and remnants of once common plant community types . . . National preserves may not contain any 'spectacular' scenery and are not necessarily attractive to the casual tourist."[15] Describing the role of preserves in the national park system, Carls notes: "They are important as a concept and as a prototype for the management of similar areas. They represent the protection of environmental resources under less than optimum conditions and recognize, too, the value in protecting natural areas that may be less than pristine. Rather than a lowering of standards, the national preserves are an acceptance of the need to acquire and reclaim certain altered landscapes."[16]

Greenline Parks—Paths Not Taken

In Europe and to a lesser extent in the United States, greenline parks are well developed examples of ways to protect landscapes that are not pure wilderness.[17] A greenline park is defined in this way: "A large, scenic landscape area which is protected by law and regulation from being overtaken by unplanned development to the extent that it retains its natural, scenic, or historic attributes; the area is often in productive use by traditionally low-impact, land-oriented industries, like fishing, farming, ranching, or timbering; the protections for such a landscape are cooperatively arranged and managed by citizens and agencies on the local, state, and federal levels, usually through a joint commission."[18] The goal is to protect not just ecology but also culture, not just land but also traditional residents. The method rests on cooperative development of land use plans governing both private and public property, rather than full ownership and management of the area by federal agencies. In Europe, the idea is quite common; national parks in the United Kingdom and France are specially regulated landscapes rather than nature preserves.[19]

In the United States, greenline park examples include New York's Adirondack State Park, the Pinelands National Reserve in New Jersey, the Cape Cod National Seashore, and the Columbia River Gorge National Scenic Area.[20] In all of these cases, there was significant development pressure on the area from urbanites and other in-migrants as well as from second-home construction. In each case, either federal or state government in partnership with local residents and their elected officials developed local and regional land use regulations that protect the natural and scenic qualities of the land while allowing some economic use of the land by traditional residents. The Adirondacks is the only one that was a state-local partnership; in the rest, it was federal-state-local.

Much of the difference between the greenline models described above and the Mojave is the act of reaching out beyond park boundaries. To implement a greenline park requires creating partnerships with the local communities, working out land use plans that will meet the needs of local residents as well as secure environmental protection. That sort of partnership building requires environmentalists to release some control over the process of protection, and to have some trust in local residents. Greenline approaches might have been more acceptable to local residents and to their representatives and thus prevented some of the ongoing ill will between those opposed to protection and those in favor. Creating local partnership and preventing ill will might have prevented the intense governmental infighting the preserve experienced. Perhaps because the federal landholdings in the Mojave were so extensive, there was less perceived need to collaborate with communities. This is a topic to which we return in Chapter 6.

The Mojave's Fit to the Criteria

To determine whether the Mojave fit the criteria for inclusion in the park system, the NPS conducted a "Resource Assessment for Features Proposed in the California Desert Protection Act," dated January 1987. This report does not provide a yes-or-no answer; instead, it details the features of the land and management considerations. A cover letter from Howard Chapman, director of the NPS's Western Regional Office, that accompanied the report stated that the Mojave area met the criteria and ought to be included in the park system.[21]

The resource assessment found that the Mojave had significant biological, scenic, recreational, and cultural (historical) values. However, the report's authors indicate that most of the ecosystem types and historical values the Mojave offers are already well represented in the national park system, in that other California desert areas are already in the system. They find that while there are some adverse effects to the area from the BLM's policies of allowing mining and ranching, the BLM already has sufficient authority to protect the East Mojave. Additionally, they find that the area would be difficult and expensive to administer. Overall, the report is ambivalent regarding the importance and value of the Mojave as an addition to the national park system.

The report did not specifically consider using national preserve status among its alternatives.[22] However, if we understand the goal of preserve status in the way suggested by writers Carls and Bratton, the Mojave fits the suggested goals of preserves very well. Much of the area is disturbed (although other than roads, this is largely not visible to the casual visitor), and it has a long history of human use. While some of the scenery is spectacular, most of it is not. Moreover, the area is unconducive to casual visitation, because those places of great beauty tend to be difficult to access (and now that many are in designated wilderness areas, access will be particularly difficult). Because it is home to representative ecosystems and populations of flora and fauna that are becoming less and less common, the area meets the biologic goals described by Carls and Bratton. In addition, the overall desert region is under intense development pressure, which could indicate a need for NPS management.

The BLM's Mojave

The lands that became the Mojave National Preserve have been federally owned ever since California joined the union. Prior to the establishment of the BLM in 1946, the Southern California deserts were part of the vast reservoir of federal lands held open for settlement.[23] As early as 1968, BLM State Director Russ Penny was concerned with the management of the California desert. According to Ed Hastey, powerful California state director of the BLM, in the late 1960s and early 1970s the bureau began pushing for official legislation that would allow them to more actively manage the desert, including having a uniformed ranger force. On a separate track, legislation was making its way through Congress to provide the bureau with its own "Organic Act," the Federal Lands Policy and Management Act of 1976 (FLPMA).[24] It was convenient to merge the two legislative actions, and so Section 601 of the FLPMA was written to create the California Desert Conservation Area.[25]

FLPMA

Section 601 of FLPMA required the BLM to develop a plan to "provide for the immediate and future protection and administration of the public lands in the California Desert within the framework of a program of multiple uses and sustained yield, and the maintenance of environmental quality."[26] Multiple use under FLPMA was given a long and complex definition, much of which amounts to providing for "a combination of balanced and diverse resource uses that takes into account the long-term needs of future generations for renewable and non-renewable resources."[27] To meet these goals, the BLM was to prepare a comprehensive, long- range plan for the California desert—twenty-five million acres of land including over twelve million acres of federal land. The California Desert Conservation Area Plan (the 1980 Plan) was the discharge of that duty.

The 1980 and 1988 Plans

The 1980 Plan for the California Desert Conservation Area (CDCA) was a massive undertaking, prepared over four years by a panel of experts that included eminent planner Harvey Perloff.[28] The goal of the plan was to "provide for the use of the public lands and resources of the California Desert Conservation Area, including economic, educational, scientific, and recreational uses, in a manner which enhances wherever possible—and does not diminish, on balance—the environmental, cultural, and aesthetic values of the Desert and its future productivity."[29] To accomplish this, the plan divided the public lands into four multiple-use classes, laying out goals for each sort of resource or use ("plan elements") to be considered, along with implementation procedures.[30]

The 1980 Plan was created with extensive public participation, including fifteen public hearings held between 1977 and 1979, feedback meetings with groups who provided comments during the initial process, three public opinion polls on a desertwide, statewide, and national basis, advertising the availability of and free mailing of a first draft of the plan to any who requested it, and finally, during the first part of 1980, holding still more hearings locally and in the major metropolitan areas of California. The result was about nine thousand individuals providing about forty thousand separate comments. These comments were then integrated into the final plan through a formal process of tabulation, analysis, development of options, and development of recommendations.[31]

Virtually as soon as the 1980 Plan was published, the BLM significantly amended it, with continuing amendments through 1990. These amendments were quite controversial, with environmentalists claiming that they significantly weakened the plan.[32] A review of amendments to the plan for the whole desert region suggests that while the record is mixed, the effect of the amendments overall appears to weaken some of the environmental protections in the plan. For the whole desert region, the results of the plan's amendments included the following:[33]

- Changes in the land use classification of specific parcels increased protection in fourteen cases, and decreased protection in twenty-three cases.
- Changes to motorized access increased protection in five cases, and decreased protection in seven cases. Two of those changes included allowing the resumption of the Barstow to Vegas off-road motorcycle race and expanding an existing open-play off-road vehicle area—the sort that almost permanently devastates natural processes. The BLM had little choice in resuming the motorcycle race; off-road motorcycling enthusiasts had successfully sued to force resumption of the race.[34]
- Seven Areas of Critical Environmental Concern (ACEC), which were subject to strong regulation, were deleted; nine other ACECs were

added. Of the changes to ACEC boundaries, four diminished the area protected, and three enlarged the area protected. One of those boundary changes deleted 47,520 acres from the Mojave National Scenic Area. These acres are the sites of Cal Coal and Molycorp mines.

* Grazing adjustments weakened environmental protection in eleven of thirteen identifiable cases.
* In several areas, allowable burro populations were reduced to zero.

The 1980 Plan also designated the East Mojave as a national scenic area (NSA).[35] There are no clear guidelines on how NSAs in general ought to be managed, but the implication is that they are to be oriented more toward tourism and preservation than other BLM lands. The 1980 Plan provided that a follow-up plan would be written to guide management of the East Mojave National Scenic Area (EMNSA).[36]

Eight years later, the BLM produced the 1988 Plan for the EMNSA.[37] The 1988 Plan described the goal of the NSA designation as: "to ensure continuation of the uses and occupations which give the region its character, and yet give special emphasis to retaining the area's natural scenic qualities in evaluating and permitting changes and new uses."[38] Generally, the 1988 Plan provided for more environmental protection than the 1980 Plan. The two plans provided for higher percentages of protected lands in the NSA as compared to the rest of the BLM's desert area (the California Desert Conservation Area, or CDCA).

The 1988 Plan's only comment on public involvement is the following: "Responses to over 400 comments received from the public during the review of the draft Plan are included in the Environmental Assessment. Several changes were made to the final Plan as a consequence. On the whole, commentators approved of the Plan's direction, but many favored stricter environmental controls and increased enforcement efforts."[39] That the "400 comments" resulted in only "several changes" seems telling. For the 1980 Plan the bureau sought and accommodated a very extensive public participation effort, but was rewarded, as we shall see, with continued environmentalist efforts to transfer the Mojave to the National Park Service. By the 1988 Plan, the Bureau of Land Management seems to have turned to a defensive inward posture. It was under this 1988 Plan that the BLM administered the Mojave until 1994, when the land was transferred to the park service.

The Mojave under the NPS

The 1994 Bill

On October 31, 1994, President Clinton signed the California Desert Protection Act (CDPA) into law.[40] The CDPA designated approximately 7.7 million acres of Bureau of Land Management and National Park Service federal lands as wilderness and added approximately 3 million acres to the national park system by expanding Joshua Tree and Death Valley and upgrading their status from national monuments to national parks. It also created the new Mojave National Preserve. Upon signing the bill, President Clinton said, "Few Presidents have the opportunity to preserve so valuable a piece of this Nation's heritage . . . The broad vistas, the rugged mountains ranges, and the evidence of human past are treasures that merit protection on behalf of the American people . . . This Act is proof that the common good and the will of the people can prevail."[41]

The 1,419,800-acre Mojave National Preserve (MNP) is designated in title 5 of the act; later calculations indicate that the actual size of the preserve is 1,589,165 acres.[42] According to the act, the need for the MNP is indicated by its unique ecosystem, its outstanding natural, cultural, historical, and recreation values, and the fact that the Mojave area was previously "afforded only impermanent administrative designation as a national scenic area."

The bill specifically permits a wide variety of uses; these are described in some detail in Chapter 5. Hunting, fishing, and trapping are permitted in the area, and the State of California retains jurisdiction over fish and wildlife. Grazing continues at current levels with no time limit, but the secretary of the interior can purchase base property and respective grazing rights if the seller is willing. The act withdraws the preserve lands from new mineral entry under the mining laws, although claims with existing valid rights can be exploited subject to the Mining in the Parks Act. These claims cannot be patented for surface rights; in other words, claim holders cannot buy the surface land over their mineral claims.[43]

Utility rights-of-way receive in-depth treatment in the act, basically permitting existing pipelines and transmission corridors and allowing utilities to upgrade pipelines within the existing rights-of-way. The act permits military flyovers throughout the CDPA lands, including low-level and sonic overflights. Two research establishments, the Granite Mountains Natural Reserve and the Soda Springs Desert Study Center, located within the preserve boundaries, remain the properties of the University of California and California State University, respectively.

The act limits the secretary of the interior's land acquisition powers. State lands within the preserve boundaries and lands owned by the Catellus Company, a real estate subsidiary of Santa Fe Pacific Railroad, can be acquired by donation or exchange for other surplus federal lands. The park service may acquire private land only from a willing seller, unless the secretary determines that a use or proposed use will create a threat to the preserve. Property owners are assured that "the construction, modification, repair, improvement, or replacement of a single-family residence shall not be determined to be detrimental to the integrity of the preserve." No in-holdings can be subject to federal regulations resulting from the act, and in-holdings "may be used to the extent allowed by applicable law." Private property owners are also guaranteed reasonable access to their lands. The previously described exclusion of private properties within the Lanfair settlement area is not addressed in the wording of the legislation; instead, it appears in an attached map.

The CDPA designates an enormous amount of wilderness on both BLM lands and park service lands—7.7 million acres total. Within the MNP, the act designated seventeen different wilderness areas, totaling 695,200 acres, or fully 49 percent of the preserve. The Wilderness Act of 1964 defines such areas as usually at least five thousand acres of "undeveloped Federal land retaining its primeval character and influence, without permanent improvements or human habitations." All wilderness areas, regardless of the managing agency, must be managed to retain their wilderness character, with no roads, no use of motorized vehicles, and no structures or installations. Grazing and mining are permitted in wilderness areas, but are subject to regulations minimizing vehicular ingress and egress from the sites.[44]

Funding authorization covers the whole CDPA area, including both BLM and NPS lands. Congress authorized a total of $300 million from 1995 to 1999 for land acquisition and $36 million for administration and construction over and above current appropriations. While these authorizations appear quite generous, authorizing appropriations in a bill is no guarantee of actual dollars being budgeted in the annual federal appropriations bills.

Planning the Mojave—The NPS's General Management Plan

With this legislative history and mission in place, the National Park Service is creating a general management plan for the Mojave National Preserve. According to the terms of the legislation, a fifteen-member advisory council was appointed by the secretary of the interior to cooperate in developing the plan.[45]

The park service has a regular pattern of preparation of general management plans (GMPS), because these are prepared for each unit in the park system. Typically, early in the process the NPS will publicize several management options for the most critical resource decisions in the plan, and elicit public comment on the alternatives. The park service then decides which options to pursue, and these decisions, including the alternatives that have been evaluated but not selected, are contained within the draft GMP. The GMP usually includes the following sections:

- Statement for Management—a presentation of the goals of the unit;
- Resources Management Plan—the strategy for protection, preservation, and perpetuation of the natural and cultural resources
- Visitor Use Plan—interpretation, visitor safety and use, and the means of supplying visitor information
- General Development Plan—the development (i.e., infrastructure and buildings) needed to accomplish the above goals
- Draft Environmental Statement, if required by the National Environmental Protection Act

After a period of thirty to ninety days designed to allow for public comment on the draft GMP, the park service considers the comments it has received, revises the draft, and publishes the final general management plan.[46] For the MNP, the final plan consists of minor amendments to the revised draft GMP.

It is worth quoting the cover letter of the revised draft GMP at some length to provide a sense of the compromises the park service had to achieve in creating their preferred alternative:

The proposed action envisions Mojave National Preserve as a natural environment and a cultural landscape, . . . where the protection of native desert ecosystems and processes is assured for future generations. The protection and perpetuation of native species in a self-sustaining environment is a primary long-term goal. The proposal seeks to manage the Preserve to perpetuate the sense of discovery, solitude, and adventure that currently exists. This means minimizing development inside the Preserve, including the proliferation of signs, new campgrounds, and interpretive exhibits. The National Park Service would look to adjacent communities to provide most support services (food, gas, and lodging) for visitors. The proposal also seeks to provide the public, consistent with the NPS mission, with maximum opportunities for roadside camping, backcountry camping and access to the Preserve via existing roads. The proposal would seek funding for the complete historic restoration of the Kelso Depot and its use as a museum and interpretive facility.

For this National Park Service unit, a balance must be struck between the NPS mission of resource preservation and other mandates from Congress, such as maintaining grazing, hunting, and mining under NPS regulations, and continuing the existence of major utility corridors. The proposal would maintain the ability of landowners in Mojave to maintain their current way of life, while also seeking funding to purchase property from willing sellers where proposed uses conflict with the primary mission of preserving resources. Nearly 230,000 acres within the preserve were in nonfederal ownership until the recent requisition of 80,706 acres of Catellus lands.[47]

The management team at the MNP has made significant decisions, and progress toward those decisions, in the years since the preserve's designation. One key activity has been to reduce the cattle grazing within the preserve. The NPS's nonprofit partner, the National Park Foundation (NPF), purchased three ranches—the Granite Mountain Ranch, the Kessler Springs Ranch, and the OX Ranch—from one local family, plus a fourth grazing allotment at Crescent Peaks. With these ranches come the grazing and water rights, which were permanently retired when the NPF donated the land and the rights to the park service.[48] As a result, grazing in the preserve has been reduced by 65 percent.[49] For those still grazing cattle in the preserve, restrictions have been put in place to respond to concerns that the cattle compete for forage with the desert tortoise, federally listed as threatened. During key spring grazing periods, cattle may be kept out of critical tortoise habitat unless the area has certain levels of available annual plants. Additionally, ranchers will not generally be able to use trucks to get to cattle grazing in wilderness areas, and instead will have to walk or horse-back ride in.[50] In general, protections for the desert tortoise are significant, but largely achieved through site-specific projects to protect its habitat.

Another of the most visible activities by the NPS has been the burro roundup. As further described in later chapters, feral burros are quite a problem for the desert ecology and have a high reproductive rate. At the same time, they have a certain level of support from animal rights groups, so that simply killing them is not politically possible. In a compromise solution, the MNP rounded up all the burros it could find on preserve lands and had them moved to specific wild burro facilities. The first roundup was held in 2001, and be-- cause the burros are likely to move back into the preserve from neighboring BLM lands, regular roundups will be required.[51]

Kelso Depot is on its way to becoming the primary visitor center for the preserve as the NPS rehabilitates this historic structure. Other than this, for visitors, much will not change–roadside camping remains permitted, and the existing improved sites will stay in operation. The Mojave Trail will remain open for four-wheel drivers, but some road closures were enacted in response to wilderness designation. Some rock climbing will continue, but no new anchors will be permitted. Hunting and trapping continue without much change, except that the rabbit season is shortened to reduce hunter-days during key tortoise periods. However, the large amount of the preserve that is designated as wilderness, and the restrictive access rules of wilderness, will continue to have a limiting impact on vehicle-based recreation to some of the traditional sites in the preserve.[52]

Ecosystem Planning for the California Desert Region

The MNP planning process was complicated, and perhaps strengthened, by the decision of the Department of the Interior to initiate an ecosystem planning effort for the whole of the California desert. In 1991 the major federal and state land management agencies in California signed an agreement called the "Memorandum of Understanding: California's Coordinated Regional Strategy to Conserve Biological Diversity" (the Agreement on Biological Diversity). With this document, the agencies endorsed moving from the protection of individual species and sites to protecting and managing ecosystems and biotic communities. The document's goal was to officially institute a policy of coordination among agencies and emphasize regionwide approaches to regional issues.[53]

The Agreement on Biological Diversity established a council made up of executives from the major land agencies to "set statewide goals for the protection of biological diversity, recommend consistent statewide standards and guidelines, encourage cooperative projects and sharing of resources, and cooperate in . . . program areas."[54] Regional participation is through "bioregional councils," with membership from the field staff of the involved agencies plus county governments and local environmental and industry groups. These bioregional councils are to develop regional memoranda of understanding that align with the goals of the Agreement on Biological Diversity. At the local level, the agreement suggests that the bioregional councils should support the development of watershed and landscape associations made up of interested citizens and interest groups. Such was the intent in 1991.

With the passage of the CDPA in 1994, the agencies felt it was necessary to prepare and sign a "Statement of Intent by Federal and State Agencies to Participate in the Implementation of the California Desert Protection Act." In this one-page document, the principal federal and state agencies indicate their support for ecosystem management, shared data collection and assessment, and bioregional planning and management of the California desert area, and their intent to "participate to the fullest extent practicable in the implementation of the California Desert Protection Act."[55] That such a statement was necessary points to both the power of an independent civil service and to the interagency strife created by the CDPA legislation.

On December 7, 1994, Secretary of the Interior Bruce Babbitt designated the entire California Desert Conservation Area a "laboratory" under the National Performance Review, a part of former Vice President Albert Gore's Reinventing Government initiative. The Desert Conservation Area, which stretches across much of southeastern California, is a test of interagency cooperation in achieving ecosystem planning and management, as was set forth in Babbitt's and Gore's policy goals.[56] The desert-region state and federal land management agencies formed the Desert Managers Group (DMG) to "deal with desert-wide operational issues in a collaborative forum."[57] Along with the agencies who signed the Statement of Intent, the DMG includes participation by Department of Defense military installation managers, who bring to the group funding, technical expertise, and equipment not generally available to the Department of the Interior, as well as a pressing interest in managing endangered species and land protection.[58] The DMG also includes the six southern California counties that are part of the Desert Conservation Area. The MNP is located in the combined Eastern and Northern Mojave Desert bioregion planning area, one of seven identified ecosystems in the planning effort. The Mojave preserve staff directed the overall ecosystem planning effort for the Eastern and Northern Mojave Desert bioregion.[59]

Despite the presumably good intentions of this effort, the result was frustration. As described in a sentence written by NPS staff for the website of the ecosystem planning effort: "After about two and a half years of scoping, public meetings, data gathering, interagency meetings and staff work on alternatives, the Bureau of Land Management decided to pursue preparation of their plan amendment as a stand-alone document. The National Park Service proceeded to extract relevant information from the combined draft environmental impact statement that was being prepared, and began assembling separate draft environmental impact statements for each park unit" (i.e. Joshua Tree National Park and Mojave National Preserve).[60]

Summary

The Bureau of Land Management began requesting authority to more closely manage the desert as long ago as 1968. Based on interviews for this study and written materials, it seems clear that the BLM acted from a genuine concern for the unique environment, as well as frustration with the agency's limited management powers and a desire to increase the professional stature of the organization. They were finally able to implement that concern with the development of the 1980 Plan. This was the agency's, and perhaps the federal government's, first true ecosystem management plan, covering millions of acres, providing for both human use and environmental protection, and created with both science and public participation. When it was time for the BLM to implement the plan, times had changed. The Reagan/Bush administration, with its philosophy of economic development over environmental protection, was in power, and secretaries of the interior were determined to follow that direction. The amendments to the plan that ensued weakened protections and increased development opportunities—an appropriate response to the directions that no doubt flowed from above.

As shown in later chapters, these amendments had the effect of breaking the trust of the environmental community, and provided an impetus for removing the land from the control of the BLM, an agency that environmentalists have never trusted. The 1994 bill, as enacted, provides that most of the activities that occurred previously in the national scenic area continue in the preserve. Accordingly, existing mining claims can be exploited, and hunting, trapping, and grazing continue, albeit somewhat abated. It is under this in effect multiple-use mandate that the National Park Service must manage the Mojave.

CHAPTER 3

Legislating and Designating the Preserve

A myth endures that the park service alone preserves the national parks. That is its aspiration, but not the reality.

If one reads the journals of the citizen conservation organizations, one may conclude that they preserve the parks. That is their objective, but not the reality.

There are even some romanticists who suggest that the park service and the citizen conservation organizations, together, preserve the parks. That, certainly, is their endeavor, but not the reality.

The reality is that the people through their elected representatives in the Congress preserve the parks—or destroy them.

—GEORGE B. HARTZOG, *Battling for the National Parks*

This chapter entails a narrative account of the designation of the Mojave Desert as a national preserve—who did what, when, and to the extent that they have reported it, why. I compare that to the typical park designation process. The MNP fight proves to be reasonably representative of the legislative and political process for park designations in general, which suggests that these findings may be generalized to other park debates. This chapter describes central questions in the debate regarding whether the Mojave should move to National Park Service jurisdiction, and if so, whether it would become a park or a preserve. The next chapter discusses the more specific questions of whether hunting, mining, and ranching would continue in the new park service unit.

The Mojave designation account derives primarily from a set of interviews with major participants in the drama, most of whom work in or near Washington, D.C. To protect my sources, in this chapter I use aliases unless credit is clearly possible without harm or bias to the source. The story of the legislation's origins and process is an amalgam of the reports of my various sources, and again to protect them I do not cite them directly unless it is clearly necessary to support my findings. By and large, this story is theirs. Those involved recognized one another and while they often disagreed in their evaluation of events and policies—this is, after all, an account of conflict—they did not differ significantly in their understanding of the plot, and even shared uncertainties. This perhaps is not surprising, in that the Washington lobbyists form a long-term community; the most important organizations, if not the individuals, work with and against each other on many issues. They have in common a past, present, and future, and they form in effect a discourse community with a shared understanding of the goals and means of legislation.[1] For the MNP debate, the narrative focuses on events in the 103d Congress, the Congress in which the legislation was finally enacted, but brief trips into the longer history of the grass-roots organizing for the legislation are necessary.

Typical Park Designation Processes

A park designation must start with a person with a dream, someone who looks out across a land and cares for it so much that he or she cannot bear to see it change through human development. But to go from the dream to the reality is a long and complicated process. Someone must have sufficient political power and savvy to build a constituency for that designation, do the hard work of determining appropriate initial boundaries and management goals, secure the interest and support of elected representatives, and, often, initially craft the legislation.

Traditionally, some of the primary instigators for land preservation have been among our country's social and political elite, people able to provide both land and funds to create many of our national parks.[2] Presidents such as Theodore Roosevelt and John F. Kennedy have been instrumental in creating new park lands. Under very activist directors such as Stephen T. Mather and George B. Hartzog Jr., the park service was an advocate for new units, particularly when it meant appropriating land from another federal unit, such as the Forest Service. In the 1970s, the secretary of the interior, and by reflection the NPS, was required to develop a "park of the month" list, culminating each year in a list of twelve potential additions to the national park system. The Reagan/Watt administration halted this practice, because it generally opposed such additions.[3] Greenline-type parks developed through public/private partnerships did, however, gain the support of the Reagan/Bush administrations,

as those parks coincided with the administration's political philosophy.[4] In recent years, the instigator for park proposals has often been a preservationist
group such as the Sierra Club, the Wilderness Society, and others.

Historically, state representatives were generally unconcerned about preserving federal land; so long as the land was "worthless" and did not reduce
economic development potential, they did not oppose park designation. Beginning with the 1960s,[5] however, the park process became much more politi-
cized as legislators turned to parks as a source of local benefits for their constituents, and henceforth became potent advocates for particular parks.[6] In recent years, the NPS's ability to either seek out desirable new additions or fight
off inappropriate proposals appears to have weakened, while congressional
initiative has grown. As a result, political considerations rather than system
planning or ecological representativeness increasingly determine new additions to the park system.[7]

Not surprisingly, then, substantial politicking is involved in obtaining approval for any proposed park. The primary participants are the home-state senators and representatives, preservation and environmental interest groups, the
secretary of the interior, the NPS (which usually, but not always, falls into line
with the interior secretary), development interests and industry groups (if the
land has any development potential at all), and the president (if he has any
particular interest for or against the park). Local interests are generally expressed through elected representatives or senators, although it is usual for a
bill's sponsors and opponents to be sure that at least some constituents attend
and testify at hearings so as to evince local support or opposition beyond that
of the elected representative(s). Other government departments may be involved, including the Forest Service and Bureau of Land Management, particularly when the land is being transferred from them to the park service (and
they are often in opposition).[8]

The participants with the most consistent positions in park designation debates seem to be the preservationist groups; not surprisingly, they generally believe the more preserved land, the better, and so they will usually support park
designation. Occasionally, however, a park proposal is so clearly politically
motivated and an area so undeserving that the National Parks and Conservation Association and other environmental groups will actively oppose the proposal.[9] Industry groups tend to be split; natural resource extractors and the like
are usually concerned to minimize "lock up" of land;[10] the tourism lobby usually favors federal designation.

The position of local interests varies. We can understand this in terms of the Old West / New West split. Where local economies and lifestyles are dependent (or are perceived to be so) on resource extraction, and where individual culture remains Old West, local interests are likely to be anti-designation.[11] Where local economies are either tourism dependent or more service and manufacturing based, and where the culture has become more like the New West, local interest is likely to be pro-park.[12] This is, of course, a generalization, and local interest in any area is likely to be split, with people weighing both their pocketbooks and other values in their decisions, such as a desire to preserve open space[13] or a desire to prevent increased bureaucratic control. Because national park designations are locally high-profile events and generally well covered in local media, most congressional representatives will fall in line with the general weight of local opinion in supporting or opposing legislation.[14] Yet, because senators are elected statewide, they may not be as responsive to local desires; instead, they may adopt the position of other state constituencies, such as their urban voters. While this idea has been best developed for the western region of the United States, the general concept is applicable nation-wide.

For the Department of the Interior, a major consideration is under whose jurisdiction the land was before; if it is a transfer of land from another interior agency, internal politics can become quite divisive, as was the case in the Mojave. Much of the direction stems from the White House, and presidential support or opposition can be crucial. Because the process is political, it is not that uncommon that the NPS must administer a new park that it considered not particularly desirable.[15] Even so, to speak of the NPS as having *a* position is a simplification, since individuals within the park service have their own sense of the appropriateness of a new unit. Hence, internal campaigning goes on while the service's power elite determine what the official institutional position will be—if the NPS chooses to take one.[16]

Three different sorts of factors go into the deliberations over whether the NPS will officially support a designation. The first is the basic fitness of the park—how well does the park fit into the selection criteria, including how well it fits into the general goals of the Department of the Interior and the NPS, how difficult it will be to purchase needed private land, and the complexity of administering the park. A second factor will be the ever-present desire to expand the importance of the park service, with more parks being better. Offsetting this is the reality of the appropriations process. Park designation is not directly

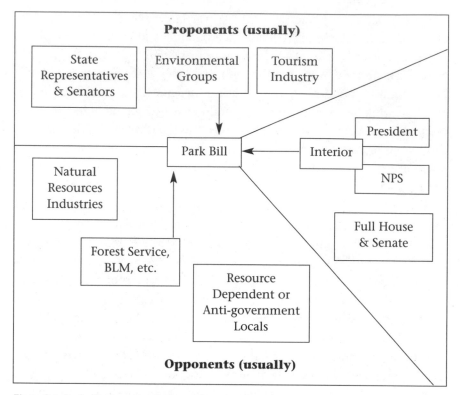

Figure 3.1: Parks Designation Interest Groups

tied to appropriation of funds; in fact, appropriations have not been sufficient to keep up with acquisitions of new land for designated parks.[17] Each new park competes with all old parks for appropriations, so adding a new park usually means spreading already-thin current resources. All of these concerns seem to have been in play during the Mojave designation.

While the participants and interest groups involved in the initial effort to get a site declared part of the park system have varied across time, the basic legislative process itself usually is the same. Someone, often either the director of the NPS, the president, or a home-state congressional representative, brings a bill before the Parks and Recreation Subcommittee of the House Interior and Insular Affairs Committee, the subcommittee and committee that have jurisdiction over most of the activities of the NPS. The park bill is first considered in the subcommittee, which takes testimony from supporters and opponents of the bill. After the hearings, the subcommittee reviews the bill, considers

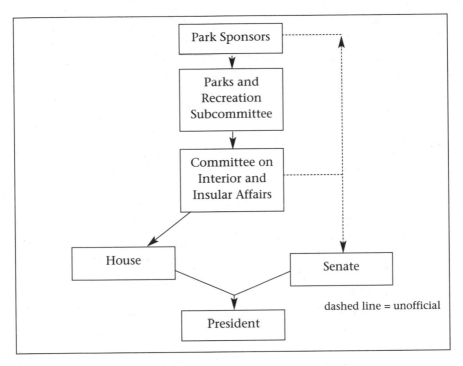

Figure 3.2: Movement of a Park Bill

amendments and revisions, and then marks up the bill with its changes. The subcommittee then reports to the full Committee on Interior and Insular Affairs, which takes a vote on whether to approve it for consideration by the House. Usually only bills approved by the full committee may be considered by the House.[18] Powerful congressional representatives can, however, bypass this process.[19]

The House then votes on the bill. At some point in the process, the bill's sponsors will request that an associate in the Senate sponsor a similar bill. If both Senate and House bills pass but are different, a subcommittee will meet to work out the differences, and if a compromise is reached, the final bill is passed on to the president for signature or veto. Once the president has signed the bill, the site is officially part of the national park system. The Senate process is in outline not much different from that in the House.

In the case of the California Desert Protection Act, a handful of individuals loosely associated with the Sierra Club did much of the initial organizing work. Later, other environmentalist groups stepped in with their support. Unlike many park proposals, however, local representatives strongly opposed the designation. The proponents had to find support from senators, who as representatives of the whole state also represent urban interests. It was in the Senate that the CDPA was first raised and the House followed, because the strongest political support for the CDPA was with a senator.

Legislating the Mojave National Preserve

Local Origins of the CDPA

The idea of a desert bill goes back as far as the 1950s, when a group called the Desert Protection Council began to work to raise public awareness of the values of the desert. This council ran tour trips, trying to show people that the desert was not just a dumping ground and wasteland, but rather a place of beauty and ecological importance. It also sought to recruit and train leaders for the future of environmental activism in the area. The Southern California Sierra Club began to take an interest, and started drafting wilderness maps as early as the mid-1970s. Serious Sierra Club efforts on the desert, however, had to wait for Congress to pass the California Wilderness Bill, which dealt with Forest Service lands. That occurred in 1984.

In the meantime, Barstow resident Peter Burk began a campaign to make the Mojave area a national park. He developed a slide show and a fact sheet, taking these on the road and presenting them to various Barstow area groups such as the Chamber of Commerce, the Rotary, the Kiwanis, and garden clubs. One group who viewed the show was the local chapter of the Sierra Club, which passed a resolution supporting the park, and created a task force of which Burk was chair. In 1976 Burk sent a copy of the proposal to Congresswoman Shirley Pettis, who passed it on to the National Park Service for evaluation. The Sierra Club chapter was advised by Pettis and later by Senator Alan Cranston that they should first work within the 1980 California Desert Conservation Area planning process being undertaken by the BLM, and so national-level organizing went into a hiatus. Local organizing continued, with Burk promoting the new park to other Southern California environmental groups and forming the Citizens for Mojave National Park.[20] Clearly, at least some environmentalists never had much trust in the BLM, and participation in the 1980 planning process may have been in less-than-full faith.

Throughout the California Desert Protection Act process, the Southern Cal-

Peter Burk is a tall, lanky resident of a small ranch house in Barstow, California. He is a high school librarian, passionate about big ideas and about citizen activism. He and his wife moved to Barstow to escape the sprawl and congestion of Los Angeles. He has been described as the "father" of the Mojave National Preserve, and worked on the issue since 1976. To hear him tell the story, "I started it on July 4 in 1976, when my wife Joyce and I took a walk around the block like we do most nights, and we were thinking about the bicentennial. And I used to say that there are only two great ideas that America has given the world: the idea of the national park and the national constitution. So we started the idea [of the Mojave National Park]."

ifornia chapters of the Sierra Club provided the grassroots support and organizing for the overall bill. Three activist individuals—Judy Anderson, Jim Dodson, and Elden Hughes—get particular credit as leaders on the bill. Anderson, for instance, began working on the bill in 1980. Through their efforts and the leadership of other environmental organizations, a larger coalition for the bill was created that included many Southern California environmental groups as well as the local Sierra Club activists.

Local pro-park activists between 1982 and 1994 continued the hard work of grassroots organizing. They presented slide shows to public groups, attended field hearings and lobbied in Washington for the bill, prepared and distributed newsletters detailing their progress and the goal of a Mojave National Park, took important political people for tours of the area, and garnered resolutions of support from cities and counties. Urban areas were the first to express support. One example of the extent of effort and skill that went into the process is the "picture books" developed by Elden Hughes. His books of photographs detailing the virtues of each proposed wilderness area were more persuasive than words alone, and generated support among key legislators.

Washington-based Participants and the Coalitions

While local activists were important in generating the initial energy for the CDPA, much of the action occurred in Washington, D.C. A wide variety of lobbying organizations were involved both for and against the legislation. The CDPA coalitions basically split into two groups, for and against the bill. The pro-

Judy Anderson was one of the three key citizen activitists working on the CDPA as a whole, along with Elden Hughes and Jim Dodson. She lives in a townhouse complex in the suburbs of Los Angeles, and teaches high school math. She moves slowly, talks slowly, but is forceful and clear and hospitable. She is a long-time activist with the Sierra Club, and worked as a volunteer on variousprojects before the CDPA. When the desert protection bill came along, she saw an important and valuable project that she could make her own, take control of, and bring to reality. She worked on everything from developing grassroots support to defining the boundaries for wilderness areas in the final legislation. That work took longer than she ever expected—fourteen years, altogether.

CDPA camp was generally strongly united, and shared a commitment to having the Mojave be a national park. Opponents to the CDPA were less united, as each opposed the bill for individual reasons. As a result, the opponents broke into factions.

The Wise Use Movement (WUM) was apparently not involved at the Washington level. When asked, all of the Washington-based park opponents denied that they worked with the WUM closely, although they acknowledged occasional contact. Even the staffer to Congressman Jerry Lewis did not claim the WUM as a supporter. He did, however, draw a link between the Wise Use Movement and the CDPA, declaring that the CDPA was an example of Clinton's "War on the West," and that opposition to it had a strong relationship to the Sagebrush Rebellion and other "Western independence movements." The WUM was active locally, however. WUM leader Chuck Cushman paid periodic visits to the desert area, which were reported to have first sparked and then inspired the opposition to the park.[21]

Legislative Origins

The first attempt at legislation goes back to 1976 when Senator George Brown (D-Calif.) put forward a bill without expectation of passage or even significant action on it.[22] The mantle was taken up by Senator Alan Cranston (D-Calif.), who was convinced of the importance of the bill.[23] Cranston, however, faced two immovable roadblocks—first Republican Senator Pete Wilson, then Republican Senator John Seymour. Without support of both California

Table 3.1 *Active Groups and Their Acronyms*

Organization	Organizational Acronym
National Audubon Society	Audubon
Bureau of Land Management	BLM
California Department of Fish and Wildlife	CFW
Department of Interior	DOI
International Association of Fish and Wildlife Agencies	IAFWA
National Cattlemen's Association	NCA
National Mining Association	NMA
National Park Service	NPS
National Parks and Conservation Association	NPCA
National Rifle Association	NRA
Sierra Club	n/a
Wilderness Society	n/a
Wildlife Legislative Fund	WLF

senators, the CDPA experienced the long, lingering limbo of bills that have been introduced but clearly lack the support necessary for passage.

Important groundwork for the bill was laid in this period prior to the 103rd Congress. The BLM and the NPS conducted resource evaluations as described in Chapter 2, both of which were moderately favorable about the Mojave. In 1987, the NPS's Western Regional Director Howard Chapman testified to Congress that the Mojave met the criteria for inclusion in the park system.[24] Meanwhile, CDPA proponents drew, redrew, and drew again maps and boundaries to eliminate conflicting land uses and respond to Capitol Hill staffers' concerns. The longevity of the CDPA effort created some presentment of legitimacy for the bill. As Henry M. put it, "it had been around, it had been debated, we had made accommodations." The issue of accommodations is a contentious one, to which we will return.

The Mojave specifically was the focus for debate throughout the CDPA designation process. As described by one environmental lobbyist, "[The Mojave] served as the lightning rod to draw all of the fire, so that while folks were fighting over the Mojave . . . [the rest of the bill] went through almost without a peep. All of the fire gathered around the Mojave. If you will, it was the symbol of the bill . . . So it took pressure off of everything else. But as a result it paid a price. One of the prices is that it doesn't get to be a national park, which it should have been."[25] CDPA opponents focused on the Mojave because, as one opponent noted, "[it] was the only thing we felt like we had any kind of a shot

Table 3.2 CDPA Coalitions and Legislative Leadership

Position	Political Representative	Lobbying Groups
Pro-CDPA	Senator Feinstein led in the Senate, supported by Senators Bennet Johnston and Barbara Boxer. In the House, Representatives Richard Lehman (D-Calif.), Mel Levine (D-Calif.), George Miller (D-Calif.), and Bruce Vento (D-Minn.) shared management of the bill.	Environmental Groups: Sierra Club as lead; Wilderness Society, NPCA as second tier; Audubon and others supportive. NPS and DOI under Clinton administration supportive.
Anti-CDPA	Representative Jerry Lewis (R-Calif.) led in the House, suppported by Representative Larry LaRocco (R-Calif.) and others (Hunter, McKeon, McCandless, and Thomas (R-Calif.) from the area. In the Senate, Senator Malcom Wallopp (R-Mont.) led for the opposition.	Industry/Interest Groups: Hunting (NRA; WLF; IAFWA; Congressional Sportsmen's Caucus) Mining (NMA) Grazing (NCA) Off-road vehicle (AMA) Local interests—California Desert Coalition as lead; other local groups in supporting roles.

at." Both Joshua Tree and Death Valley were already in NPS management, so the Mojave was the largest change.

For the Mojave to be a national park meant that there would be no hunting. Prior to the 103rd Congress, there were several attempts by representatives sensitive to the issues of pro-hunting groups to ensure that in the CDPA the

Henry M. is one of a strange breed, the beltway environmentalist. He wears a suit and tie, but badly, as if to show that the uniform is not the man, and has more facial hair than is the norm in the Washington, D.C., circles of power. Despite this unprepossessing appearance, his knowledge of how to get things done in Washington is apparent. He worked on the CDPA essentially full time from 1992 to 1994, lobbying Congress and generating grassroots support. He worked closely with the local Southern California activists, and speaks with affection of the entire team for that effort. It was, after all, a victory. When I met him in 1995, he had already moved on to the battle over Utah wilderness.

Fred F. works for a pro-hunting interest group. Fred grew up hunting and fishing in the South, and keeps quite a bit of the accent, giving him a pleasant down-home aspect and occasionally a colorful turn of phrase. He came to Washington directly after college as a political intern, and stayed as a lobbyist. He clearly takes pleasure in his status as Washington insider, enjoying discussing the importance of fat rolodexes, and the ways his and related organizations were able to quickly organize responses to environmentalist initiatives and manage the flows of information and power in the legislative process.

Mojave would be a national preserve which would allow hunting.[26] Senator Cranston and later Senator Feinstein accommodated many of the economic interests in the Mojave by realigning the boundaries to get mines and other existing uses out of the proposed park and by explicitly permitting continued grazing, military, and utility uses. But they continued to insist on national park status. As a result, while other interests were appeased, the hunting community was not. For opponents, the hunting issue also provided "the wedge we needed to divide our opposition and ensure that Park status for the Mojave could be defeated."[27]

1992 Elections

With the 1992 elections of Senators Dianne Feinstein and Barbara Boxer (D-Calif.), the CDPA prospects changed dramatically. Fred F. reported:

We had a completely different political environment in the 103rd [Congress], what with two new Senators from California, Boxer and Feinstein, singing from the same sheet of music on the CDPA. And that's what the traditional roadblock had been all along, you had a Republican and a Democrat who did not agree on the legislation. Traditionally in the Senate, if two Senators agree on a land issue in their state, other Senators are not very willing to interfere with that issue. I mean even though there were a lot of Western Senators who thought the CDPA was a bad bill, they were very hesitant to enter the fray when they had two Senators who agreed on the issue. That's Senatorial deference, is what they call that.

Feinstein was elected for a two-year term filling the seat of Senator John Seymour. As part of her election campaign, she pledged to do what it took to fi-

Kathy Lacey, Senator Feinstein's main staffer on the CDPA, became one of the most hated people in the Mojave preserve area. Local residents swear that Lacey never once visited the area, yet held the future for it in her hands. She was the gateway to the senator, and in local opinion, that gate was shut. A curious, and perhaps intended, outcome from this was that many people viewed the senator as a victim of her staffer, and felt that if only the senator knew the whole story, she would be on their side. Lacey is a long-time Washington insider, having served Senator Cranston as a lead staffer on the CDPA and other issues. Senator Feinstein does not allow her staff to be interviewed.

nally get the CDPA passed. The election promise became a priority item as soon as she arrived in Washington. With elections in just two years, she had little time to waste, as described by an environmental lobbyist: "This was an issue she would grab and she would solve. [She felt] this had been sitting, languishing, for so long, all this uncertainty, nobody knows what's going to happen with their land, and it's time for the uncertainty to end. If you elect me, we will finish this, and you will know one way or the other what is going to be happening to this land . . . You may or may not like the decision, but there will be a decision." Or, in the words of a park opponent, the Mojave was a "big green trophy" for Feinstein to take to her urban constituents in an election year.

Feinstein's reelection was a top priority for the Democratic Party. As a result, Democratic leadership took an intense interest in getting the senator her needed victory. The bill was debated for the whole session and not passed, until the last day of the Congress, at the last hour of the 103rd Congress. In the House, the leadership refused to let Congress go into recess until the bill had received a floor vote. Henry M. asks with understatement: "I mean, would George Mitchell have kept the Senate in an extra day to get this bill done, and made it known that he was going to keep them in until the Desert Bill was done . . . if Senator Feinstein wasn't up for reelection and her ability to deliver on this campaign promise wasn't important? I'll never know. But one would suspect that played a role in that decision."

Like most blessings, however, the conjunction of Feinstein's reelection with the passage of the CDPA carried its own curse. Republicans hoped to unseat Feinstein and replace her with Michael Huffington. If they could show that

Laura S. is not the usual sort of face associated with the National Rifle Association. Her idea of hunting involves horses and hounds and the rolling Virginia countryside. She is part of the Washington revolving door, having spent some time with the NRA early in her career, then moved over to the Department of the Interior and then back to the NRA for a "second tour of duty" as a lobbyist. Highly polished and well-groomed, she is a very effective public speaker. Her familiarity with being interviewed was so great she would pause mid-sentence when a tape needed to be changed, wait, and then restart without missing a word when the new tape was recording. She is a thoughtful, intelligent participant in the Washington corridors of power, and a careful interview respondent. The NRA's invovlement in the CDPA was so quiet, environmentalists could only see the shadow of their most politically powerful opponent at work. One environmentalist told me that if I found out how the NRA had worked this issue, to please let him know—the tone was joking, but the content was not.

Feinstein was ineffectual at achieving one of her main election promises, Huffington's case would gain credence. There was no one in the House of Representatives with a strong interest in getting the CDPA passed, and so it was there that the strongest challenges to the bill occurred. Early in the life of the bill, Representative Mel Levine (D-Calif.) provided leadership, but he had lost his seat by the time of the 103rd Congress. The task of spearheading the bill in the 103rd went mostly to subcommittee chairman George Miller.

Clearly, the passage of the bill was possible only because Congress was, for that brief term, majority Democratic. Minority Republicans such as Representative Lewis felt "steamrolled" by the process, as reported by one of his staffers. The NRA's spokesperson described it this way: "Their interest, [Representative] Jerry Lewis's interest, was to take down the entire bill, but he did not have the votes, because you know it was Democrat majority and they were hanging tight to what was now a party position. Secretary Babbitt, Democrat, weighed in in support of the bill, so the Republicans, especially the Republican members representing that area, were frozen out. I can tell you it would be a completely different story if the bill came in this [104th] Congress."

Pro-parkers had a different view of the Republican's position. An environmental lobbyist commented: "[Lewis] was critical of how the process worked and of how he and his fellow locals were ignored. But I think it's one of those things: you're given the opportunity to present testimony, you work with your colleagues; no matter how much access you're given to the process, if what you are asking for does not end up in the bill, then you're ignored, you're slighted. And I think it's more politics than anything else."

The timing of the Feinstein/Boxer election coincided with the election of the Clinton administration. The Clinton administration did not take a particularly strong leadership role in the 103rd Congress on this legislation. This might have been a strategic decision on the part of the administration in response to its difficulties with the Congress. As described by parks lobbyist Jack T., "For whatever reason, the administration never piped up on this. At times it was frustrating because it made us feel like we were flying blind, but my guess is there was good reason why they didn't, and they were probably asked by the Democrats on the Hill to stay the hell out of it."

Secretary of the Interior Babbitt's support for the Mojave is unclear. Opponents argued that Babbitt did not support the Mojave park designation until the president told him to support it as a party-line issue; proponents claim they never had any indication that Babbitt's support was lacking. Bill F., who worked for the park service in its desert parks, was an informal internal supporter of the CDPA. Now retired, his assessment of the position and politics of the DOI is worth quoting at length:

> The park service under the Bush administration officially opposed it [the CDPA], because that was the position of the Bush administration. The park service under the Clinton administration was officially in favor of it, because that was the position of the administration. But, during the Bush administration there were some park service people who were informally in favor of it, namely Howard Chapman, the former regional director in San Francisco . . . And the symmetry is, when the Clinton administration officially supported the bill and the park service officially supported the bill, there were some people in the park service who were unofficially still against it.
>
> In fact there was kind of a battle for the heart and mind of the secretary in April of 1993, when the new administration came in. There were some people, primarily in the BLM, who tried to convince the secretary to oppose Senator Feinstein's proposal, at least insofar as the Mojave National Preserve went. And there were tremendous rumors and discussions that the park service leadership at

Table 3.3 Pragmatists and Staunch Defenders

Pragmatists		Staunch Defenders
Accommodators	Hunters	
Various mining corporations	Wildlife Legislative Fund	California Desert Coalition
American Motorcycle Association	National Rifle Association	Representative Jerry Lewis
National Cattlemen's Association	California Department of Fish and Widlife	Various local user groups
	Congressional Sportsmen's Caucus	
	International Association of Fish and Wildlife Agencies	

that time . . . would have been quite comfortable if the Mojave had not been created.

There were some park service people who probably would have loved the secretary not to endorse the Mojave portion of the bill . . . But that was all informal, there was no formal [opposition]. What finally happened in late April of 1993 was Secretary Babbitt made up his mind and decided to endorse Senator Feinstein's proposal. And therefore the [NPS] administration became a supporter of Senator Feinstein's CDPA.

This account suggests that the statements of both opponents and proponents about Babbitt's position are true, and that his support changed over time. It also reveals, however, that the NPS's leadership was never strongly committed to the merits of adding the Mojave to the national park system.[28]

Despite a lack of NPS enthusiasm, the change in administration was crucial to the role played by the Department of the Interior. One of the main antagonists to the CDPA had been the California director of the BLM, Ed Hastey. As explained by one environmentalist, "Ed Hastey . . . has been openly hostile to this whole thing [the CDPA] for a long time, and for many years had an administration that backed him. When the Clinton administration came in, all of a sudden they supported the bill, and now Ed sort of lost his platform, and credibility in terms of being able to publicly oppose it; he did not like that." Hastey was, by all accounts, a powerful figure in the Interior Department, and with his silence on the issue, another roadblock to designation fell.[29]

After the 1992 election, with the increased likelihood of enacting some sort of CDPA, opponents split into two camps—those who would "negotiate the size

of the truck which was about to run [them] over," and those who would continue in "kill mode." Let us call these the Pragmatists and the Staunch Defenders. The Pragmatists can be further divided into two groups. One group included the various interests who basically went their own ways, negotiating
individually with Senator Feinstein and her staff to generate reasonably acceptable accommodations (Accommodators). The other one consisted of those
who worked together with one goal in mind—securing national preserve designation rather than national park designation for the Mojave. The primary
characteristic this latter group shares is a desire for maintaining hunting in the
area, for their own individual reasons; I call them the Hunters.

Accommodating the Accommodators

Some accommodations were fairly easy for Feinstein to make. Early in the
CDPA history, utility rights-of-way were assured for the Southern California
power companies, and military flyovers were granted to the Department of
Defense. Many of the most valuable mining claims were located at preserve
boundaries, and those companies were appeased through boundary changes
excluding their sites. Other groups were more difficult. Perhaps the most vocal
of the Accommodators was the American Motorcycle Association, who was finally slightly appeased by boundary changes that removed some favorite trails
from wilderness.

One of the early issues to surface was the continuation of grazing in the Mojave and the Death Valley addition. The original text of the bill allowed current grazing practices to continue for the next twenty-five years, at which time
all grazing would cease.[30] Local ranchers' groups, assisted by local elected officials, reached out to Feinstein to remove the time limit so that ranching could
continue indefinitely. As described by grazing lobbyist Mike B., "The High
Desert Cattlemen's Association and the California Cattlemen's Association
asked her to come out and see what they were doing there, give her a sense of
the historic ranching practices in that area, and I think she was persuaded by
that . . . She did a helicopter over-flight of the area to see how much we were
talking about, which is not a great deal of ranching out there, and was persuaded that it would be important to grandfather that in.[31] And we were able
to get that . . . And you know it was very important to the passage, I think. And
I think the senator understood that."

Describing the same event, Henry M. credits the change primarily to Feinstein's reluctance to be seen as taking away a right or privilege any of her con-

stituents had enjoyed. He explains it this way: "Senator Feinstein [went] out to the desert the weekend after [the bill] had passed the Senate committee, sat down with [names some ranchers], and essentially got the American cowboy pitch. And I mean it's legitimate. 'We've been here, we've raised these cattle, our kids take the school bus fifty miles to school, it's seventy-five miles to the nearest grocery store.' So she . . . bought in on not taking away from these people what they've been doing for a long time." The result is that the legislation specifically permits grazing to continue in perpetuity.

The picture presented above is one of Senator Feinstein actively seeking or at a minimum accepting the compromises necessary to quiet opposition to the bill. Henry M. indicated that there had been some two hundred changes to the legislation since its original introduction in 1986. Three different environmental lobbyist reported they believed that Feinstein accommodated a great deal, perhaps too much, while acknowledging the political necessity of most of the compromises. Anti-park interests have a different memory, largely one of Feinstein as insulated by her staff and unresponsive to their claims. Some of the Accommodators issued letters of support for the bill, while some simply silenced themselves on the issue. Given how close the final vote was, it seems likely that these accommodations were necessary for any bill to pass.

The Hunting Fight—A Park or a Preserve?

While the Accommodators worked individually to secure the interests of their constituents, the Hunters came together early in the 103rd Congress to develop a coordinated strategy to get the Mojave designated as a preserve. Of particular interest is that this strategic session included staffers from several powerful senators and representatives. This is described by one Hunter lobbyist:

> You were asking about how we got to preserve designation. We had a meeting . . .
> back on May 5, 1993, and we invited people from the House Natural Resource Committee, the Congressional Sportsmen's Foundation [Caucus], the NRA, various senators on the Hill, the Safari Club International, a representative from the Energy and Natural Resources Committee in the Senate (two of them), somebody from the International Association of Fish and Wildlife Agencies, somebody from Senator Shelby's office, somebody from Senator Rakowsky's office, and then folks here . . .
>
> And I think that was the point in time when we decided the national preserve designation was our best bet. We were negotiating the size of the truck that was about to run us over . . . We had to dilute this down to something we could live with.

The Hunters' first move was an amendment sponsored by Ron Marlenee (R-Mont.) to change the Mojave from national park to national preserve. This amendment failed in the Senate Energy and Natural Resources Committee (ENRC) in a party-line vote. The CDPA thus got out of the ENRC with the Mojave intact as a national park. It had been "worked tightly," with few amendments allowed into the bill. Credit for that management goes to Senators Feinstein and Johnston.

The question then for the Hunters was whether to attempt another amendment in the full Senate vote, or whether to let the bill pass the Senate as is and go for national preserve designation in the House, where hunting support was greater (or leadership less strong). In Fred F.'s words: "In contemplating trying to attach it [the preserve-designation amendment] on the floor, we just realized that . . . if it went to the floor and we didn't get the votes . . . we might end up losing there. And if we could attach it successfully in the House, then you've got a no vote in committee and a no vote on the Senate floor, and in a conference situation, when you have two bills go to conference, that can only hurt you. So we decided to cut our losses in the Senate, let the bill go through the Senate, and we'll take a bite out of this apple in the House." The CDPA passed the Senate on April 13, 1994 by 69 to 29, with the Mojave National Park intact.

The House Resources Committee began consideration of the CDPA in the spring of 1994, bypassing initial consideration by the subcommittee. Representative Larry LaRocco introduced an amendment that would again have changed the Mojave to a national preserve; that too failed.[32] Fred F. notes: "We lost—again, politics, heavy-handed politics on the part of the chairman, George Miller. He was twisting arms on both sides of the aisle, and we lost . . . which was a pretty embarrassing defeat for us."

The strength of the management given by Miller cut both ways, however, creating some resentment over "excessive" pressure. The House Resources Committee reported the CDPA out with the Mojave National Park intact. The preserve designation battle was, however, far from over; in the House, local representatives who adamantly opposed the bill would have much more impact. The full House began consideration of the bill in July.[33] Another preserve amendment was offered on the floor of the House, and eventually passed 298 to 128,[34] in what a hunting lobbyist described as an "overwhelming victory."

Because the House's CDPA included the Mojave as a preserve while the Senate's bill designated the Mojave a national park, the final designation would have to be worked out in conference. As pro-park Henry M. explains: "Once we lost [the LaRocco-Lewis amendment making the Mojave a preserve] I knew it was over, because in conference in the Senate they weren't going to fight that; you've got too much pro-hunting sentiment in the Senate to hold."

While the vote to allow hunting in the Mojave was surely a demonstration of the continued strength of hunting interests in both the House and Senate, it was confounded with more general issues of the NRA. As Henry M. describes the situation:

> We had unfortunate circumstance[s] [regarding] why we lost on the hunting issue in the Mojave, not once, but twice—in 1991 and then again in 1994. It was really for very similar reasons. We had the bad luck to come on the heels of a very major gun bill. In 1991 the California Desert bill was up on the floor of the Senate . . . within twenty-four or forty-eight hours of the Brady bill [a controversial gun control law]. Folks who had gone against the NRA on that and then were trembling in their space boots didn't want to do it twice in a row . . . In the 103rd Congress, we were not as close on the heels, but still close enough, to the assault weapons ban, another big gun vote, same dynamic. What you had is a situation where you've got a bunch of members very nervous, they had just voted against the NRA on their biggest issue, and bam, here is another one, what am I going to do? And so, they go against you.

Or, in the words one of Representative Lewis's staff: "The LaRocco-Lewis amendment vote was a freebie to many members who went south on the NRA in a key vote earlier in the year. That clearly helped the final outcome of the vote to our advantage."

Laura S. of the NRA chose not to respond directly to a query on this question.[35] That lobbying was intense and feelings ran high on the issue is clear. As Jack T. notes, "One Republican told Feinstein before the vote . . . that he had never had more lobbying done and more pressure put on him to vote in one thing."

Showdown at Lanfair Valley

The Staunch Defenders, led by Representative Jerry Lewis, had been working this entire time to kill the bill, but given the makeup of the House Committee it was clearly going to go to the floor. Republicans introduced a key amendment, the Wallopp amendment, which will have lasting implications for the MNP. The amendment was supposed to minimize the effect of the bill on private property by removing from NPS management all nonfederal land located in Lanfair Valley. This amendment came, according to parks advocate Jack T., "out of the blue at committee, and we lost a vote we did not expect to even have."

The story of Lanfair is, however, nowhere near as rational as that brief account indicates, and suggests how randomly amendments can be created and how with time they are adjusted. Only 4 percent of preserve land is privately held, and Lanfair Valley Township is roughly two thirds public land and one third private land with the in-holdings (nonfederal land) concentrated in the geographical valley itself. In-holdings in Lanfair Valley Township include

- state school lands ceded during settlement,
- railroad lands ceded during the construction of the Santa Fe Railroad and now owned by Catellus Corporation, a Santa Fe spin-off corporation,
- private lands.

Park opponents, with votes from others concerned with private property rights, worded the Wallopp amendment to state that "Lanfair Valley" would be excluded from the CDPA and the Mojave. What was missing was a map. As Henry M. describes it: "Once they made the vote, and it won, somebody asked, 'who's got a map?' And they went tearing around . . . Minority [Republican] staff were digging around for a map, and majority [Democratic] staff knew that their map would probably look something like, you know, this half of the park is Lanfair Valley. So the majority staff pulled [out] . . . a map [previously] drawn by the Interior Department [for other purposes]. This, then, became Lanfair Valley, . . . and it was just that haphazard."

This might not have been such a problem for park supporters, except the map they found showed the entire township, an area that included a large amount of federal land and some of what the pro-parkers considered the finest sights in the area. Park proponents realized that attempting to restore the private lands was a lost cause. Instead, their focus would be on the public lands excluded in the amendment, but reinstating them would prove both easier and harder than anticipated. They first had to convince Feinstein that the amendment as written seriously compromised the preserve. Feinstein looked at pictures and maps of the Valley, and became convinced that, in Henry M.'s words, "this was far more [land] than she [had] thought, was far more than was even close to reasonable." That was the easy part.

Feinstein was prepared to introduce an amendment to restore Lanfair Val-

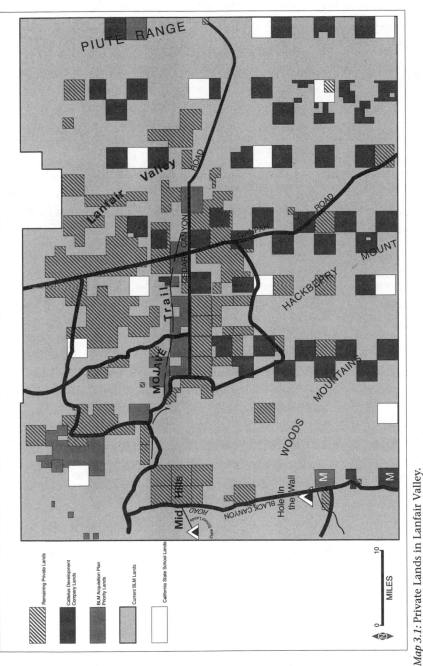

Map 3.1: Private Lands in Lanfair Valley.
This map was used in the preserve's legislation to identify which lands would be excluded from preserve boundaries. The excluded parcels are those in the cross-hatching marked private.

ley during the full Senate hearing on the bill, but Wallopp and his colleagues thought otherwise. As Henry M. describes it: "They threatened that if Feinstein tried to put Lanfair Valley back in, [they would] throw so much at this bill, it'll make your head spin. They would throw takings at it, they would throw all sorts of non-germane controversial amendments at it, to try to muck it up, drag it down, kill it. If you don't offer Lanfair . . . we'll stop right now . . . and you have your bill out of the Senate today."

According to Jack T., at that point Feinstein's staffers came out to the environmental lobbyists waiting in the lobby, and asked what they thought. His and his colleagues' response was: "We had been waiting for eight years for the Senate to pass the bill. We said go ahead and do it [laughs]." She agreed, dropped the Lanfair issue, and the bill passed that day.

It was in the House Committee that the majority of the land deleted by the Wallopp amendment was restored to NPS management. Representative Wingman offered an amendment putting all of the federal lands, all of the state school holdings, and all of the Catellus (railroad) property back in the bill. Private land-holdings were left out of the preserve, but willing land owners who so wished could sell their lands to the federal government, an option that was disallowed under the Senate bill. The rather odd result of this is a preserve with one area resembling Swiss cheese, wherein the many units of private property are the holes in the surrounding NPS land. The amendment ended up having some benefits for the standing of the overall bill. Explains Henry M.: "What it did was very effectively blunted the wise use / private property rights arguments, because it left private property out of the park . . . Politically it worked very well."

High Noon for the Staunch Defenders

At this point, a CDPA had passed both the Senate and the House, but with the Mojave as a national park in the Senate and a national preserve in the House and with different treatment of private property in the Lanfair Valley. The bill was to go to conference to resolve the differences. But, rather than letting it proceed to conference, Republicans began a last-ditch effort to prevent final passage. Lewis's staffer describes their strategy: "Our goal was to build a filibuster strategy based on amending the bill to death. We insisted on an open rule, and once granted, introduced over one hundred amendments to bog down the process. While we lost in the end [barely], we had far greater success than we ever imagined."

This was the first preconference filibuster in Senate history. The motivation was primarily timing. The session of the Senate was almost over, and the next Congress would be majority Republican. Opponents hoped to run out the clock so that the final bill would come under consideration in a new Congress with a much more conservative makeup. Jack T. was on the Hill during the last votes, and describes the last few hours of the bill:

> The Republicans in the House spent ten hours one day [when] they were trying to go to conference, calling for every conceivable vote they could under parliamentary tactics. It was exceedingly frustrating, but boy, you have to hand your hat to them, because they used process, and they killed the bill for an entire day. Something that normally takes five minutes to do took like eight hours. There was a Conference Committee that was supposed to meet at noon, at two, at four, at five, at six, six thirty, seven, I can't remember what time they met . . . While they were delaying the conference, staff is actually *doing* the conference . . . [so that when the conference finally met with George Mitchell as chair] it took five minutes [and the conference report was reported out]. And all of a sudden about four or five Republican members of the Conference Committee show up to find out the thing has already been called.

The Republicans, not surprisingly, were displeased, but by then the cards had been dealt. They could not kill the bill, but the final outcome looked more like the House than the Senate version. The CDPA passed the Senate and the House with the Mojave as a national preserve, hunting and grazing allowed in perpetuity, and private in-holdings in Lanfair Valley excluded. President Clinton signed the act into law on October 31 of 1994.[36]

Anti-climax—The Joshua Tree Ceremony

The CDPA received its public ceremonial initiation at Joshua Tree, where Senator Feinstein, Secretary Babbitt, and local representatives such as Jerry Lewis and Al McCandless joined forces to announce the reality of the CDPA. An environmental lobbyist describes the scene with a fine political edge:

> Babbitt was there and he [told me something] like "I guarantee you I'm going to have Dianne Feinstein, Jerry Lewis, and Al McCandless up here shaking hands and smiling in a spirit of reconciliation." And he did. Lewis could appreciate the political jab, that was Babbitt getting back at him for everything he was saying, I'm almost certain. Feinstein was loving the moment, and McCandless had this look on his face like, "This is why I retired, I hate this crap." It was really funny . . .

The amusing thing, though, [at] this Joshua Tree ceremony, Jerry Lewis was there and he talked about what a great place this was . . . He was talking about Joshua Tree specifically; he never mentioned Mojave, which is also in his district. [Lewis said] "Now it's my job to bring home as much money as I can for it, regardless of the fight we had on this bill."

Denouement—The Appropriations Fight

When the Republican-majority 104th Congress took their seats, they came into office with a strong ideology and little interest in working with the Democratic administration—and perhaps vice versa. The 1996 appropriations fight was the most difficult in our nation's history up to that time, with multiple shutdowns of the federal government, stopgap funding under continuing resolutions, and final appropriations achieved in April—seven months after the start of the fiscal year. Representative Jerry Lewis was on the Appropriations Committee, which gave him the opportunity to resume the Mojave fight in a different venue. He promptly inserted language into the 1996 appropriations bills that provided the NPS with only $1 to manage the Mojave while giving the BLM the remainder of the money it was accustomed to getting for Mojave management. The DOI budget was one of the most controversial budgetary items for Congress, and within that the funding of the Mojave funding was one of the last issues to be resolved.[37]

The final funding resolution saved some face for both parties. Attached to the 1996 appropriations bill were three provisions. The first was that the preserve be managed under the BLM multiple-use regulations in effect prior to the passage of the CDPA. The second was that a one-year management plan be developed and submitted to both authorizing and appropriations committees (i.e., Representative Jerry Lewis's committee). These two would clearly have had significant impact on the way the preserve was managed, were it not for the third provision. The third provision was authority for the president to waive the first two provisions if he found such recision appropriate "based upon the public interest in sound environmental management, sustainable resource use, protection of national or locally affected interests, and protection of cultural, biological, or historic resources."

President Clinton wasted little time in waiving the first two provisions, doing so by a memorandum dated April 26, 1996, and the National Park Service was given the authority to allocate money to manage the preserve.[38] The reality of ongoing appropriations fights is the difference between designing a plan and getting it implemented. In the end, as long as federal land protection is bitterly opposed by local forces, getting a bill passed is just half the battle, with the second half—appropriations—being a fight that must be won every year.

Summary

The CDPA Designation vs. Typical Designations

How closely did the CDPA designation follow the typical process outlined at the start of this chapter? In fact, fairly closely. The CDPA began as the effort of a grassroots environmental coalition; this coalition remained strong throughout the designation battle. While historically the designation of a new park was often the work of a member of the rich or politically connected, the CDPA was largely an effort of middle-class environmental activists. This is consistent with more recent trends in park designations, such as the greenline parks.[39]

The interest groups' alignments for the designation generally conforms to generic designations as described in the first part of the chapter. The NPS followed the lead of the Interior Department, which followed the lead of the White House; the designation was supported under a Democratic White House, and opposed under Republican administrations. In the weak stance taken by the NPS we see a shift from the clear positions and strong leadership provided by early NPS directors such as Mather and Albright to leadership that is more politically aligned. It is questionable whether it is appropriate for a federal agency to lobby legislation. Thus, the NPS's current tendency to be less active in support or opposition may be entirely appropriate. Because the bill was a reduction in BLM authority, the BLM opposed the bill albeit largely informally. The full House and Senate voted along political lines, with Democrats lining up to support the bill and Republicans to oppose it. The environmental community and tourism industry supported the bill while resource-dependent industries opposed it.

In some ways, the national-level CDPA debate was as a fight among family. All of the lobbying organizations rely on the existence of open space for their existence. Hunting, off-road motorcycling, and wildlife management are all done on open lands, and often on public lands of some sort. Grazing and mining rely on public lands. So do nature tourism and environmental interests. Guaranteeing the continued availability of federal lands, as well as their federal funding, is in the interest of each. In the transition of the Mojave from BLM to NPS management, some groups benefited to the detriment of others, all of whom have interests in the public lands. This is perhaps part of what made this debate so bitter—there is little that is less forgivable than fights within the family.

For the lobbying groups involved in the debate at the national level, their alignments matched their interests—conservation groups supported the legislation, resource-based industries opposed it. Environmental groups have members who expect them to achieve action on conservation issues, and who believe that more land protected is better. Hunting, gun, mining, and off-road vehicle enthusiasts want to preserve maximum access to the land necessary for their activities. Much of this is motivated from manufacturers; without the land on which to hunt, for instance, fewer guns would presumably be sold. This is hardly news, but is a basic fact of how the debate unfolded.

The tightest coalition was that of the environmental groups, who work together on many issues. Their management of the issue was practically seamless. At no point in the 103rd Congress could the public positions of the Sierra Club be differentiated from that of the Wilderness Society or that of the National Parks and Conservation Association. Other pro-environment groups, such as the Audubon Society and the League of Conservation Voters, fell into line as well, having their endorsements included in many of the letters sent to the Hill.

This is particularly interesting in that some of the environmental organizations are patently anti-hunting, while some of them are neutral on the question. This was a particular sore point for some of the park opponents who felt that if an organization was not anti-hunting, a stance against hunting in the Mojave was inexplicable. But to the Sierra Club, NPCA, and other pro-park groups, the question was whether the Mojave deserved national park status. If it did, and they thought that it did, then hunting would have to be excluded to gain "justice" for the Mojave.

Alliances outside of the environmental community were much more tenuous. The alignment of those opposed to the CDPA splintered when the strength of political will to pass the CDPA became clear. Even for the Hunters who remained in coalition, differences in the emphases of the various groups were visible among the interviewees and in the papers they sent to Capitol Hill. Much of this tenuousness is no doubt from having a more disparate set of interests than do the environmental groups. According to a hunting lobbyist, some is also attributable to competition over members with each group wanting to show that they have achieved results. Presumably, this same sort of competition exists between environmental organizations, but none of the lobbyists commented on it.

In evaluating the Washington-level coalitions that developed during the CDPA, one question is why the Californian senators supported the bill and local congressional representatives largely opposed it. The most reasonable answer seems to be that offered by grazing lobbyist Mike B.: "I have to assume it's because senators are elected on a statewide basis, and they know that their votes are coming from urban parts, like L.A. and San Francisco . . . Where urbanites want to have playgrounds to go to, you're going to vote to establish playgrounds. If you're a congressperson, however, from any of the fifty districts that are in California that are not in the urban areas, then you're saying, no, we don't want our district turned into an urban playground."

Not surprisingly, in the 1994 senatorial elections Senator Feinstein lost the Mojave's local county, San Bernardino, by a large margin while her Republican challenger lost in his own more-urban district, Santa Barbara, but carried San Bernardino. The political reality suggests that the elected officials probably fairly represented their constituents, both New Westerners and Old Westerners. We will return to the question of why local opposition was so strong and the theme of rural vs. urban interests in the following chapter.

The MNP: An Exemplary Case of Park Designations?

So, is the California Desert Protection Act in general and the Mojave National Preserve in particular a reasonably representative case study of park unit designation in the United States? Park designations are highly contingent on local as well as national peculiarities of both place and historical time, and generalizing about them is therefore to be approached with caution. With that caveat in mind, however, let me venture a few generalizations. The answer regarding representativeness is both yes and no. Historically, parks were (generally speaking) created from land that was viewed as worthless, not contributing economically to the community. As a result, local representatives supported park designation as a way to increase tourism and federal funding and thereby improve the local economy. Clearly the Mojave does not fit this mold.

What it does fit is the class of designations whereby the local community and industry does not view the land as worthless, but instead as economically valuable, whether for agriculture and industry or construction of second and retirement homes. In these cases, increasing protection and thereby decreasing use is not in the economic interest of many local area residents. Examples of this type of debate abound as well, from the creation of the Adirondack State Park in New York to the recent designation of the Tallgrass Prairie National Preserve in Kansas or the fight over the appropriate extent of wilderness in Utah.[40] The timbre of the Sagebrush Rebellion, with its emphasis on state's rights and decreasing federal presence in the western states is also evident in the Mojave and in the Utah wilderness debate.[41] The relationship of local residents to the land may also make a significant difference, as explored in Chapters 6 and 7.

We can expect that these sort of local conditions, both economic and ideological, will continue to create two classes of designations, those supported or opposed locally. But, I suggest, there is a time element involved as well. When the country was metaphorically speaking larger and literally less populated, it was easier to find new park land with few local residents and little economic value. As our country becomes more crowded and resources more intensively developed, fewer and fewer lands proposed for new park designation will meet the criteria for inclusion in the first, locally supported category.[42] Instead, we can expect that, as in the Mojave case, much of the land that is newly proposed will have a reasonable level of resource value and use. Additionally, we can expect to find fewer and fewer lands where nobody lives to complain about the restrictions involved in becoming part of the park system. Residents of sprawling urbanized areas near undeveloped land will be increasingly concerned with assuring that there are some lands with breathing space available to them—national parks—no matter what the local residents of those lands may happen to feel. While both types of designations will probably be undertaken, more and more of them are likely to fit this second class.

The gist of this argument, then, is that the Mojave is a prototypical case, one that presents many of the issues which will have to be faced in future designations, assuming, of course, that Americans continue to create national park units. The final legislative decision to make the Mojave a national preserve rather than national park is, in this argument, exemplary of the responses to these pressures. In the way it has come to be used, a preserve suggests an area where human use and ecosystem protection must find a coexistence, however uneasy—and that coexistence is the topic at hand.

CHAPTER 4

Narratives of the Preserve Debate

My Way or the Highway

If one is inclined to wonder at first how so many dwellers came to be in the loneliest land that ever came out of God's hands, what they do there and why they stay, one does not wonder so much after having lived there. None other than this long brown land lays such a hold on the affections.　—MARY AUSTIN, *Stories from the Country of Lost Borders*

And now, after I had been there only three days, I was to experience my first sand storm. When the desert does things, it seems to do them in a great big way. It may only have been doing what it conceived to be its duty, but sometimes I have felt that back of it all there was a sort of resentment toward human beings who dared to come in there and meddle around in a puny way, to make things more comfortable for themselves. The longer I lived there, the more I felt this Spirit of the desert, sometimes benign, but often the opposite, as though it must make up for those heavenly days of smiling sunshine by a tremendous blast which would show those humans their absurd significance.
　—FROM THE DIARY OF SADIE MARTIN, IN RUTH MOYNIHAN, SUSAN ARMITAGE, ET AL., *So Much to Be Done: Women Settlers on the Mining and Ranching Frontier*

Introduction

The particular steps lobbyists, citizens, and elected officials undertook to either pass or block the CDPA legislation are clearly actions—events with outcomes. But the way these participants debated the issue—the stories or narratives they used pro and con—are actions as well. The narratives we are concerned with here were undertaken primarily for the purpose of persuasion, and so they are rhetorical narratives.[1] The way participants' narratives construct an issue affects the outcome of the debate; the narratives also provide a window into the reasoning and motivations of participants.

In this chapter I present the major and minor narratives told by both proponents and opponents to the designation regarding why the Mojave should or should not be transferred from the BLM to the park service. In the next chapter I use a similar analysis on the particular uses that were important in the debate—hunting, mining, grazing. The specific elements of each narrative are complex because the issue is multifaceted, and many of the elements came into being in response to opposing positions rather than as initial parts of that side's story. To reflect this complexity, I will present the narrative elements separately in the body of this chapter as individual themes, and bring the themes together to form true narratives with past and future, causation and moral reasoning, at the end of the chapter. With a very few exceptions, I do not include outside references in this section. My purpose here is to as far as possible present the ideas of the participants themselves without significant mediation from external sources. Most of the data comes from respondents who are local to the Mojave; commentary on the differences between the emphasis among Washington-based respondents and local respondents is included where applicable. The interviews with participants were conducted with a year after the passage of the CDPA, and so are fairly fresh reflections on the process.

I have identified six particular major themes and one minor theme in the debate.[2] For major themes, multiple participants addressed that story in one way or another—whether to promote it, adjust it, or deny it. Occasionally, there is a theme that is peculiar to one particular position on the issue, which I call a minor theme. Such an occurrence is itself interesting, and I provide some commentary describing why it was a one-sided topic when relevant. These themes are as follows.

Theme 1: The Land—The park proponents' first job was to show that the area ought to be a unit of the park system. By claiming that it met the park service's criteria for inclusion in its system, they could establish that the area deserved increased protection. Opponents disagreed, claiming that the land did not have sufficient value to merit inclusion. Opponents argued that the environmentalists' mistake was to believe that the land should not include people and the signs of their use of the land, when in fact an appropriate understanding of landscape in general and this one in particular includes people.

Theme 2: Issues of Management—The park proponents also had to show that a change in land management was needed. They built a case against the Bureau of Land Management, claiming that the BLM could not or would not give the land the protection it deserved. Opponents countered by arguing that the

BLM's 1980 Plan was a good, balanced plan which environmentalists had participated in developing, and that to override it was unjust, unfair, and unwise.

Theme 3: No Reduction in Property Rights!—At its heart, the opponents' argument was that the CDPA would interfere with their right to use their property as they desired. Opponents strongly distrusted the government, in contrast to the positive view of the government held by proponents. When proponents chose to address this theme, which was not very often, they would argue that federal ownership of the land meant that it should be managed for the good of all the public and not just the good of a few local residents.

Theme 4: Past and Future Economies—A significant part of the debate focused on the area's economy and economic future: should it be a traditional-resource economy or postindustrial service economy? The advent of the park service would increase tourism while decreasing traditional uses of the land. Proponents focused on the economic growth from tourism, while opponents were not convinced that such growth would occur, and even if it did, they would not consider those types of jobs as constituting progress.

Theme 5: Likely Futures—By the time the legislation passed, opponents and proponents' stories had converged on at least one thing—the current condition of the land was good and the goal was to keep it that way. However, just what the current conditions were and what it would take to keep them were understood very differently, and so both sides, while agreeing in words, had very different suggested solutions. Opponents looked to the recent past and the relative stability of the area over the last decades, and argued that it should be managed similarly to the past. Proponents instead looked to the extensive growth in neighboring metropolises, and suggested, privately at least, that an important motivation for the designation was controlling the incursion of growth from these areas. This view represents a localized aspect of a larger, and also usually unexpressed, reason, which was simply that given the enormous growth in human population and pressures on the environment, more protected land anywhere is good. In a similar vein, environmentalists argued that the designation would complete protection of the whole ecosystem, with the preserve area serving as a migratory and evolutionary bridge between Joshua Tree and Death Valley National Parks. Not surprisingly, given the extensive scale required for ecosystem preservation, it was this proposition that scared opponents the most.

Theme 6: Political Aspirations—Certainly the most direct reason that the Mojave became part of the NPS system is that the political conditions were right. Whether the act constituted an appropriate political action depends on who is discussing the politics of the bill.

Theme 7: Characterizations of the Other Side—In general the picture each side holds of the other is unflattering, and I briefly describe some of these characterizations. Included here is a minor narrative I became aware of only at the community presentation. In this, opponents argued that the United Nations was the power behind and the intended recipient of the benefits of reducing use of the desert.

I present the themes beginning with the theme that generated the most public discussion and move to the ones that were usually discussed only privately. For my uses here, a "private" story is one that appears in conversations with debate participants, but does not usually appear in the public debate as represented by talking points memos, testimony, and other documents, while a "public" story is one that appears in official memos or letters and also appears in interviews.

The reader will meet a number of people in this chapter; some are the Washington-based lobbyists discussed in Chapter 3, and some are local people who have not previously been presented. Not all the interview respondents are quoted here. Instead, I limited the number of persons quoted so that a richer, fuller picture of those presented can emerge. Quotations are only from interviews that were taped to assure accuracy; from among those taped interviews I selected the most articulate quotations that expressed a representative view. The Appendix contains a discussion of the selection of interview respondents, the interviews, and the general research method.

Theme 1: The Land

It Fit the Criteria

The proponents' job was to justify a change in management regimes. To do this, they first had to establish that the Mojave fit in the NPS system. For an area to merit inclusion in the NPS system, it has to have national significance, suitability, and feasibility, and it helps if it is an underrepresented type of ecosystem. In 1979, the BLM conducted a study of the area and found that it met the NPS criteria, and in 1986 the NPS's Western Region confirmed that conclusion in its own study of the Mojave.[3] This finding of merit became one of the major

At the time of our interview, Bill F. was working at one of the NPS's desert units. After a full career with the park service, he was articulate and close to retirement and therefore had nothing to lose by speaking his mind; hence, he was an excellent source. A compact, energetic man who appeared far too young to retire, Bill has been a passionate supporter of the desert parks, and land protection in general, within the park service, and was an active inside promoter of the CDPA. When working at the MNP when it first opened, he and the other rangers made it clear that they wore guns and bullet-proof vests; they enfoced regulations that prevented visitors from putting up campfires wherever they camped; they closed roads and otherwise annoyed local residents. These actions may have been necessary, but they were not popular with local residents. In comparison, the accommodative style of the next superintendent, Mary Martin, seemed like a cool breeze.

talking points for park proponents, particularly in Washington.[4] As Bill F., a park service employee who previously worked at the MNP and was an informal promoter of the park within the NPS, noted: "The park service's own study determined that the area merited inclusion in NPS system because of the unique primarily natural values. It was a part of the California desert which contains the joint points of three major North American deserts. So, for its own value it should be part of the park system. And too, placing it in the national park system would normally afford it the highest level of protection you can receive under law."

As discussed in Chapter 3, despite the official "merit" studies, a determination on the official stance of the NPS is based on the decision of the secretary of the Department of Interior, who instructs the NPS as to what position it can present in congressional hearings. While the NPS was under Republican administrations, the DOI/NPS opposed the CDPA. When the NPS came under Democratic administration, the DOI/NPS supported the bill. Yet even within the NPS under the Clinton administration, there was dissension about the Mojave,[5] as Bill F. indicates: "The [NPS] people who informally opposed the bill, even after the administration had endorsed it, a large part of their thinking was [that] the place is not worthy of being protected by the NPS. It just doesn't have the quality."

At the time of our interview, Renata W. was an employee of a big limestone mine outside the preserve's boundaries. The business was originally started by the family of her husband, and was later bought out by a foreign corporation. Since her husband's death, a big part of her job has been monitoring legislation that affects the mine and being a voice for its interests. She is a life-long resident of the desert region who in some ways was just beginning to discover the desert—at the time of our talk she had just gone with a group on her first visit to Joshua Tree and Death Valley National Parks and spoke flowingly of the experience. Nevertheless, she was a strong proponent of the company's right and duty to mine a limestone claim that lies within the boundaries of the preserve under a rare ecological community. In her local knowledge and strength of beliefs, she was a good spokeswokman for the opposition to the CDPA and for those generally supportive of property rights.

Congressman Lewis, the local Republican representative, used this lack of quality as his main objection to the MNP. Landscape quality was an issue that bill opponents returned to time and time again, noting the area's extensive reminders of human use. Renata W., a mining company representative, provided a typical comment: "The Mojave preserve, it really doesn't qualify for park, because you've got your big overhead power lines going through there, you've got gas lines going through there, you've got railroad track going through there, and you've got quite a few lines in there. So it doesn't qualify."

Park proponents' rebuttal rested on the enormous size of the preserve, as explained by Charles H., a former upper-level manager for the NPS:

I think one of the reasons [former Secretary of the Interior] Bill Mott was opposed to the area was, as he put it, there are two interstates, I-40 and I-15; one's on the north end and one's on the south end, then right through the middle of it you [have] this railroad [going] through. Then you have the power lines crisscrossing it, and their power line lands associated with them. So he said those three reasons right away eliminate it from being a national park—one that we would want to administer. But yet, to draw within the confines of the interstates, taking into account the railroads, taking into account those areas that would crisscross it north and south, you could still find an area within those that was almost 200,000 acres, two or three of them, and that is larger than a lot of parks.

Melinda and Mark S. sold their Southern California business and retired to the desert after witnessing several crimes in their neighborhood. The land they bought is virtually surrounded by federal lands, much of it in designated wilderness, and is very, very private. Melinda reports having seen a mountain lion on the property. They built a suburban-style home with all the conveniences and grow tomatoes and flowers in their desert garden. Their only complaint was that telephone service has been slow to get established, since laying line out to them is very expensive; thus emergency response was not all one would hope—although it does seem to me that this trade-off should have been obvious when they chose to move there.

Now that wilderness access rules are being enfoced, visiting friends is more difficult since some jeep tracks are closed, and Melinda is not supposed to take her dog with her on her daily desert hikes. Her husband Mark has less physical mobility and thus does not hike, and talked very little in the the interview except to test my politics—a test I imagine I failed when I described what would usually be considered a centrist view. Both were passionately, adamantly opposed to the designation.

Often the opponents' comments would focus on the perceived lack of scenic quality of the land as the reason it did not qualify for the NPS system. As it was put by Melinda S., a local homeowner, "This park doesn't have anything magnificent like Yellowstone or the Grand Canyon. But [it has] a lot of little places, you know . . . " For many, outside of those lovely spots, the land is "just plain desert."

Bill F.'s comment, above, clearly addresses the ecological fitness of the area, while opponents would focus on scenic quality. As discussed in Chapter 3, the NPS's criteria include both scenic value and ecological importance, mirroring the NPS's dual management goals, as well as administrative feasibility. Because of the dual nature of criteria and the complexity of the landscape, both sides can argue from that same landscape and come up with different conclusions.

People Are Part of the Landscape

Park opponents had their own argument about the land, largely based on the claim that the character of the landscape was improved by people's using the land. For Mal Wessel, former mayor of Barstow, for instance, the landscape is made more meaningful by having cattle visible on it; this reminds him and other viewers of our nation's cowboy history. One of the claims made by both hunting and ranching supporters was that those activities improved the habitat value of the landscape for all species. For example, the water holes that hunters and ranchers maintained for their chosen species of interest also provided water for many other thirsty desert fauna. Mary J., owner of a small land mining company, sums up this position, saying that "the real goal of the legislation . . . was to get rid of all the land users," and that "people are a legitimate part of the environment, and that is what the environmentalists don't see."

This argument generally contrasts the land user's position with that of the environmentalists, a construction that makes sense in that environmentalists, by attempting to change the current rules of American life and land use, forced the land users to reconsider just what their own position was. This idea was expressed by Kevin K., lobbyist for the mining industry: "I think the whole issue over land use, particularly as regards public lands, boils down to those who would use the land responsibly and those who do not want the land to be used for anything. They do not want anybody on it. I think that's the basis of the argument." Similarly, a motorcycle lobbyist commented: "We don't want to see those [recreational] opportunities lost simply because the environmentalists want to lock up the land so nobody can use it." Clearly this argument is aligned with the argument from property rights, discussed further in Theme 3.

Environmentalists responded that they are not locking up the land but opening it up for recreational use. Glen R., who headed a California tourism association, characterized the local opponents as wanting to keep the desert to themselves. While "locking up the land" was a common cry among antipreservation forces, it was really more a question of access for whom—traditional local residents and users, or urbanites and visitors. Whether or not visual reminders of human industry are interpreted positively, as by park opponents, or negatively, as by park proponents, was obviously based on the preconceptions of the viewer as much as on the character of the visual reminder itself.[6]

Theme 2: Issues of Management

Judgment on the BLM

Arguing that an area deserves inclusion in the NPS did not say why designation needed to happen today, or even soon; it was a very static argument, without a crisis to overcome. To create a persuasive account of a need for action, park proponents had to create a sense of threat to the area. So, they argued that the current management of the area, the BLM, was not the right one for the land. Why this was so could be understood in two ways. The first was that the BLM's multiple-use mandate was the issue, not the ability or willingness of the agency to manage for environmental protection. We can call this the polite argument. Public documents, not surprisingly, used this approach, phrasing the problem in such terms as: "The NPS is uniquely qualified to protect the Mojave."[7]

While this reasoning may have been valid for the Mojave as a national park, it is difficult to reconcile with the final bill. Based on language written into the bill, the Mojave remains a multiple-use land area even under the NPS. Grazing and hunting on the land will continue in perpetuity. Miners can work existing mining claims, although new exploration was halted. The BLM had already stopped the infamous Barstow-to-Vegas off-road motorcycle race, which at any rate did not really affect the area that would become the MNP because the route largely skirted the East Mojave Scenic Area.[8] Perhaps the major legislatively required change resulting from NPS management prohibits collecting rocks or plants by human visitors—not exactly a big change.

Conversations with the participants provide clues that it was an issue of trust, not of congressional mandate, that made getting rid of the BLM important. Robert P., a local pro-park activist, discussed his unsatisfactory experience working as a volunteer with the BLM on land planning for the Mojave in the early 1980s, and concludes: "So, you know, I never trusted BLM after that . . . California is one of the most urban states in the nation, maybe Connecticut is more urban, but we're not a bunch of cowboys out here; we're not reactionaries, we're urban people. And the Bureau of Land Management, which catered to—sometimes people would call it the Bureau of Livestock and Mining—they just lost it."

His disillusionment with the BLM stemmed from his sense that the BLM was not responsive to urban interests—his interests. The NPS, on the other hand, has a reputation for being responsive to the environmental community, which is a largely urban community. In the end, it may not have mattered how the BLM was doing in its management; environmentalists wanted a land management agency they could trust, one that listened to their perspective. A comment Robert P. made earlier in the interview refers to this issue of trust. Describing his sense of the bill's outcome, he stated, "So our dream came true. We lost to the NRA, and we lost to the grazers, ranchers. [But] I think now what we can see is there is a park service here."

Park opponents had a concise rebuttal to these charges of poor management. If the BLM had managed it so badly, how could the land qualify for national park status?[9] That the area was in good enough shape for the park service was proof that local residents and the BLM had been good caretakers. This was a point of considerable frustration for the BLM employees, who received the brunt of the proponents fire.

The BLM Plan was a Good, Balanced Plan

Park opponents had their own view about the appropriateness of BLM management—namely, that it was very appropriate. They would usually first point out that the 1980 BLM management plan for the California Desert Conservation Area was a good, reasonable compromise between various interests in the desert and that the environmentalists had participated in that negotiation. It had been developed over a long period of time, with a great deal of study going into reaching its conclusions. It had extensive public involvement by local residents, unlike the CDPA, which was viewed as largely forced on the locals by urban interests and approved by eastern senators. Renata W. captures much of this argument:

> [The BLM undertook their studies and found] there were places they said should be wilderness areas, which were of special interest, and we set those aside. And there have been studies on the mineral deposits, and [the deposits] were to be kept out [from wilderness designation] where they could be used. And we had the California Desert Conservation Act [the 1980 Plan]. It was ten years putting that together. People from all over worked on that, and when it was finished, no one was completely happy, but it was something most everyone felt they could live with. But then just right after it was finalized the Sierra Club goes to [Senator Alan] Cranston and says we don't like it, we should do this. [But] there was a lot of study, a lot of man-hours that went into that [BLM plan], it was about the best that could be done.

Laura S., a lobbyist for the NRA who previously worked for the BLM, expresses similar sentiments in her comments on the NRA's position on the bill:

> In those earlier years the NRA supported the efforts of the BLM through its wilderness designation process. I personally feel too, because I had been in Interior at that time, that the [CDPA] legislation preempted that process. Then, secondly after that process was completed, recommendations made, the [CDPA] legislation dismissed the ten years worth of public involvement that lead to the recommendations. So, if you take it beyond the specific hunter interests, to the bigger issues of good policy, it swept aside I mean hundreds of thousands of dollars if not millions and countless hours of administrative time as well as countless hours that the public either as interest groups or as individuals applied in either reviewing the proposals or commenting on the proposals, and swept that completely aside.

Ralph N., an environmental lobbyist, in contrast considered the designation of the national scenic area to be "a political response without any guts," and believes that if the BLM had actually managed for recreational and ecological needs, the preserve designation would never have occurred. The problem, according to Robert P., was with the character and rapid pace of amendments to the 1980 Plan: "It was pretty good in 1980, but then in 1982 BLM started their plan amendment process. They should have implemented the plan before they amended it, and so, it's a textbook case on how not to do land use planning. If you start amending it all the time, whatever consensus you had will [evaporate]. Well, [after] the 1982 plan amendments, that's when we decided to incorporate the area as the Mojave National Park, because of those plan amendments."

Ironically for planners, that amendment process was the idea of eminent planner Harvey Perloff, according to the BLM's Ed Hastey.[10] It was a point of pride for Hastey that they had this proactive way to address changing conditions through having the static plan adjusted by the amendment process. The plan amendments do not appear in opponents' narratives.

Theme 3: No Reduction in Property Rights!

No Reductions in Property Use Rights!

At bottom for many opponents was the sense that the act would reduce their property rights, rights they had developed in using the federal lands.

Lydia H., an eighty-plus-year-old activist and long-time property owner living between Barstow and the preserve boundaries, discussed with great emotion how the act threatened the Jeffersonian ideal of the small property holder, to our shared societal peril. Mary J., mine owner, similarly appealed to the Jeffersonian ideal, without which "the property holders' rights would be trampled." She considered the act to be a takings issue, in which property owners were not being compensated for reduced use of their private lands. Unspoken was the point that most of the land under discussion was not "private" in the usual sense of the word, and rather was federal with either open-access (hunting) or specific-use rights (mining, ranching).

This narrative was part of both the national and local debate, and figured both publicly and privately. Laura S. of the NRA, making the case for preserving hunting in the Mojave, notes: "It went back to why would you want to take away from the public an opportunity to recreate on lands the public owns. You know, the BLM and other federal agencies may manage the land, but it is the American people that own the land . . . And I think that legislators have to make a good case why the people who own the land can't use the land."

Thomas G., a hunting lobbyist, voiced a similar public-use based reason for retaining hunting, but one with a political spin: "In an effort to engender their [the public's] continuing support, it seems to me that we have to continue to provide for legitimate public uses of these lands after they are acquired. A policy of excluding or eliminating or significantly reducing public uses isn't necessarily going to engender continued public support for acquisition of these properties and for agency fiscal support to continue to manage the properties."

One of the park opponents' standard techniques was the call to a history of use, saying that good cause must be shown to change these traditional practices. Rancher Tony K. raised the issue, describing his testimony to Congress about the bill:

> At that time they had what they call a sunset clause in this bill, and the sunset clause said that [I] could be on this land with [my] ranch for twenty years. At the end of twenty years, everything belongs to the federal government. You know, these kids of ours are the fifth generation of my people right here. So that means [in] twenty years, they would be up [and out] and they would have put a lot of their sweat into this piece of land too. So everything for almost five generations just goes down the tubes, because the federal government says this is your cut off date.

Tony and Betty K. raise cattle within the Mojave preserve. Tony's family has been there for several generations now, dating back to the early settlement of the area. Tony is the picture of a cowboy, long and lanky with a strong mustache and a slow talk. Betty also expresses a certain centeredness, from her arms used to labor, to her careful comments, to her "Eat Beef" t-shirt. Ranching is both vocation and avocation for them, and apparently sometimes more avocation than profit. It must be a labor of love—they still have no air conditioning in the desperate desert heat, and only recently broke down and got a television for their children. They drive the kids for miles to a spot where the school bus comes that then takes the children on a long ride to a community school. Tony's father lives near them on the ranch, and they share duties. Their sense of the pro-park people was more dismay than anger, dismay that people who knew so little about the desert would believe that they could tell Tony and Betty about the way to manage the land they live with every day. When I visited with them, which was after the park service had been in charge for some months, they were feeling better about the outcome of the legislation. It was beginning to look like the park service might not be such a bad landlord after all.

Mike B., a grazing lobbyist, discussed why grazing should continue in the Mojave: "Well, there's been ranching in that country for many decades, and we were interested in preserving that . . . We were just interested in making sure that the historic grazing practices that had been going on for a century would be able to continue."

Mining company employee Renata W. made similar claims for mining: "Southern California depends on mining for its economy; that's what brought people here to start with, what brought people to this valley. [They] came for gold mining in the mountains, came down here to live in the winter, found gold on this side of the mountain. And other minerals." Even the motorcycle lobbyist used this argument: "We're not totally opposed to wilderness, we just don't want to see our opportunity lost, opportunity that we have had historically for, you know, tens of years." It may seem odd to call a land use that has only been popular for at most three decades historical, but in the context of the Mojave, where Anglo settlement dates back only about one hundred years, three decades becomes a significant portion of the American experience—although certainly not of the experience of Native Americans.

Environmentalists rarely chose to rebut this argument on the grounds of property rights, seeing the issue as one of appropriate uses and appropriate recipients of the benefits of the land, not previously existing property rights. They discussed how few ranchers were actually involved, the foreign ownership of many of the mines, and the many tax subsidies that support those traditional use rights. They also discussed the future of the economy and the importance of tourism for the future, as further developed in Theme 5. Environmentalists' indirect responses to the property rights issue may reflect the reality that arguing for reductions in property rights is an unwise rhetorical choice in American politics.

Distrust of Government

One of the private narratives told by local residents goes to the heart of their opposition to the act. People saw the coming of the NPS as another layer of federal government constraining their activities and controlling their lives. Melinda and Mac S., local homeowners, were among the most emotional and outspoken of the respondents on this issue. Themes of a sense of broken trust with the government run throughout their discussion of the act, as shown in the following comments from Melinda: "They made it a preserve, and then they made 99 percent of it wilderness, and what that does is make all the things that we've been able to look at and go to, all the places we've gone to for twenty years, now off-limits . . . We lost our freedom. This place out here was like a giant park to me—as far as it is a whole bunch of things to do—so it's an amusement park to me, where some people would think Disneyland. Now it's all closed down and everything is 'no.'" Later in the interview she added: "I'm just saying that this place has been like this for the last two hundred years that [Anglo] man has been on it, and I think it's survived pretty good. I think there's a lot of responsible people out there, the hunters and rock hounds and climbers and all that stuff. None of us have worked to destroy this. We don't need the government, we just don't need the government."

Melinda and Mac might sound extreme, but echoes of their views came through in other interviews. Tony K., for instance, believed that the intention of the federal government toward the ranchers was truly nefarious:

When everybody buys these ranches they buy the water rights, because that's private property. And if the federal government forces you not to use that water for three years by taking your cattle off there, you lose your water rights. And guess who gets it? The federal government ends up with the water rights so that nobody can use it. Because they [the feds] will go to the state and say, okay, we own that water right, so the water right would be null and void from thereon. That was how they were going to get out of paying us what they would owe us. They would just say, hey, you have to pull your cows off, and then say, hey, you don't even own the water rights now. So they were just going to come in here and virtually kick everyone off.

Under the original bill design, the NPS would have been able to purchase private property within the preserve in the normal NPS fashion—either from willing sellers or, as in some parks, when the original owner passed away. With the strident rhetoric and misinformation that went on in the debate, many residents interpreted this as enormous power on the part of the NPS to kick them off of their private property. As a narrative, it fits well with fears of increased governmental intervention and reduction of local control over the future.

It Was Federal Land to Start With

How did the park proponents rebut the arguments about reducing property rights and distrust of government? There were two main ways. The first was to remind listeners that the land in dispute was not local residents' to begin with. Bill F. explains:

These lands in the Mojave Desert that are federal land have been owned by the people of the United States since 1846 . . . when the United States stole these lands from Mexico fair and square [laughter]. And they never belonged to the State of California or to any private person. They have always belonged to the people of the United States as a whole. And you may not like it, but this is still one nation, not fifty, and there is a federal government that I work for, and I am happy to. So. [laughter] I'm not going to apologize for that.

Robert P. has a different understanding of the source of government distrust— a history of inept federal management:

During the California Gold Rush, where was the federal presence? There was no federal government in 1849. Why did we have all these vigilantes and claim jumping? There was no federal presence. People say they don't like government, but that's just like Jeffersonian talk. People really do want a government, but a government that works. And [during] the California Gold Rush it didn't work, and it wasn't working out here. The [1980] desert plan was a chance for the federal government through the BLM to show that they could do the job, and they failed miserably.

An Expected Argument Left Untold

A story I expected to hear from park proponents was that the designation would increase opportunities for recreation. My expectation was largely incorrect. When recreation did get discussed, it was largely as a response to economic arguments about restricting income from desert exploitation. Robert P., for example, discussed the increase in tourism-related income from visitation likely to result from the designation, but also noted, "I don't like framing the environment in terms of money." Indeed, increasing the number of visitors was largely absent from his interview narrative. Jane J. was about the only one who posited that the CDPA was about recreational access, and tied the increasing populations in Los Angeles and Las Vegas to a need for more recreational land.

There are several possible explanations for the general nonappearance of recreational need in the discussion. The first, as park opponents were fond of pointing out, was that increasing visitors was generally difficult to reconcile with increasing resource protection. Linda C., a desert biologist and a supporter of the bill, described it this way:

> Just by being a national park, it means you'll get more people here, and that means you're going to have to develop sites more. And certain areas might get more impact . . . So the idea is that we might experience increases in impact over the next fifty years. But hopefully that is going to level out; there is control over that, there will be some management of that. And then in a hundred years the total impact might be less, even though we might see these pulses in types of disturbance.

Her use of a long time frame is a point to which I will return.

The second problem with increasing recreational opportunity lies in the combination of the nature of the area—desert—and the fact that about 49 percent of the preserve has been designated as federal wilderness. The primary way most people recreate in the desert is to drive to sites, and then hike a short while to see them, and then drive some more. Long desert hikes are difficult for all but the best-conditioned hiker. Placing such a large percentage of the preserve in wilderness means that vehicular access is closed to visitors and hiking in will be the only way to see many of the area's "treasures." Given these inconsistencies, it is in retrospect not surprising that it was not a major story for park proponents. During the legislative debate the issue of wilderness received much less comment from opponents than the issues of NPS designation, but once the bill had passed and park opponents became aware of the extent of wilderness, this became a common complaint.

Theme 4: Past and Future Economies

Ranching and Mining Produce Real Wealth, Unlike Tourism

One of the points of debate was the relative contributions of traditional resource-based development versus tourism as an economic tool. Much of opponents' desire to have the land stay in BLM management was based on the desire for continued resource uses—mining and ranching—and a traditional industrial economy, or what can be characterized as Old West. By contrast, the change to park system supervision with the NPS's focus on land preservation and tourism promotion signals an economic change to a postindustrial economy and a New West. In park opponents' eyes, the wealth created from traditional land uses was greater, somehow more real and noble, than wealth that might be created by tourism. To park proponents, the opposite was true. Mike B., a Washington lobbyist for ranching interests, exemplifies this: "I don't accept as gospel that the recreation industry is the quick and easy replacement for commodities production and the creation of new wealth. Because when that heifer drops a calf on the ground, you just created new wealth [laughs], whereas the recreation services industry just keeps rolling the same dollar around and around and around."

This sense of creating new real wealth was a point of pride for Tony and Betty K., and a pride they shared with fellow ranchers.[11] Discussing the rather uncomfortable coalition of opponents to the designation, in which ranchers got "lumped together" with off-road vehicle users, miners, and landowners who opposed the designation, Tony and Betty K. comment:

> TONY K.: It got to be kind of hilarious the way this whole thing got lumped in. Because the ranchers have always kind of stood by themselves.
>
> BETTY K: We're here for different reasons than the rest of the county.

TONY K.: We utilize virtually the only renewable resource here. The miners don't, they take it out one time. The recreationists don't produce anything for anybody within this desert; the landowners, they don't produce anything. So we're virtually the only producer affected by this thing, the ranching industry.

Closely aligned with the "real wealth" argument are several themes of economics and patriotism. Renata W. pointed out the multiplier effects on job creation and income from mining jobs. Mining people are fond of reminding listeners that "everything you see around you comes out of the ground. It is either grown or mined or comes from the sea." They questioned where we expect to get our minerals if we close off access in the mineralized areas of the United States; clearly, we will have to import them, with the effect of increasing our balance-of-trade deficit with other countries where mining is still encouraged. A San Bernardino County elected official representative went so far as to call the mineral exploration withdrawals "almost criminal" and "unpatriotic." His concern was the cost in economic opportunity, because according to him mining is the number one industry in the county.

To these respondents, there was no comparison between jobs from mining or ranching and jobs from tourism. Most opponents simply do not believe that visitation to their desert will increase enough to make a difference—because the area still is, after all, "plain desert." Even if they believe that the designation will increase tourism jobs, resource-based positions are preferable—higher wage, and somehow more respectable. Melinda S., expressing her solidarity with the ranchers, says: "Everything in this country now it has to do with money, and it's really sad for me. Like trying to put these ranchers out of work, you read articles saying that we don't need this [ranching] anymore, we should put them out of work. Well, I don't know how you feel about it, but I think somebody who works hard seven days a week, twelve hours a day, who loves their job and is feeding other people, I don't think that's a bad thing."

Historian Richard White provides some insight into this perspective: "The rural West feels itself betrayed by the cities with whom its fate has so long been linked. More than a century of brushing off the last bust and waiting for the next boom has left scars both upon the land and the people. Some rural westerners console themselves that amidst the explosive growth of the metropolitan areas, they alone are the last remnants of a real West, a true West. But in a region whose people have always defined themselves, for better or worse, in terms of the future rather than the past, such a guarding of the flame has an aura of defeat."[12]

Phillip J. owns his own small town, population of about five. He retired from an engineering job in the city and moved out to the desert mid-career. He still owns a house in Las Vegas, where he goes when the desert gets too quiet or too hot. I talked with him in the store/restaurant that accompanies his small hotel. The feel inside the store is like a museum general store, wood lined and carrying a great variety of goods, most of them dusty. He is ambitious for the future of his business, looking for ways to expand and improve the hotel. Global population and environmental pressures weigh heavily on his mind, and he sees the preserve as the right thing to do for the enviornment and the future. It also should be very good for his business, since his is about the only ecotourist-style accommodations anywhere around the preserve. He runs some tours into the desert, and has an outside hot tub for spectacular desert star viewing. He was one of the few local residents who was willing to give very public support for the designation both early and late in the process—perhaps because he was sufficiently disconnected from the local community that being shunned would not matter to him much.

Tolerance for this sort of argument was short among the park proponents. Phillip J. is a local tourism entrepreneur who hopes to make a major move into ecotourism with the coming of the preserve. Commenting on those who oppose the bill, he had this to say: "There is a lot of really vocal antagonism. And it's based on some kind of a 'turn back the clock' psychology to the 1900s. We want to turn back the clock to the 1900s because that's how it was and that's how we want it, and that's how it should always be. Unfortunately, it's not very realistic, not very attuned to reality." This was in stark contrast to how he characterizes himself and his tourism business: "The twentieth century is sort of an extrapolation of the nineteenth century, and now we are coming to the end of that possibility, so a new set of ideas has to develop. And we would like to be at the front line, make that our business. So that's my theory of what we are doing now."

Park proponents push the tourism-based economic development potential of the preserve, describing the park as the best of both worlds, the best economics and the best means to live. This potential was enough to eventually win over the Chamber of Commerce (COC) of Barstow. Prior to World War II,

Barstow had a mining- and transportation-based economy, which has changed to a transportation, tourism, and military-based economy. Initially, the town and its Chamber of Commerce opposed the bill, as a representative of the Barstow COC describes: "We don't have that much development. If somebody wants to come in, we don't want to shut that off . . . We believe in managed use." Once the future of the bill was clear, tourism-related businesses stepped forward, arguing that there would in fact be local benefits from the bill. The Barstow representative responded to my probe about tourism jobs not being good jobs with the following comment:

> They are not high paying, you're right. Most of them are 5, 6, 7, 8 dollar an hour jobs at most. If the tourism gets big enough, then we will have people that own the hotels, own the bigger facilities, that run the malls, that run the tourist at-tractions . . . Not that we're going to become a little Anaheim or Disneyland, but not only do you have entry level jobs, you've got lower management and middle management jobs, and we would certainly like to push those. It also is excellent for the economy. The tourism dollars with the sales tax they generate, the bed tax they generate, that comes back into the city to help fund other projects in the city. It will be a springboard for economic development.

Clearly, tourism wealth is real wealth to her. Are the environmentalists doing the local people a favor by bringing them into the twenty-first century, albeit kicking and screaming? That was Robert P.'s view: "Most of them [park opponents] are the ones who think they are going to make money off the old ways, and they don't. It's their dream that they think is real, but if you know they won't, you're not really hurting them. I look at it as kind of an action of love." Environmentalists did not address the troublesome ethical and envi-ronmental costs resulting from shifting mining to other countries where environmental controls may not be as strong, nor did they discuss the cost in energy consumed to ship the minerals, while U.S. resource consumption con-tinues unabated.[13]

On the following pages I include maps that opponents used in the debate to show the extent of reductions to land access.[14] Map 4.1 shows nonfederal (multiple-use) land across the whole desert region prior to the 1980 Plan. Map 4.2 shows the land that was closed from mineral exploration and other private sector uses after the BLM put in effect its wilderness study areas, but prior to the CDPA. Map 4.3 shows the land that was no longer available under the CDPA, and Map 4.4 is the CDPA plus designated wilderness. Map 4.5 shows anticipated clo-

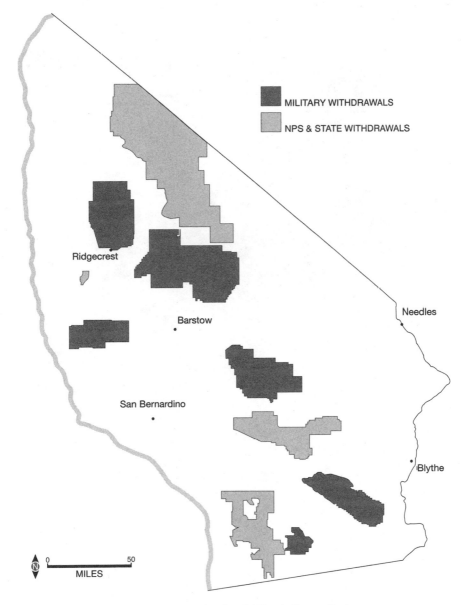

Map 4.1: Multiple-Use Lands in 1993 for the California Desert Region.
Multiple use lands as shown on this map are either private or local government lands,
and those owned by the BLM and available for mining exploration and grazing. This map
and the four that follow it were developed by property rights advocates and other anti-
park legislation lobbyists. The series of maps was used to demonstrate the extent of land
that had been withdrawn from multiple use access over the preceding decade and the
land that would be withdrawn as a result of the California Desert Protection Act. The essential message is that too little land is left for traditional resource use.

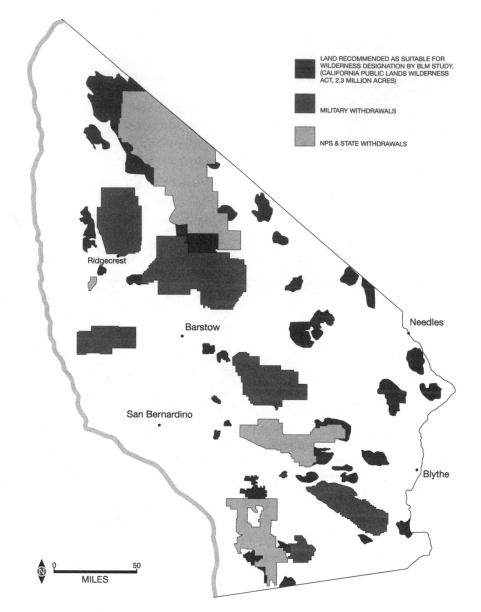

LAND RECOMMENDED AS SUITABLE FOR
WILDERNESS DESIGNATION BY BLM STUDY.
(CALIFORNIA PUBLIC LANDS WILDERNESS
ACT, 2.3 MILLION ACRES)

MILITARY WITHDRAWALS

NPS & STATE WITHDRAWALS

Ridgecrest

Barstow

Needles

San Bernardino

Blythe

0   50
MILES

Map 4.2: Land Recommended for Wilderness Status by the BLM.
The economic use of designated wilderness land is strictly managed.

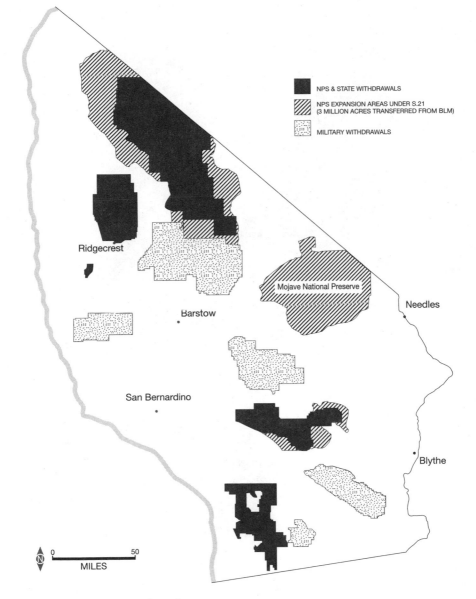

Map 4.3: NPS Expansion from the CDPA.
This map shows the approximate boundaries of the additions to Death Valley National Park in the north and Joshua Tree National Park in the south, along with the new Mojave National Preserve.

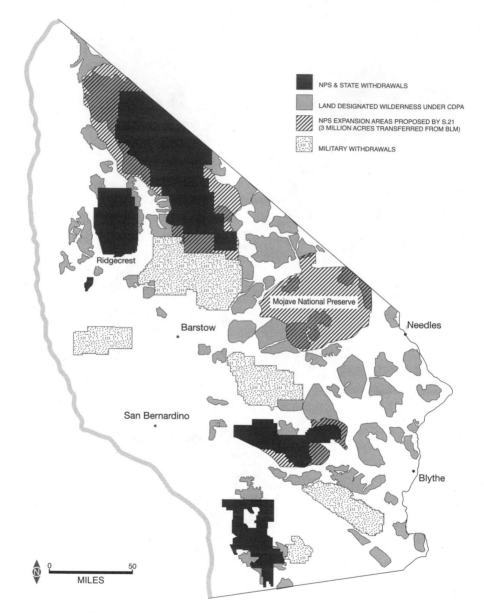

Map 4.4: Land Status after the CDPA.

This map gives a sense of the outcome of the legislation by showing the cumulative effect of the additions to the NPS units in the Southern California desert region, the areas that are designated wilderness and thus very strictly managed, and the existing military reservations. Boundaries are approximate.

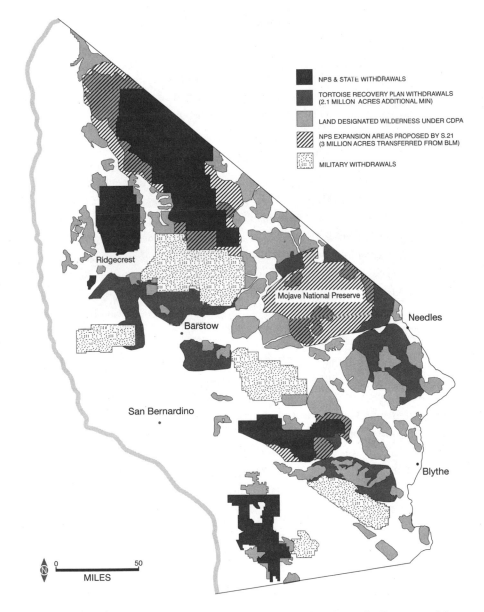

Map 4.5: Land Status after Proposed Withdrawal of Land to Assure the Recovery of the Tortoise.

Unfortunately, the boundaries of the lands designated under the CDPA were not based on the range of the region's preeminent threatened species, the desert tortoise. To assure recovery of tortoise populations, the noted BLM lands were under discussion for management that would prioritize tortoise needs rather than economic uses.

sures of land to give the endangered desert tortoise enough space to recover its population numbers.[15]

Wasting Taxpayer Money

Opponents would often point out the cost of the act to the federal government and so to taxpayers. The motorcycle lobbyist was among those who talked about this:

> The cost associated with transferring from BLM to park service is just ludicrous. When you look at the fiscal problems this country has, and the deficit that we have, not to mention the debt, why are we adding to the park service? Why are we spending money to shuffle the management of our land, our public land, from one agency to another? The signing alone is incredibly expensive, just to change the signs over from BLM, so that people know that they are on park service land instead of BLM. It's federal land. It just doesn't make sense to me when we've got the kind of demands that we have on our resources, financial resources, to be adding to the park system, to be transferring from one agency to another. I can't comprehend that.

The issue of cost was a complicated one, because it was a line-item transfer between federal government units. There were start-up costs for the NPS in taking over the property, and there was also an increase in cost because the NPS manages more intensively than the BLM. The BLM reported that about $600,000 of that desert area's budget went to managing the East Mojave National Scenic Area (EMNSA), but some sources suggest this was an underestimate.[16] The NPS's first-year budget for managing the Mojave National Preserve was $1.1 million, while the 2002 appropriation was just under $3.7 million.[17]

Theme 5: Likely Futures

It's a Nice Area, Let's Keep It the Way It Is

This was to me the most poignant story of this land use fight—park opponents and proponents both want to keep the area roughly as it was prior to the designation. When I asked Renata W. what she would like the area to look like in the future, she responded, "I would like to see it stay the way it was." Other opponents answered with virtually the same words. Robert P., in discussing the need for the park, said, "I guess the question . . . is how do you keep a nice area the way it is?" Environmental lobbyist Ralph N. described this as the most effective argument that the park opponents used, and that having the area not change was a goal both sides shared.[18]

This conflicts rather starkly with another story proponents told—that BLM management was harming the land (see Theme 2). By the end of the conflict, proponents focused more on the positive aspects of the area, in response to concerns that the land would not be perceived as qualifying for national park status.[19] Thus, by the end of the conflict, there was story convergence for both sides. How both sides could agree on this premise of retaining the current quality of the landscape but come to such differing conclusions on how it should be accomplished was closely related to the next story theme, and is further discussed in Chapter 6.

Stop the Los Angeles-ization of the World!

What follows is a subtext of the debate which became evident only through interviews with local proponents, and which, I argue, provides an additional emotional and ideological power to motivate the proponents during so long and hard a battle. Let us listen again Robert P.: "Personally, my wife and I moved out to this desert to get away from the Los Angeles invasion, that's pretty much wall-to-wall people. I guess the question, one question in land use planning, is how do you keep a nice area the way it is. And isn't it sad that the national parks are the only real alternative?" Later in the interview: "Do we have to be Los Angelesized? Look at all the beautiful areas in Southern California that are wall-to-wall people now, like San Bernardino Valley, Orange County, San Diego valley, wall-to-wall people. Is that what we want?" Or, with apologies to North Dakota, we can listen to Bill F.:

> I think many people who oppose the park say, we love it just the way it is, we love living out here in the desert and we want to be left alone. And we don't want the park service coming in and changing our lives. The problem is that if you don't protect it now, forces over which they have no control and the public generally has no control, will come in and change their lives, whether they like it or not . . . It doesn't stay that way, nothing stays that way, except maybe if you live in North Dakota, where nobody wants to move anyway. So here we are between one of the biggest population areas in the country and one of the fastest-growing populations in the country, which is Las Vegas and the Colorado River corridor, that's only fifty miles from the eastern part of the preserve.

This sense of national parks as growth control measures was evident to some of those who lobbied in opposition to the MNP as well. A pro-hunting lobbyist saw environmental education as one role of the national parks, and went on to note that generally national parks "keep it [open space] from being encroached upon by urban sprawl, which is a new paradigm this [pro-hunting] community is going to really have to take a look at. Right now we are not at odds with the Homebuilders Association or with the golf course people or any development type folks, but that is the paradigm when you consider the population growth and what it means to this land, this finite landmass you call the United States of America. And you've got more people coming onto it, and I think the parks can certainly serve a role in staving off any encroachment there."[20]

Or, we can listen to Brian R., former BLM staffer who went to the Department of the Interior and worked on the transition of the area from BLM to NPS. Prior to his appointment at interior, he was not in favor of the MNP designation:

I feel the CDPA was about growth in Southern California. And the reason I feel that is this corridor, this access, controls the utility corridors into Southern California. Pipelines, power lines, highways, and all the accesses to Southern California. If you look at this [points to a CDPA map], there are not very many places to put a pipeline, another highway, another utility corridor to get into Southern California without hitting a wilderness area or a park . . . It is based on this chunk of territory being the key, and if you can control the access to this, you get control on the growth end . . . You'll never find anybody, I think, in the Sierra Club that may even understand that, but the powers that be at that time in putting that together, I'm almost positive that's what they had in mind . . . My personal feeling is that the wilderness and parks were surrogates for growth control.

There are some problems with this hypothesis on utilities, given changing power generation technologies as well as opportunities to increase urban water allocation by decreasing agricultural allocations.[21] Nevertheless, there was great consistency in these views, that the real problem was growth in Southern California and Las Vegas, and the inability to manage that growth.[22]

One problem with this hypothesis was that in fact it is relatively difficult to get the BLM to turn land over for private real estate development. By law, the BLM is allowed to exchange land or to donate land for the achievement of public purposes, but not sell it for development purposes. Public purposes, however, can include both sanitary and nuclear dumps, airports, and military base expansions, all of which have been proposed for BLM land in the Mojave area (see chapter 2). Also, if a developer offered to swap private land of high habitat quality for BLM land of low habitat quality, the BLM will often favor the trade, so there remains a real possibility of private development on what had been federal land.

Another consideration was the timing of the CDPA. It was first proposed during the Reagan/Watt years when privatization of federal land was seen as a distinct possibility.[23] Were privatizing to become official policy, it seems clear that BLM lands would likely be the most vulnerable.[24] Imagine the position of an environmentalist working during the Reagan/Watt years, concerned about sprawling growth from the megalopolis of Los Angeles as well as Las Vegas, and hoping to create the regime least likely to be breached given the vagaries of politics. It makes perfect sense to work very hard to get a greenbelt, or in this case more descriptively a brownbelt,[25] between the two metropolitan areas, and to be sure that the brownbelt had, as Robert P. put it, "the highest possible level of protection."

More Protected Land Is Better

A related story line we might expect to hear was simply that more protected land is better, wherever it may be. As Bill F. of the NPS put it, "I also have a personal philosophy that every square inch of land we can put under some type of protection now is land put in the bank. We can always un-protect it. But once it goes under concrete you can't protect it anymore." Aaron H., an activist for the CDPA, describes it this way: "We're trying to save a world, a habitat, an ecosystem." Why this was important now was clear to local resident Phillip J.:

> The overwhelming reality of today's world is the number of people who live in it . . . When my mother was born, we had 1 billion, and it had taken 400,000 years to get to 1 billion people. Now, within the last hundred years we have gone to 6 billion people, and we're going to double that in forty years. We're getting to be a very crowded planet, and we've got to begin thinking in terms of conservation of resources. And the Mojave is an example of that, and the Mojave National Preserve—that's all the justification it needs, in my opinion.

This fundamental value could inspire local park proponents, volunteers all, to the effort needed to see the legislation through. It was also the sort of rhetoric that many environmentalists have learned to avoid in public because it is so easily characterized as radical and anti-human. This may be why it did not appear prominently in public debate, but it clearly informed the motivations and thinking of supporters of the bill.

Ecosystem Management

The MNP needs to be seen in the context of the entire California Desert Protection Act, which increased protection for Joshua Tree and Death Valley desert areas. Jane J., one of the key Sierra Club volunteers working on the act, commented on the connection of the MNP to the other parks: "There were some people who looked at Death Valley and Joshua Tree and saw that if we don't protect the land between them, it may take fifty years, but we'll stop species exchange and migration, for species diversity as well as for wide-ranging species." The Mojave, then, was a linchpin in assuring that the entire ecosystem would remain functional. As noted by Rob Fulton, however, most desert species do not migrate, so the science behind this argument is questionable.[26]

Secretary of the Interior Babbitt also argued the importance of ecosystem management, but from a financial rather than an ecological perspective. In a letter from Babbitt to Senator Feinstein and intended for wider distribution, he argued that the costs of the bill have been inflated, and that "I anticipate that the Department of the Interior will be able to fully implement S.21, and will do so more efficiently and in a more cost effective manner than ever before by managing the California desert as one ecosystem."[27] This economic incentive was not one of the primary narratives used by environmentalists in describing the importance of the MNP, as indicated by its relative rarity during interviews as well as in talking-points memos and similar written documents. Nevertheless, it was apparently important to Secretary Babbitt, and thus to the outcome of the debate.

Ecosystem management and coordination of management among various federal land agencies was one of the goals of Vice President Al Gore's Reinventing Government initiative.[28] Secretary Babbitt followed up on the goal of ecosystem management. Under his direction the various federal agencies with land within the desert region, including the Bureau of Land Management, the National Park Service, and the Department of Defense, undertook ecosystem wide integrated planning—and this process created yet more fear and dismay among local residents concerned about property rights and their access to the land. It is important to note here that this new planning effort was based largely on the habitat of the desert tortoise, a federally listed threatened species. The tortoise is often considered an indicator species for the desert.[29]

Unfortunately for local residents as well as the federal agencies, the boundaries of the CDPA and its wilderness areas were drawn up with no attention to tortoise habitat. Thus tortoise protection was not assured just by virtue of the CDPA, despite its increased land protection. To residents, this round of large ecosystem planning constitutes a third wave of land use controls—first it was the CDPA, then it was the wilderness areas in the CDPA, now it's the tortoise habitat ecosystem plans (see the maps in this chapter). To people who already feel their use rights are at risk, this third wave of planning felt like a threat indeed.

Theme 6: Political Aspiration

Politics, Politics, Politics

In searching to understand why the preserve came to be, park opponents most often ascribed it to political aspirations. MNP ranchers Tony and Betty K. give voice to this idea:

> TONY K.: But to go back to this park, why we didn't want it to be a park . . . Every-
> thing we have worked for we would have lost, our home, our way of life, our
> livelihood, our roots that we've put down in this old desert, and all that would
> have been washed away by a national park. For what?
>
> BETTY K.: Yeah, for what?
>
> TONY K.: That's it, for what. People can come and visit this preserve, they could
> visit it under blm. It's not like it wasn't open, people could come and visit it.
> And so it was all for somebody's political aspirations, this national park.

Virtually all parties to the designation agree that the bill passed in 1994 because it finally had the support of both California senators, along with White House muscle for both the bill and the senators.[30] To say, however, that a bill had Senate support says that either it is something that a senator feels very strongly about personally, or it is something that a senator's constituency, generally a vocal interest group, wants very much and the senator therefore obliges. Senator Feinstein, the lead in the bill, no doubt cared personally about the environment and was generally in favor of actions to benefit the environment. But did she really care personally about the desert area of the East Mojave? The senator made two documented trips to the area during her first term, only one of which was to the East Mojave. The first she undertook after significant pressure from opponents, as Renata W. relates: "Then when Senator Feinstein came in [to office], we couldn't get her to the desert. So, finally after I had been back to D.C. with the [local] government group, she did agree to come out. They picked her up in a helicopter, flew her over some of the desert, stopped at a rancher's and had barbecue, and then she flew back out. That's all she saw. When they had the dedication of the Joshua Tree National Park, once again she flew in by helicopter; when the dedication was over, she flew out."

While the tone was of course different, park proponents tell a similar story of offers to guide her around the area and difficulty getting her to accept. While her actions may simply reflect the time pressures of being a new senator, it seems unlikely that she acted from personal love of the East Mojave.[31] By contrast, Senator Cranston became famous in part for hiking through the breadth of California to publicize the need for land preservation. One reason reported for Senator Feinstein's support of the bill was her desire to honor Cranston's legacy. Another reason no doubt was constituent pressure. The Sierra Club committed itself to the passage of the CDPA, as did other California environmental groups. In her election campaign Feinstein promised to get the CDPA passed, and in that difficult election she received significant support from the environment lobby.

Theme 7: Characterizations of the Other Side

Fat Senators and Urban Meddlers

It was particularly irksome to local opponents that the people who wanted to increase desert land protection in their view knew little about the land. Renata W. described the debate as "the people who don't know the desert against the people who do." The fairness of such a characterization depends on the criteria for "knowing." Renata W. certainly knows the desert, but lives a long way from the Mojave National Preserve. Does she know the Mojave? Rob Fulton "has lived in the Mojave since 1986, worked here, studied here, read volumes of research (more than most people). I've walked it, driven it, flown over it, sung to it, cursed it, . . . and I don't know it yet!"[32]

Aaron H., one of the primary CDPA activists, has traveled the desert extensively, as has Jane J. None of the main activists, however, actually lived in the preserve. At the Washington level, most of the respondents I talked with had not visited the Mojave for any extended period of time, if at all, even though they were working on the bill—and this was true for both sides of the debate, mining and off-road vehicle lobbyists as well as some of the environmental lobbyists. The feeling among desert residents was that, as one respondent put it, "we don't try to tell the bay area what to do with the bay, so why should they tell us what to do with the desert?" Lack of clarity about the criteria for knowing does not change the salience of the point for park opponents. Many people interviewed commented that the act was "an easy green vote for eastern senators," which in fact for Democrats it was.

One motivation of environmentalists, according to some opponents, was simple jealousy because the environmentalists did not get to live in the desert and see it every day or personally manage it. In point of fact, the four environmentalists who are credited with originating and pushing the CDPA lived in modest houses or townhouses in suburban Los Angeles or Barstow, houses without much land. Of course, as citizens of the United States, they owned the federal lands, including the land where the desert cattle run, in which all citizens have a common interest.

Proponents Response—Largely No Comment

The environmentalists tended to be more discreet about characterizing their opposition. Hints of their view come through in comments such as Robert P.'s on the changing of the economic base as an act of love for misguided opponents (quoted above). Often proponents pointed out just how few people would actually be affected by the act. Others characterized the ranching and mining industries as taxpayer-subsidized; these are activities that a local park proponent described as "unacceptable uses of beautiful public lands."

Bitterness and Demonization

Some degree of demonization of the opposition took place on both sides. Environmentalists were often portrayed as "elite" and "obstinate," the opponents to the park as "reactionaries." Both sides accused the other of being "selfish" and "unreasonable." Both sides felt the other benefited improperly from government action—park proponents seeing the miners and ranchers as federal subsidy recipients, opponents seeing the environmentalists as federal dollar spendthrifts using tax revenues to achieve their personal goals of recreation. Both sides saw the other as political powerhouses, opponents, as noted above, pointing out the Sierra Club's influence with Senator Feinstein, proponents pointing out the national power of the hunting, ranching, mining, and the motorcyclists' lobbies. It suffices to say that another thing the sides shared was bitterness.

An Outsider Narrative

After completing the interviews, analysis, and preliminary write-up of my research, I presented my findings to a small group of local residents, as further described in the Appendix. During that community presentation I became aware of a narrative I had not previously recognized. Three different participants suggested or supported the idea that the entire California Desert Protection Act was a cover for a very different sort of goal:

> PARTICIPANT 1: There is a pattern developing, and has been [developing], wherever there is a resource in the U.S. that's being taken away from the users of today, and you're going to laugh at me, but it's going to the U.N. [United Nations].
> PARTICIPANT 2: That's true.
> PARTICIPANT 3: [later] The one-world army is really behind this [the CDPA].
> These opponents really believed that deep in the desert, helicopters would soon land with blue-helmeted U.N. troops set to begin a takeover of the country.

After hearing this one-world army narrative and reflecting upon the interviews that I originally conducted, I realized that this story had been hinted at in several interviews but I had simply dismissed it out of hand. My own biases prevented me from recognizing it as a significant story among some traditional-use advocates. As a narrative, it fits well with fears of increased governmental intervention and reduction of local control over the future. This finding suggests the importance of narrative research—it is only by taking the residents and their beliefs seriously that planners and policy analysts can really understand the source of a conflict. And only then can the planners/analysts begin to address these fears.

Commentary

Proponents' Narratives: Tragedy Averted

When dressed down to the bare bones, there are essentially three proactive elements in the narratives told publicly by park proponents to justify the need for the new park. First, the Mojave fits the established criteria for new units of the NPS, and thereby deserved the increased protection that the NPS could provide. This sets the scene and creates moral entitlement—the land was deserving. Second, BLM management provides insufficient protection. This argument has two formulations. One was the public story that the problem was the BLM's multiple-use mandate; the second was a more private story, that because of the BLM's constituency orientation (mining and grazing), it could not be trusted to provide sufficient protection for the land. In either case, this part of the narrative provides the historical flow of action and suggests that without a change, the land will not get the kind treatment it deserves. Third, the flow of action was carried into the future, as the legislation was predicted to create a better world. A better protected Mojave allows for management of the larger ecosystem, reducing costs and improving environmental conditions for the entire desert region. Less publicly, proponents suggest that one of the long-term goals was growth control, and the Mojave designation was important because it places a brownbelt between the sprawling metropolitan areas of Los Angeles and Las Vegas. Designation not only protects the immediate lands, but improves the future for the entire Southwest.

The picture thus painted was a land that is important and deserving of increased protection (static view), a land threatened by its current management and by external metropolitan growth, and a land that could help protect and sustain other areas (dynamic views). It was the picture of a tragedy in the making, with an honorable main figure (the Mojave) which through no fault of its own was destined for a bad end (exploitation and development). Yet, this story provides the opportunity for lawmakers to step into the plot and avert the tragic outcome, ensuring that for all time the worthy protagonist is saved from the risks in its environment. As a bonus to legislators, action in the Mojave will prevent similar tragic outcomes for other areas—in fact, for the whole California desert. The safety and prosperity of the wider kingdom was thus assured by one small action—designating the land as protected under the national park system. This formulation sufficed in persuading lawmakers to enact the CDPA—but watered down to accommodate existing land users.

Opponents' Narratives: In Search of a Plot

Opponents to the designation had multiple reasons why the designation was unwise and necessary. These basically came down to the common sense point of "if it ain't broke, don't fix it"—and in opponents' current view, the area was being managed just fine.[33] The essential elements of this position were as follows. The 1980 BLM Plan for the desert was a balanced compromise that had been worked out with extensive public involvement and represented fairly the interests involved in the desert, including environmental protection. In this version, the past was not a problem; rather, it was an enlightened example of participatory management for multiple use, including recreation and ecological protection. There is some irony in this, in that prior to the threat of NPS management, many residents thoroughly disliked the BLM and complained bitterly about them. Nevertheless, once the legislative threat was real, the BLM looked pretty good to residents.

Given that the current situation was both equitable and satisfactory, the proponents need to show very good reasons why property and use rights should be compromised, and in opponents' view, there were no such very good reasons. The opponents argued that increasing protection of the land would reduce development of resource-based industry and force residents instead into relying on tourism, which was a less-valued economic base. The coming of the NPS heralded an increase in governmental intervention in their lives, with little or no positive outcomes for the residents.

At the local level these elements coalesced into a powerful plot. This story essentially tells of the little guy run over by the power of the government gone amuck. This little guy had been quietly living out his life, contributing to the environment, loving the land as he used it, and living the western tradition of ranching, mining, and minding one's own business. With the park designation, government was trying to come in and substitute a distant and ill-conceived idea of what ought to be for local direct knowledge of the land, destroying our hero's livelihood along the way. This is a classic story, deeply rooted in American consciousness and history and able to draw on central myths of yeoman farmers and Thomas Jefferson. Unfortunately for opponents, this story did not get much play at the national level.[34]

At the national level, opponents arguably had no narrative, because they had no plot.[35] Instead, they spent the entire debate in a reactive mode, rebutting arguments that the proponents put forward, and seeming not to believe that the proponents' arguments could ever be persuasive enough to create a perceived need for change. In this, they were wrong. Opponents' rebuttals did not form a persuasive enough whole to counteract the power of the potentially tragic situation the proponents were able to project. What the opponents did accomplish was to bring attention to specific points of inequity within the bill, which were then addressed by permitting ranching and drawing the boundaries of the preserve to exclude active mines.

The major problem with the opponents' story, as I see it, was that they could not change the fact that the Mojave was federal land to begin with, and federal land is to be managed for the good of the whole United States people. Proponents were able to create a perceived situation in which the interests of all Americans were at risk from local development and local BLM management. Opponents attempted to show that there was no risk and the broader interests were not being impaired, but they were unsuccessful. Instead, the local arguments of inequity were largely addressed via specific changes to the bill.

In the end, how things were said mattered. Legislators responded to the tragic structure suggested by the park proponents, but delivered only the minimum required to avert tragedy; the land transferred management, but not at the high protection level requested by proponents. Opponents achieved consideration of the specifics of their position but not the whole, as appropriate given the structure of their non-story. The lessons here for future policy issues are clear—attention to the rhetorical structure, the quality of story, is important in forming policy arguments. To get the votes of a majority of legislators, the bill had to have good political timing, solid grassroots organizing, strong environmental lobbying, and the dedicated support of the home-state senators with support for them from the White House. But given that elected officials make decisions based on substance as well as on political packaging, the issue also had to be persuasive—it had to be a good story. In the end, environmentalists were able to tell a better story than multiple-use advocates. The irony of the designation, however, is that under the terms of the legislation, many of those traditional uses continue. It is to this debate that the next chapter turns.

CHAPTER 5

Of Miners, Cowboys, and the NRA

And then there are the stark, hostile deserts of the interior, a landscape
that even today people find hard to love, one that has often drawn the
angry, the misfitted, the rejected, the alienated. Everywhere in the region
there is so much space—so much amplitude of rugged rock, soil, climate,
and vista—that the landscape, like the gods of old, can leave men and
women feeling humbled or diminished, exhilarated or threatened.

—DONALD WORSTER, *Under Western Skies*

In the traditions of the culture in which we were raised, ever firm in
distinguishing between Man and Nature, a humanized desert is a self-
canceling proposition. The traditions of Greek logic require us to dis-
criminate clearly between D and not-D, that which is deserted and without people, and that which is peopled and therefore cannot be a desert.
And the Judeo-Christian tradition requires our deserts to be truly waste,
cruel and inhuman places for the punishment and solace of sinful but
repentant mankind.

—RICHARD MISRACH AND REYNER BANHAM, *Desert Cantos*

While the question of whether the Mojave would be a park or preserve was important, so too was the potential fate of the traditional uses of the desert. The
history of Anglo settlement in the desert is a history of mining, of ranching,
and of living off the land. Would the ranchers who have been there for generations still be able to graze their cows on the sparse desert brush? Would corporations and the few remaining individual prospectors be able to look for
undiscovered minerals still hidden in the ground? Most important politically,
although perhaps least important ecologically, would people still be able to
hunt and trap? Would they be able to hunt not just the coyote and quail, but
the rare trophy big horn sheep that find a home in the remote parts of the preserve? Would there be limits on where autos, jeeps, and motorcycles were allowed? If so, how strict?

The answers to these questions would tell what sort of park unit the area could be; alternatively, deciding what sort of unit it ought to be would tell what uses could be allowed. While the answers were interrelated, here I present them separately for clarity of discussion. The arguments are particularly interesting because they crystallize much of the debate the country is currently undertaking about what sort of nation we are and will be. Are we at heart agrarian? Industrial? Postindustrial? And just as importantly, does our desired future match the directions in which we are heading?

To try to get to the center of this, I present the stories told by four major user groups that got involved in the debate over the California Desert Protection Act. I also present some basic facts regarding hunting, ranching, mining, and off-road motorcycling, and then the narratives used by the various parties regarding each of the four topics. Facts are, however, selective: Which authors do I cite on the effects of cattle on the desert ecology? Do I present the ecological devastation wrought by huge off-road motorcycle races that stopped a decade ago, or do I describe how the tracks of a jeep driven through a sand wash disappear immediately? Do I talk about the average hunter pursuing quail and rabbits, or do I focus on the more controversial and highly elite hunting of big horn sheep?

None of the issues presented here has a body of facts that all sides agree to; much of the debate is, in fact, over what counts as the facts. I present what I see as a balanced portrayal of the issues using the best science available. I am sure that local ranchers will disagree with my choice of facts regarding grazing. Others may disagree with other parts of the analysis. How facts get selected and presented in writing or in policy decisions is a rhetorical issue—this is central to the point of interpretive planning.

In the previous chapter, I kept separate the narratives regarding an issue and the facts relevant to it. This is a helpful approach when what matters is understanding the debate surrounding an issue rather than finding some external truth regarding it; the approach rests on a premise that in complicated policy questions, facts are selected for persuasive purposes and there rarely is a neutral set of relevant facts. In this chapter, I group together the facts as I see them and the arguments participants used. This will feel more comfortable to those who believe that facts are not strongly dependent on rhetorical construction and therefore a neutral set of facts can be determined, but who still recognize the need for better inclusion of narratives in the policy and planning process. This places the planner/analyst (and in this case, the reader) in a position of judging the appropriateness of narratives based on the selected set of facts. This is a midrange approach to the role of interpretation in the planning process, where fact determination neither leads interpretation and framing nor follows, but where the analysis of narratives and the foregrounding of facts occur concurrently and in relationship to each other.

There is a third approach to this issue of facts and conflicting rhetoric. In this, participants agree that what will count as a fact is whatever the group agrees is a fact. Determining what counts as a fact then becomes an important part of the community dialogue. As interpretive planning develops, this may come to be an important part of the process. In other cases, it may be as well to ignore conflict over facts and try to search for points of narrative concurrence using the framing process that I later describe.

For now, I will turn to the four main uses of the desert, and will add some commentary on pipelines and transmission lines as well as on the population of wild burros, because these are important management issues for the preserve even though they were not important issues in the debate. I close with some analysis and commentary on these particular issues of the designation process.

Hunting the Big and the Small

Background

The future of hunting in the Mojave preserve proved to be one of the most legislatively difficult issues. Hunting is one of the main differences between national parks, which never allow it, and other units of the system, which sometimes allow hunting.[1] The legislation authorizing the Mojave specifically allows hunting. Game management continues to be the responsibility of the California State Department of Fish and Wildlife. Hunted wildlife species in the Mojave include rabbits, the mourning dove, Gambel's quail, and chukar, which is an introduced species.[2] There are a few mule deer (also an introduced species), which attract a disproportionate number of hunters. An unfortunate victim of gun users is the desert tortoise; on test plots, 14.3 percent of tortoise carcasses had evidence of gunshot wounds.[3] Trapping is permitted in the preserve, as it was under BLM management. The 1988 Plan noted that there were an average of fifteen permits for trap lines issued each year in the EMNSA, with coyotes and bobcats being the most commonly trapped animals.

The prize animal for Mojave hunting is the big horn sheep. Nine permits

To understand desert hunters, it helps to imagine a ninety-degree morning where the desert sunlight is already a palpable force pressing on your
shoulders. You've come to one of your favorite spots in the desert, and
are waiting, waiting, walking, and waiting, for quail. Years of study of
the ways of quail tell you where to look, where to wait. Finally, you see
a bird. Unfortunately, it also sees you—and heads straight up a steep
desert hill. You follow it. Straight up. It is faster than you are, and needs
no switchbacks. A bullet, of course, is faster than it is. And so the contest ensues.

At the end of the day, you may or may not have killed a bird, or a few.
You stop at the water guzzler you habitually care for. It is a flat concrete
basin covering a small concrete catchment, designed to grab the swift
desert rain and keep it for game rather than for the soil, the plants, or
the aquifer. The entrance to it is just big enough for quail. You clear out
the brush accumulated since your last visit. If you didn't keep doing this,
soon there would be no quail—quail are not native to this desert, and
like cattle, rely on the water guzzlers for survival.

were issued for big horn kills in 1987, the first year hunting was allowed. An
interesting system is used for issuing these permits: all but one permit is lot-
teried off to potential hunters for a fairly nominal amount, but one permit
each year is auctioned off to the highest bidder, who typically pays around
$100,000.[4] This auctioned permit often goes to a big game hunter interested
in completing what is called a grand slam, killing one of each type of big horn
sheep in the world in one year. Funds from the permit sales were used to support research and management of the herd. The same big horn population
serves as a nursery herd, with excess animals removed most years for reloca-
tion to create new herds in historic big horn habitats. In 1987, the BLM estimated the big horn population at 550 to 600, but later reports show that the
population is declining.[5] Other than for tortoises and perhaps big horn sheep,
the environmental impact of hunting in the area appears minimal.

Hunting Narratives

As the debate was constructed, it was largely up to the proponents of park
status to show why legislators should prohibit hunting, and they failed to do

this with sufficient persuasive force to create the change. The National Rifle Association was one of the major participants in this part of the debate, and Laura S. of the NRA describes their position this way:

> Our point was, there was no reason to close this area to hunting. There was no reason to do that. That is why when the legislation came up last year, we took the position that if it's a fait accompli that you are going with this legislation, and this land is transferred out of BLM's management to the park service, that we still wanted hunting retained, and to do so then we recommended that the area be designated a preserve rather than a park, because preserve status has just come to be used to designate park units where hunting or trapping or other such activities are allowed. And that was the position that we prevailed on.

Later in the interview, Laura S. comments: "[Hunting] was an activity that had been permitted for decades on BLM lands, so it was historic by nature"—again, creating a situation in which proponents must show the need for the change. Hunting lobbyist Thomas G. described their position as concern that "legitimate forms of recreation should continue."

There were many contributing story lines. One of the most popular, perhaps because most poignant, was that hunters improve habitat for all species. Local hunting groups maintain water guzzlers, which are shallow tanks with concrete aprons designed to catch the rare desert rainfall and store it. Openings allow game to reach the water, thereby supplying a perennial source of fresh water for both game and other species. Fred F. describes it this way: "We're representing conservation. We refer to our people as sportsmen conservationists, and they are . . . They are all out there trying to enhance habitat, support organizations that are doing positive things for the environment . . . There [are] plenty of benefits for not only game species but nongame species and in many cases endangered species."

The design of the guzzlers does not accommodate all animals, however, as pointed out by Linda C.; different guzzler designs favor different animals. Biologist Rob Fulton indicated that no endangered species he was aware of would use a water guzzler—or even need human interventions for water; endemic species are highly drought resistant.[6]

Rebuttal 1: There's Nothing to Hunt, Anyway

How were the park proponents going to create a case for stopping hunting in the area? The first way was to indicate that hunting didn't really matter, because there was little to hunt. The favorite comparison by environmentalists suggested that "more deer were hit by cars on the Washington, D.C., George Washington Parkway each month than are shot during a year of hunting in the Mojave."[7] Somewhere around twenty deer a year are reported taken in the preserve area each year. This is a particularly useful story for eastern congresspersons because it gives a comparison they understand and focuses on the favored game in much of the East. It ignores the fact that deer are not the main game in the desert. In fact, several long-term residents I talked with had never seen a deer in the area,[8] although I was lucky enough to see two. Not surprisingly, however, those trying to retain hunting virtually never discussed the trapping of coyotes and bobcats, which is also undertaken in this part of the desert.

This argument over numbers of game killed also focuses on outcomes, not process, in hunting. Asked about the low numbers of actual animals taken in the area, Thomas G. responded: "That may represent only the final outcome of the individuals reduced to bag. There are hundreds of thousands of hours of opportunity out there for people. Everybody that goes hunting does not need to have a critter reduced to their game bag to consider the trip successful. In fact, if you were guaranteed that every time you went out, you probably reduce some of the adventure to it, because it's not a guarantee."

Park opponents used numbers creatively as well. The California Department of Fish and Wildlife provided lobbyists with information on the total number of days hunters spent in the area to show that hunting was important. These numbers were used in talking-points memos and position papers by opponents. What was not mentioned, however, was that those statistics were for all of San Bernardino County, the largest county in the country. The MNP is only about 12 percent of the county, and much of the rest of the county is in BLM management with hunting allowed. Proponents also questioned the validity of the survey method.

The above discussion ignores one of the key reasons why it was important to park opponents to continue hunting—big horn sheep. Environmental lobbyist Henry M., describing the outcome of preserve status and the importance of hunting in the Mojave, comments: "It was a line in the sand by the NRA and Safari Club International, those are the sheep hunters, who are actually very wealthy, most of them. This is high-dollar stuff . . . These folks are used to paying a lot of money to go get their sheep and its very important to them. And the NRA and Safari International were in there because of the sheep."

The NRA and other groups tended to focus on game hunting, not trophy hunting. This was no doubt a good strategic move for two reasons. Given that the national population of big horn sheep has experienced significant declines as their habitats have been developed, many question whether we should hunt them at all. The second reason, as shown in the Henry M. quote above, is that big horn sheep hunting is largely an elite avocation and therefore does not make the best press. It does, however, explain in part the political muscle that was expended to assure that hunting would continue in this area, along with internal NRA issues described in Chapter 3.[9]

Rebuttal 2: Managing Hunting Is Expensive

As we saw in Chapter 4, one of the park opponents' major narratives about the Mojave was that the designation should not be changed because it would increase costs. Similarly, one of the park proponents' stories was that hunting should not continue because it would increase the park service's management cost for the area—as stated by Henry M.: "Hunting is going to need increased law enforcement in the Mojave. They are going to have to monitor and enforce [in ways] they usually don't have to bother with in the national parks. So that is going to cost more money."

Sorting out the truth in this argument is difficult. Park proponents took the estimated cost of managing hunting and divided by the number of deer taken, to come up with astronomical costs per hunted animal—$20,000 each. In fact, most of the cost of managing hunting is borne by the California Department of Fish and Wildlife, which retains authority over game in the preserve, making the cost argument "smoke and mirrors" according to Fred F. He also argued that hunting should be retained for its economic benefits: "Those who go out and buy licenses, buy firearms and ammunition have a self-imposed excise taxes on that firearms ammunition and archery equipment which goes into an account. That's ten or eleven percent depending on exactly what type of firearm it is . . . About 75 percent of those moneys find their way right back on the ground . . . The whole concept of hunting is self-perpetuating, perpetuates continuation of healthy wildlife. It is user-pay, user-benefit."

Hunting's generation of income reveals why there is such support for big horn sheep hunting. The annual permit auction, yielding between $60,000 to over $100,000, is one of the single biggest revenue generators from the area for the California Department of Fish and Wildlife; thus, it is not surprising that the department was loath to give up management of hunting in the Mojave.

The truth of the costs versus benefits of hunting in the area is a complex issue with highly contested sets of facts. What is clear is that both sides could argue as suited their particular position.

Local versus National and State Concerns

One of the interesting comparisons between the narratives at the national and state agency levels versus narratives told at the local level was the importance of hunting. Hunting does not figure prominently in any of my local interviews, except in a telephone interview with a representative of the Society for the Conservation of Big Horn Sheep, a pro-hunting group. This may reflect that my local interviews happened a year and a half after the designation was complete, and hunting was then secure. Or it may reflect the fact that the Mojave is surrounded by BLM land on which small game hunting was never threatened, and that is the sort of hunting most local people actually do. Given that Mojave area residents are concentrated on the periphery of the preserve and not in the center, it is likely just as easy for them to go outside the preserve area to hunt as to go into the preserve area. If this interpretation is correct, it supports Henry M.'s argument that hunting in the Mojave was largely a symbolic issue, and particularly an issue of the NRA. It was not symbolic, however, for big horn hunters, whose access to big horn sheep would have been significantly reduced. Given that these tend to be an elite and powerful group, it makes sense that this would be a larger issue nationally than locally, since the Mojave is home to noticeably few elite and powerful types.

Grazing

Background

Grazing in the East Mojave has a long tradition. Early miners brought with them a few cattle, and serious operations began prior to 1900 in Lanfair Valley and near the Granite Mountains. The land was more heavily grazed in the past than now. In 1920, the Rock Springs Land and Cattle Company alone kept 9,223 cattle, while in 1986 fewer than 3,400 cattle were permitted for the entire area.[10] The Mojave is reported to provide some of the best grazing in the desert. "Best" is relative; the sparseness of the desert vegetation means that grazing is very dispersed, averaging one cow-calf unit per 350 to 600 acres;[11] by comparison, in Georgia it is one cow-calf unit per acre.[12]

To an easterner, the ranching business in an environment as harsh as the Mojave seems quite odd. The cattle are usually Texas longhorn or a mixture including longhorn, providing a cow which is wilder, wilier, and leaner than the more domesticated breeds popular in the East. Late one afternoon at the end of a hike, I sat talking with a friend in a small desert spring. After a while a cow with her calf appeared in the distance. It was to dairy cows what wolves are to poodles. It waited, snorted, moved away whenever we moved toward it, and generally let us know that we were invading her turf, and she did not like it.

The rancher may only see her or his cattle once a year, when it is time to separate the cows from the yearling calves and ship the calves off to their next stop—somewhere milder with more plentiful grass so that the calves become tender cows. To those who are concerned with the quality of life of livestock—the Mojave cows are the essence of free-range beef. They are also the boniest mammals I have seen this side of the Mexican border.

In the mid-1990s, there were between five and eight ranching families grazing cattle in the preserve, depending on how one defines family.[13] The ranches were generally reported to provide a moderate living to ranch families, but not the level of prosperity that can accrue to ranchers working in gentler climes. Ranching in the Mojave means producing calves that are raised in the area for about one year before they are sold to feed lots in wetter areas for fattening into a size appropriate for slaughter. The ranchers typically provide a mineral supplement to the cattle, but do not provide extra feed except in exceptionally bad (dry) years. Grazing occurs year-round, with most allotments managed by rotating the cattle around various parts of the permitted area.[14]

Grazing allotments covered 1,255,343 acres of federal land, or about 84 percent of the national preserve. There were eleven separate allotments, which accommodate approximately 3,400 cattle. This represents less than half of one percent of cows grazing on California's public range lands; the desert area as a whole produces only about 0.3 percent of California's beef production.[15] Lack of water is the main limiting factor. Ranchers, with the cooperation of the BLM, address this problem by providing artificial water sources, often by pumping ground water into tanks or by collecting and enhancing natural springs. Cattle also use unenhanced natural spring sources. Range improvement equipment is donated by the BLM to the rancher, while the rancher provides the labor to construct the water tank. The desert plan required that, where warranted and possible, "all existing water sources and those developed in the future will include consideration for wildlife. This water for wildlife is provided at the rancher's expense."[16] The rancher's expense relates to the fact that ranchers must buy water rights; some of their water rights, therefore, are used to support wildlife—whether they like it or not.

Effects of Grazing on the Habitat

Claudia Luke, a biologist and codirector of the Granite Mountain Research Station in the preserve, and others completed an extensive review of the scientific literature on the effects of human activity on the California Desert (the Luke report), including discussion of the effects of grazing on the desert ecosystem.[17] As they explain, some history helps in placing the effects of grazing into perspective. Unlike the Great Plains, "the western deserts did not evolve amidst large congregating mammals (i.e., bison, elk, deer). Most perennial grasses in the arid west grow as isolated tufts and do not have the extensive root base of grasses that evolved with large herbivores . . . Such a growth pattern makes them more vulnerable to trampling and grazing because individual plants are more easily killed."[18] Because grazing began with the first Anglo settlements, we have very little ability to compare the current desert habitat to what it would be without grazing. There are, however, hints. Two different reports, both from early in the century, indicate that prior to grazing, the desert areas of Tucson and parts of New Mexico had such a quantity of perennial grasses that they were baled for hay; now extensively grazed, those areas are currently dominated by shrubs.[19]

Changes to the desert ecology from overgrazing can be extensive. Woody perennials often replace palatable grasses and exotics increase. Moreover, reduction in grass cover along with hoof trampling may change the soils. With changes in plant cover come changes in the density of rodents, which may actually increase. Unfortunately, rodents and cattle probably compete with the endangered desert tortoise for palatable grasses—although that issue is far from settled.[20]

All of these findings are controversial, however, and the science is far from proven. Also, the term *overgrazing* should be stressed. Management strategies, such as limiting numbers of cattle, timing the grazing to when the flora can best withstand it, and using a rotation of rest and grazing periods for particular plots of land, may limit the negative effects of grazing. Despite this, the authors of the Luke report are not optimistic about grazing in the desert region: "Whether the range in the southwestern desert can ever sufficiently recover to support livestock grazing is open to speculation, but if recovery were achieved, there might be an optimum level of grazing which is stimulatory for the vegetation."[21]

Ranching Narratives

Ranching Is a Part of the Culture / The Cowboy Myth

To many local people, ranching provides a sense of continuing local history and culture. Mal Wessel, former mayor of Barstow, for instance, said concern for ranchers was his primary conflict with the CDPA. He talked about ranching in terms of John Wayne movies and living history and deep connections to the image of the West. Park proponents discussed the political power of the cowboy myth. At park opponents' behest, Senator Feinstein toured the area and stopped for a barbecue lunch with a local ranch family. The rancher described it this way: "Feinstein came here and talked to us, and saw the desert firsthand. She felt that grazing had historical value here and it was part of the culture and it was one of the things that needed to be preserved, and that's why there is grazing in the bill." Henry M. and Robert P. concur that that visit was what changed the senator's mind about allowing grazing to continue.

The NPS Can't Manage Grazing

Most opponents rejected the proposed transfer of management responsibility from the BLM to the park service, because the NPS was not skilled in the management of grazing. A grazing lobbyist describes this concern: "There was a great deal of concern that if this was in the national park system, that [continuation of grazing] would no longer be the case, because the National Park Service is not able to handle grazing. They don't traditionally lease the land for grazing, obviously, so they don't really have the regulatory scheme or the personnel in the field to handle grazing issues like the BLM or the Forest Service. And we were concerned about that." Interestingly enough, as Tony and Betty K. began ranching under the NPS, they became moderately positive about working with the agency, in part no doubt because they remember the hassles of working with the BLM. Because the environmentalists did not want to see

---

A Rancher's Story about Environmentalists:

Author Sharmain Apt Russel relates the following story, which seems to sum up what I heard from ranchers about environmentalists:

During one range tour, Doc (the rancher) got up and spoke his mind. "You enviornmental folks are phony as a three-dollar bill. All you do is moan and complain and file lawsuits. Show me one place where you've ever improved one acre of ground!"

There was a moment of silence.

"Why, Doc," replied one of the phony environmentalists. "I thought you understood. We don't have any land to improve or manage. The federal agencies and the ranchers do that. The only way we can make a change is by working with the laws that govern the land."

It was another turning point for Doc Hatfield. Suddenly, he could see why environmentalists so often seemed "uptight, frustrated, and angry." Suddenly, he felt sorry for them. They weren't lawyer-loving busybodies. They really cared about the land. *But they didn't own any themselves.*

(Russell 1994)

---

grazing in the Mojave, they did not put up an argument supporting the NPS's ability to manage grazing.

Grazing Is Natural to the Landscape

Grazing was also presented as a natural part of the desert ecosystem. Mike B. suggested that this would be one of his first arguments to a congressional representative about why grazing should continue: "The land that this park encompasses is open range land; it's natural grazing land; it's been grazed by animals for eons . . . It's very much a symbiotic natural process: the grasslands are grazed off by the animals and . . . , to use an urban analogy, it's like a lawn-mower rejuvenates the grasses on your lawn. The grazing of the livestock does the same, the scattering of seeds acting as a natural tilling process." There are many problems with this analogy, since sod and wild grasses are quite different and cows are hardly lawnmowers, but most problematic is that, unlike the grasslands Meyers was more familiar with, the desert was not grazed by large herbivores prior to Anglo settlement, as previously noted.

Rebuttal 1: It's Bad for the Ecology

Henry M. cited grazing's negative ecological impact as the main reason they wanted it removed from the park. He describes this reasoning: "What the bill originally had, which we thought was more than generous, . . . was a twenty-five-year phase out. For a quarter century, [ranchers] would be allowed to continue, and I think that most of these folks are fifty years old and older, some of them quite a bit older, and that grazing would be phased out over time. Because it does have major impacts on the ecology of that area, and will continue to do so." He added later: "In fact the grazing bothers me more personally than the hunting, because there are cows out there and the cows do a lot of damage. You can see places where there aren't cows, and look at the vegetation, as opposed to where there are, it's very striking.

Rebuttal 2: Ranching Is Subsidized and Represents Few People

Robert P. comments: "[Ranching is] a welfare program, bad economics. Cattle grazing shouldn't be going on in the desert; it's uneconomic, taxpayer subsidized . . . There are six full-time cowboys within the preserve. Why are we spending all of this tax money to keep them? With a technology that is no longer used." I asked, "Why do you think?" He responded, "The only answer is the myth of the cowboy."

Ranching: Story Consensus

Unlike many of the issues discussed in the Mojave debate, there is a close correlation between the ranching narrative as presented at the national level and the issue as understood at the local level. Debate centered on equity to hard-working people, the salt of the country, some of the few people left who live the cowboy mystique. Perhaps because this is such a bedrock value in American society, there was little need to change the story for public consumption. Ranching was a large issue in my interviews with the park proponents. They were unhappy with the compromise, and hoped that eventually they would be able to stop ranching in the area.

The pro-ranching outcome may reflect the fact that the science-based argument about the impacts of grazing did not have the same kind of emotional charge as those that could be drawn on by ranching people. Or perhaps the science was too inconclusive to be persuasive. It remains, however, impressive that a national policy decision was significantly adjusted to accommodate between ten and twenty people, and people without great financial means at that. Whether this is a sign of hope in the ability of our process to respond to valid individual needs, the simple power of the cowboy mystique, or a reflection of interest-group power gone wild no doubt depends on the reader's particular ideological bent, and whether the reader has been convinced by the stories told here of the rightness of one particular set of claims.

Mining

Background

The Mojave area has significant mineral deposits, both developed and undeveloped. Under the Bureau of Land Management, deposits were readily available for exploration and development. Under the National Park Service, future mineral exploration is halted and existing claims will be subject to significant restrictions.

The Mining Law and Regulatory Authorities

Although it has been adjusted by many administrative and procedural changes over the years, mining on federal lands still operates under the Mining Law of 1872 (the Mining Law). John D. Leshy's *The Mining Law: A Study in Perpetual Motion* provides probably the current authoritative text on the history, development, and implications of that law.[22] He describes the Mining Law as resting on a policy of free access by individuals to any minerals that exist on federal lands. This policy assumes that "mineral development is the highest and best use of any land where valuable minerals are found and may be extracted . . . Free access must embrace both the right to explore and the right to develop, and mining must be placed at the pinnacle of possible uses of federal lands and resources."[23] Over the years more and more limits to free access have developed, through regulatory changes and through action by the secretary of the interior to officially "withdraw" lands from availability for mineral exploitation.[24] Military lands are also withdrawn. Unwithdrawn federal lands are primarily managed by the Bureau of Land Management and the Forest Service.

Prospectors may explore any unwithdrawn federal lands to find minerals. Validity of a claim is determined by the land management agency and based on whether it is economically feasible to mine and sell the minerals—thereby preventing fake claims designed not to mine the land but to move the land from federal to private ownership. "A properly located claim, if valid, gives the claimant a property right to the minerals in the claim and the right to use as much of the surface and its resources as are necessary to extract the minerals." The prospector can also apply for title to the surface rights of the claimed land, at either $2.50 or $5.00 an acre.[25] By comparison, land in the Mojave under private sales was valued in the early 1990s at an average of $266 per acre to $305 per acre—and that is land without demonstrated mineral value.[26] Between the time of applying for the claim and receiving title, the prospector must pay $100 per year to the federal land agency to retain the claim.[27] If the claim holder fails to file the annual fee, the claim is dropped. Claims are about twenty acres in size, and claimants may locate as many claims as they wish, including contiguous claims.[28] The Mining Law of 1872 also provides an implied right of access for claimants to their claims, which may include building roads to reach their claim sites.[29]

Mining in National Parks

Active mining claims occur in only approximately twenty-four units of the National Park Service. The claims in these few units result either from specific action of Congress to allow mineral exploration and development at that unit or from property rights that existed at the time the park was established. The two primary units with mining in the lower forty-eight states are Death Valley and the Great Basin National Park. Even where the park service allows mining of existing claims, it prohibits exploration for new claims. Where mineral claims exist, the park service regulates them in a variety of ways, ranging from purchasing mineral rights to regulating access, processing, and reclamation of the mine.[30]

Of specific interest for the Mojave debate is the Mining in the Parks Act (MPA), which was passed by Congress in 1976 in reaction to a major expansion of talc strip mining in Death Valley National Monument in the early 1970s. Leshy describes the MPA as "the so-called Mining in the Parks Act, which was practically a 'no mining in the parks act,' though existing mining operations and claims were afforded some protection."[31] The MPA closed the last six units of the park system that had been open to exploration for new mineral claims and placed significant restrictions on mining of existing claims.[32] It requires that all existing mining claims within the national park system be registered and that the secretary of the interior must determine their validity.[33]

The result of the MPA has been a vast reduction in numbers of claims outstanding at affected parks. In Death Valley National Monument, about 50,000 unpatented claims existed in 1976; 863 of these were recorded by their holders; of the 486 recorded claims the park service had reviewed by 1981, only 44 were deemed valid. "In other affected areas of the national park system, only 1 of 179 claims reviewed was held to be valid."[34] At the time of its designation, the Mojave preserve was estimated to have about 2,000 mining claims.[35] Once these claims are registered and validity is determined, the numbers will no doubt drop even more.

The MPA also empowers the park service to regulate existing claims to protect the integrity of the park system unit. The park service requires

- an approved plan for operations for all mineral activities;
- that the claimant post a bond to ensure that activities will conform to those required in the plan; and
- that the claimant reclaim the site.

If the park service still thinks a claim is causing unacceptable environmental harm, it can purchase the claim and extinguish it.[36]

BLM Plans for Control of Mining

Under FLPMA, the Bureau of Land Management was specifically enjoined from withdrawing lands from mineral exploration and development except by executive or congressional oversight.[37] BLM does have significant authority to regulate the activities of prospectors, although in practice the outcome is often less strict than the regulations appear on paper. Plans for a majority of BLM claims have not been filed, and the GAO found the BLM was "reluctant to impose extra costs on mine operators," and generally had "done little to enforce" its regulations.[38]

In preparing its 1980 California Desert Conservation Area Plan (1980 Plan) and the 1988 East Mojave National Scenic Area Plan (1988 Plan), the BLM laid out very specific guidelines on mining in the area. Prior to 1980, 41,125 acres of the East Mojave National Scenic Area (EMNSA) were withdrawn from mineral entry, about 3 percent of the total 1.3 million acres under BLM management. Based on the 1988 Plan, the BLM had withdrawn over 25 percent, or 389,000 acres, of the area from mineral entry.[39] Almost all of these were designated wilderness study areas, for which mineral withdrawal is federally required.[40] For areas that are not subject to withdrawal, the basic provisions of BLM management described above applied. According to local BLM staff, while the BLM could slow down a claim by increasing environmental requirements, as long as the claim was economically viable it would eventually get permitted.

Mining in the Mojave

The California deserts in general and the Mojave Desert in particular are re-ported to be some of the nation's most heavily mineralized areas.[41] Histori-cally, the richest mine in the area was the Bonanza King, a silver mine in the Lanfair Valley area that was worked in the 1880s, and gold was mined in the area through the 1910s.[42] The traditional way to mine these minerals used deep pits, essentially digging a tunnel to find the desired minerals. The visible signs of such mines were not extensive—generally some tailings (unused earth hauled out of the pit), a few housing and lift structures, one or several cavelike openings in the earth, and usually piles of trash and old vehicles left by the miners.[43] More recently leach-heap mining has been employed in two separate Mojave Desert locations, using cyanide to extract ounces of gold from literally tons of earth carved off the tops and sides of mountains, creating very exten-sive environmental and aesthetic impact.[44] The implications of leach-heap mines are very significant, but because these gold mines were excluded from the preserve's borders, they are not further considered here.[45]

The other sort of mining proposed for the Mojave that has extensive impact is limestone mining. Pleuss-Stauffer, a Swiss corporation, had a claim on a high-grade limestone deposit in one of the most scenic mountain areas within the preserve. Extracting the limestone would require stripping many tons of earth out of the mountainside. Particularly troublesome was the fact that this area has relict populations of coastal mountain vegetation, remnants stranded there after the climate changed with the retreat of glaciers from the last ice age.[46] Few details were available on the claim, but Pleuss-Stauffer asserted a value for it in the billions of dollars.[47] According to local BLM sources, while the BLM did not want to permit the mine, if the claim proved valid they would have had little choice; under the NPS, much more control and opposition was expected. Other minerals in the Mojave include decorative stones, mining of which also tends to be very extensive in scale; mining of one of the natural cinder cones (a relatively rare geologic formation) for cinders; and rare earth metals.[48]

In 1990 the Bureau of Mines (BOM) conducted a mineral investigation of the EMNSA, which identified mineral resources with a total value of $5 billion.[49] In

Mining, in most people's minds, is part of the Old West—a tradition of the lone prospector wandering through badlands, testing soils, and staking claims. Some Mojave area mines are like that. One crisp (relatively—it was under ninety degrees) May morning, I went with a friend out to an old mine site he periodically hiked. We drove a bit of the old Mojave Road and then up into the canyons. Under the CDPA, the area had been designated wilderness, so we should have stopped the jeep a couple of miles from the hiking trail site. Instead, we lifted the chain and drove the usual rocky path. Eventually we stopped the jeep and hiked in, past sand and cactus and boulders, and came to an area with an old shack, an outhouse, abandoned vehicles, and an antique deep-pit mine. The silence of the site was a force of its own. This time, however, we found a weathered paper declaring that the mine was indeed not abandoned, and that we should keep out.

Most of the money from mining now, however, is from New West–style mines. The Pleuss-Stauffer limestone mine in Lucerne Valley is a huge industrial enterprise actually owned by a Swiss corporation. To mine limestone means slowly but surely cutting up a mountain and dragging it away, complete with bulldozers, semi-trailers, and trains.

Somewhere in between are the people who own small mines of one sort or another, have a few employees, and hope to be able to pass their businesses along to their kids. For them, increased regulation, particularly if they are mining land designated as wilderness, can make the difference between a business that supports a family and economic strangulation.

that study the BOM identified twenty-four mines as profitable under 1990 economic conditions. The report suggested there would be a huge decrease in area revenues and jobs because "without access to lands for exploration, less than a 30-year life is expected on about 60 percent of current mining reserves, with most remaining desert mines depleted over 50 years." Omitted from the calculations are minerals that might in the future become economically valuable as production technology and end-uses change.

Several observations regarding this report seem to be in order. The cumulative numbers are not discounted for the time value of money, so dollars from minerals earned in the next twenty years enters the calculation at the same value as dollars that would be earned this year. If values were discounted for present-value, the totals would no doubt be significantly less. One may also wonder why, if the minerals are locatable and the mines would be profitable as implied in the report, there are so few active mines in the preserve area. Very few of the jobs the report projects would actually be held by residents of the preserve, and the numbers seem quite optimistic compared to the small numbers of jobs currently in the preserve area.[50] Problems with this report were widely noted. A representative of the U.S. Geological Survey summed up the analytical quality of this report, as well as the information that federal agencies and mining lobbyists sent to Congress on the issue, in the following way: "These gross and insupportable values should be judged by the mild words of the Menlo Park (U.S.G.S.) report: 'The prospects for further mineral discoveries in the East Mojave National Scenic Area are relatively poor. This does not appear to be an area of world-class deposits.'"[51]

In the resource assessment prepared by the National Park Service for the Mojave area, the mineral activity in the Mojave is described in the following way: "The current level of mining activity in the area is not extensive, but there are some modest mining operations extracting cinders, clay, talc, gold, and sericite. The area also includes a large number of mines with past production histories, and there is substantial continuing interest by prospectors. Some additional mining activity could no doubt occur in this area if market conditions were to change."[52] Because estimating values of unexplored or undeveloped mineral claims includes so many unknowns, the opportunity for variance based on choice of assumptions is great, to put the case mildly. As with grazing, both sides strongly contested and carefully selected facts for their rhetorical power.

Mining Narratives

Because mining is site specific and likely mine sites are largely already well identified, the issue of mining is somewhat different from that of extensive uses such as ranching, hunting, and off-road vehicle use. The National Mining Association (NMA) is the Washington representation of the mining corporations and related manufacturers and banking interests. In principle, the NMA opposed the transfer of the lands from the Bureau of Land Management to the park service because the park service is more restrictive in its management. In practice, the NMA was not very active, in part because Cranston and later Fein-

stein accommodated most major mining sites through boundary changes excluding the sites from preserve boundaries. Once these boundary changes
were made, the individual corporations removed their opposition to the bill.

While the major corporate claim sites and active mines were mostly accommodated, many of the smaller, individually held claim sites were not.
Local people I interviewed were in this latter group, people whose mining
claims for various reasons remain within preserve boundaries, people who as
a result were still particularly bitter.[53]

Access, Access, Access

At the national level and for some local people, the fundamental mining
issue was a general concern that the CDPA restricts already limited access to
mineralized lands. The lobbyist for the National Mining Association stated it
this way: "It was a straight access issue, withdrawal issue. You are taking all of
these lands—you are going to have five million acres of wilderness, three national parks, [although] one of them was not available for exploration anyway.
We said that we can explore and we can develop in a responsible manner. This
is overkill, this is too much land." The reason land withdrawal is critical to the
mineral industry is that prospectors need to be able to explore large tracts to
find the localized deposits; once the deposits are located, the amount of land
that is actually used by mining is quite small. A manager of a local mine noted
that mining itself only affects 0.35 percent of land in the United States. Despite the industry's needs, there has been more and more federal land withdrawn from exploration. (See the map series presented in Chapter 4 for a
graphic presentation of the withdrawal concern.) As technology changes, access to exploration becomes a particularly important issue. The rare earths
were discovered during the 1950s, but it took until the 1980s for them to become economically valuable. If we stop exploration of future sites, we prevent
this kind of flexible response to technologic and economic change.

Rebuttal 1: All the Mines Have Been Boundaried Out

One of the most effective rebuttals for park proponents was the argument
that mining issues were irrelevant because all mines had been accommodated
by being boundaried out. Henry M. indicated: "In terms of mining activity,
there wasn't that big a debate on the park. The other side would throw out
how important all the mineralization was, but the fact of the matter is that all
active mines were drawn outside of the park, so there wouldn't be that con-

flict." This was a very persuasive story, and one that was widely shared by park proponents. But, as the testimony of local mine owners indicates, clearly not all the mining sites were boundaried out. All large, corporate, active mining sites were drawn outside the boundaries, and many large corporations' claims were boundaried out as well. But, sites not in current use and sites owned by smaller organizations often remained within preserve boundaries. And, in fact, it would have been impossible to achieve exclusion of all two thousand of the area's mining claims.

To be accommodated in the bill required that the mine representative make a special request to Senator Feinstein or her staff, and get it approved generally in return for halting active opposition to the CDPA. Even so, some who requested boundary changes did not receive them, according to local miners. A sense of special treatment for the more powerful no doubt increased the bitterness of those who did not receive accommodation, and leaves a lingering anger, which the Mojave preserve management will need to overcome or work around.

Rebuttal 2: They Can Still Mine

Henry M. followed up his argument about all the mines being boundaried out with the following comment: "If you have a valid existing right, i.e., a legal mining claim, you are allowed to work that in any national park, under the Mining in the Parks Act. The difference between the Mining in the Parks Act and the 1872 mining law is really very simple. You have to clean up your mess. 1872 you can just walk away."

Renata W.'s take on the Mining in the Parks Act was that it increased regulation so much that it made mining economically impossible, and that other miners whose claims became part of national parks had simply been forced to close up shop. Mining lobbyist Kevin K. concurred with Renata's assessment, explaining that the problem is less the requirement for reclamation than that difficulty in accessing the site makes the claim effectively worthless. Horror stories abound of being required to bring in mining equipment by helicopter or horse.

Technically, the restrictions on access are only for sites located within designated wilderness areas. Within park units, the issue is reclamation. One of the difficult aspects of the mining debate is that wilderness areas tended to be conflated with park service management, when, in fact, in wilderness areas BLM and park service management are based on the same congressional mandate, with similar restrictions. Because those I interviewed discussed the park service management and wilderness designation interchangeably, it was difficult to be certain which one was being discussed at any one time—probably because the difference was of little relevance to the speaker. This was a problem not just for the mining issues, but for almost all access issues.

Mining: Different Stories, Different Concerns

Overall, for the park proponents mining was not a big issue. Jane J. discussed mining largely in terms of its impact on wilderness quality, indicating, "Mining doesn't particularly bother me. My personal preference of course would be to force the people who dug the holes to go back in and fill them up again, but obviously most of those people are long gone, dead." Proponents could be fairly sanguine about mining because many claims were boundaried out, and because under the Mining in the Parks Act ongoing mining is heavily regulated. For the mining industry, the withdrawals the CDPA represented were presented as fairly desperate signs of the country's lack of commitment to this basic industry, and a virtual death knell to local resource use. This was perhaps the area in which statistics were marshaled most aggressively for each side.

The difference in environmentalist and mining industry perceptions of the Mining in the Parks Act seems to reflect the management latitude that exists within the boundaries of legislated acts. The NPS is mandated to allow mining of valid existing claims. But what makes a claim valid? What qualifies as existing? What sorts of impacts from transportation of materials to and from a mine are acceptable? What sorts of bonds guaranteeing reclamation will be required, and what extent of reclamation? The uncertainty resulting from these questions left local miners imagining worst-case outcomes.

Off-Road Vehicle Use

Background

Off-roading comes in two forms in the Mojave. The first is jeep access to the interior of the preserve, usually along existing roads. The second is off-road motorcycle (dirt-biking) access, which can be on almost any terrain. During the debate, the motorcycle lobby weighed in heavily regarding the overall California Desert Protection Act. They had less to say about the Mojave, since the BLM already limited open access to areas designated for intensive motorcycle use, and all of these areas fell outside the MNP boundaries. During the debate, the off-road vehicle lobby was fairly silent. However, once the park service began management, the extent of wilderness within the preserve became obvious to local residents, as the NPS was required by law to close roads within designated wilderness areas. Road access then became a very heated topic. Because both motorcycle and jeep access were not significant issues during the Mojave designation, our discussion here is fairly brief.

The Mojave area has an extensive road system; 50 percent of the land area is within one mile of a road and more than 95 percent is within three miles of a road.[54] The reason for this is twofold: prospectors carved tracks to even the remotest mountain areas in search of minerals, and there is very little foliage to block anyone who wishes to create a road through use. *Road*, however, is a relative term in the Mojave; the vast majority of roads are unpaved, and of the unpaved roads which appear on maps for the area, many are ill-suited for passenger cars.[55] Most of the extensive road system known to locals does not even appear on the maps. The majority of the roads, then, are only accessible by four-wheel drive vehicles (generically speaking, jeeps). Prior to wilderness designation, the most scenic sites in the Mojave were reachable by jeeps.

As anywhere, the construction of paved or graded roads in the desert has significant environmental effects. Erosion accelerates as runoff from the road creates gullies that change drainage and disturbs alluvial soils some distance from the road. On the many unpaved and ungraded roads, even light levels of off-road vehicles (ORV) use can adversely affect plants: "One pass of a Bronco truck or five passes of a motorcycle on wet soil were sufficient to significantly decrease the number of annuals and grasses in the vehicle tracks the following spring."[56] Many factors, however, determine the severity of vehicles' impacts, including the soil wetness at the time of the driving and the level of rain the following year. Fortunately, the soil is not wet very often.

Light ORV use can break the soil crust that prevents erosion. Once the soil crust is broken, "stabilization of soil and recolonization by small perennials can occur in 10 to 30 years, depending on soil productivity. Longer time periods of hundreds to thousands of years may be required to fully restore plant communities to pre-disturbance conditions."[57] The tank tracks left by General Patton's World War II troop practices are still visible. In recognition of these conditions, the BLM officially restricted driving to previously used tracks and sand washes, which do not have the same environmental sensitivity as many desert soils.

When I first got off the highway to go to Zzyzx, the site of the California Desert Studies Center which was to be my home during my research in the desert, I could not tell which way to turn. By city standards, neither direction counted as road for long. The correct road proved to be four miles of complete washboard, a not unusual condition for desert roads. The good news was that after several passes, I knew that anything that was going to fall off my car already had. The jeep tracks, of which there are many, are often of similar quality as the official roads—their mapping and marking is just worse.

There is great temptation in the desert to go off-road and off-trail. Beside the quality of the official roads, the floors of the many desert valleys are relatively flat and sparsely vegetated. Looking from one's fancy new sport utility vehicle (SUV) across an open plain, knowing that you are here and want to be there and there is no one around to see you, the lack of a road directly between those two points probably does not seem much of an obstacle—particularly when you've seen hundreds or thousands of television ads showing SUVs blithely running through deserts, mud, and foliage with no bad outcome. It was illegal under the BLM to go off-trail except along sandy washes, and it remains illegal under park service rules. But for some the temptation becomes too great. Local residents who see this happen generally recognize a city dweller who has come to visit the desert. Most residents seem to know the fragility of the desert and its slow pace of healing, and stay on the beaten tracks, or at least the sandy washes.

Dirt motorcycling tends to be much more environmentally damaging than jeep touring, as the design of the motorcycles (and dune buggies) allows them to travel in areas inaccessible even to four-wheel drive vehicles. Motorcycle tire treads are especially harmful to plants in their path. Nonetheless, as a sport, it is increasingly popular. The impacts, then, tend to be both extensive and intensive. Land managers at multiple-use agencies such as the BLM and the forest service have responded by identifying specific areas for "free play" of motorized vehicles, environmental sacrifice zones designed to focus damage onto one piece of ground and thereby prevent damage to others. Few plants or animals survive in these areas, and if dirt-bike use were stopped, it would take hundreds or thousands of years for these areas to recover to predisturbance ecological health.

Because the NPS manages for environmental protection, free-play areas directly conflict with its management mandate; there are, therefore, no such areas in any NPS unit. Several existing free-play areas and favorite motorcycle trails were boundaried out of the preserve. Off-highway motorcycle use is still available in the Mojave, on the same roads or trails that jeep users drive. The largest change in road use resulted from the wilderness designation, which specifically requires roadless areas. Some of the wilderness areas in the Mojave have existing jeep tracks. These have been closed from continued use, with reclamation either through specific action or through the slow but dependable workings of nature.

Vehicle Use Narratives

The American Motorcycle Association (AMA) and off-roaders in general were described as "the loudest opponents of the legislation . . . the primary interest group screaming against the bill." They continued opposition to the bill even after the CDPA passed, working closely with Congressman Lewis to prevent funding for the preserve in the budget battle of 1996. Like other users of the desert, they received some accommodations from Senator Feinstein during the designation process, when the senator agreed to remove some areas from wilderness boundaries.

In its arguments, the AMA draws a picture of the sides in the debate in which the motorcycle rider is the generous but downtrodden average Joe, and the environmentalists are selfish elitists. The elements of the argument are demonstrated in Burt R.'s comments:

> We [off-road motorcyclists] kind of have the whole multiple-use ethic. The land is there for people to use, not for it to be locked up, not so people can extend their backyards so that from their cabin they have got a nice view and don't have to hear those pesky motorcycles through there either. Because wilderness to me is a very exclusionary experience, only for the hiker and the horseback rider. There's not too many other types of recreations you can do in wilderness areas, you know, our types of recreation.
>
> I think you need to be innovative sometimes in terms of how you think about sharing the trail. There are a lot of ways to share a trail . . . we need to think of ways of sharing them and get away from, well this is only for motorized users, or

this is only for hikers. There are a lot of different ways you can share without having those kinds of problems.

Environmentalists, not surprisingly, did not see it this way. In their perspective, the noise of the motorcycles made them a clearly conflicting use for
hiking and other passive, quiet recreation. Park proponents had little sympa-
thy for a group they perceived as interested in only a highly consumptive use
of the land, given the detrimental ecological effects of intensive off-road use.
Still, off-road motorcycle use within the MNP was never a real issue because it
was never permitted—although it was a large issue in the national debate over
the CDPA in general and wilderness designations in particular.

Management Issues

Wild Horses and Burros

One of the ecological problems the Mojave faced was increasing populations of wild horses and, particularly, burros. The burros were first brought to
the area by miners, who would release their beasts of burden when need for
them was through; some burros no doubt also simply escaped. Burros are especially hard on desert riparian areas, because they tend to congregate there
for long periods of time, browsing on the few green shoots growing there,
defecating in the water source, and generally scaring away other wildlife.[58] The
burro has been implicated as the "single most important factor in the decline of
the bighorn; the burros out-compete the sheep for watering and grazing sites."[59]

The Bureau of Land Management is required by the Wild Horse and Burro
Act to "achieve and maintain population levels that insure healthy herds and
animals," but they are to do so in a way that does not create adverse impacts
for other wildlife.[60] The NPS, by contrast, is not bound by that law, and usually
attempts to rid its lands of burros. The burro population in the Mojave was significant and well over the BLM's prescribed limits. In 1986, the BLM estimated
the burro herd in the EMNSA as 315 animals, with a proposed target population
of 174; thirteen wild horses were found in the area, with a prescribed herd
level of six. Between 1977 and 1988, the BLM removed almost a thousand
burros from the EMNSA.[61] One of the ongoing issues for the park service in
managing the MNP is the burro problem. It must first remove the burros without raising the ire of animal rights groups. Then preserve managers will have
to continue to remove burros; the Mojave National Preserve is surrounded by

BLM land where burros thrive, and they will periodically migrate into the preserve area.[62]

Pipelines and Power Transmission Lines

The MNP is bordered by major pipelines on the north (two separate corridors, one with a gas line and two transmission lines, and one with four transmission lines and a buried fiber-optic cable) and the east (two transmission
lines). The 1988 Plan identified a contingent corridor as well, designed for
three future transmission lines, which ran through the center of the EMNSA,
traversing Cima Dome and the Devil's Playground, two of the most notable
scenic and biological features in the entire area. Other utility lines, including
buried telephone lines and oil pipelines, cross the area as well, but are outside
the official pipeline corridors. There are also seven commercial and/or public
service communication sites—radio towers set high in the desert mountains.[63]
The pace of construction of these sorts of facilities seems to have been heating
up; since 1992, utilities have built two major natural gas pipelines and one
electric transmission corridor through the MNP area.[64] The California power
crisis of 2001 will no doubt contribute to pressure to build further energy lines.

In the early drafts of the legislation, power companies would have lost the
right to upgrade power lines running through the Mojave; as a result, the
power companies originally opposed the legislation. Reversing this seems to
have been an easy accommodation for Senator Feinstein, who supported
changes to allow continued access and upgrading rights. With this, the power
companies, such as Southern California Edison, withdrew their opposition to
the bill. Accordingly, under the 1994 act, preexisting utility rights-of-way are
acknowledged, and utilities can upgrade their facilities in some corridors. Otherwise, no new pipelines or transmission lines can be built (108 Stat. 4492–93).

Environmental effects from pipeline projects in particular can be extensive.
Howard Wilshire examined the effects of the Kern River pipeline, which was
developed to the north of the MNP. He found that to build that pipeline, construction corridors averaged between 89 feet wide on gentle slopes and 131
feet on steeper terrain, while the pipe itself is only 42 inches in diameter.
Drainage was not reconstructed properly. Whereas in eastern forest lands, the
recovery of the ecosystem might take a few decades, Wilshire points out that
in the desert it takes centuries.[65]

Military Flyovers

The military is a huge presence in the Southern California desert, with Twenty-nine Palms Marine Corps Base, the Army's Fort Irwin, and China Lake Naval Weapons Center all located in the greater Mojave Desert region. The desert provides the perfect space for tank and aircraft practice without interference or risk to civilians. Because the CDPA limits residential development of the desert, it is very good for the military—with one exception. The military needed assurance they could continue flyovers even across wilderness. This accommodation was quickly reached under the CDPA, with the result that while the DOI gets wilderness, the DOD gets continued access to special-use air space encompassing much of the desert. The Federal Air Administration owns the airspace over the Mojave, and will manage it to benefit both the DOD and wilderness. As a result, visitors to the CDPA see numerous military flyovers, many of which include sonic booms.

Commentary

Bad Data and Rhetoric

There was almost no uncontested data pertaining to the issues of the Mojave. The ecological significance of grazing was poorly understood, much less proven; data on the extent and value of usable minerals were hotly contested; people could not even agree on how many mines operated in the area. Much of the information used during the debate was produced by very interested parties, and included assumptions designed to promote one side of the story. This is particularly troublesome because the BLM, the agency with the database and history of managing the area, was politically involved in the debate, and basic information appears uncollected or perhaps just undistributed.[66] While much of this may just be the result of limited administrative budgets, political agendas appear to have been at work as well. Throgmorton (1996) has shown how surveys become parts of rhetorical strategies, designed to persuade by achieving desired outcomes. The Mojave designation experience shows that all kinds of data became part of rhetorical strategies, and that institutions are deeply implicated in that data management.

Given that most uses of the desert will continue, the largest change in management for the land will come from the change in management philosophy, with the NPS's preservation mandate suggesting more careful regulation of on-going activities. The use that appears to cause the greatest environmental degradation—grazing—continues under the legislation. The level of flora and fauna extant in the area today, however, reflects one hundred years of grazing. The ecological quality was judged to be good enough to qualify for NPS status, so while not removing grazing probably prevents some improvement of the ecological soundness of the area, retaining it may do no additional harm.[67] The park service has the right to buy out willing ranchers and their grazing rights. Already, such buy-outs have been a priority, and ranching is diminishing throughout the preserve.

Other environmental benefits can be expected from the bill. A less noted but possibly significant ecological benefit of NPS management is the park service's ability to remove the highly destructive burro population from the area, something that the BLM was legislatively prevented from doing. This will cause its own management difficulties, however, and no doubt be an ongoing issue as herds cross back from BLM land into the preserve. Under the BLM, new mines, some likely very large, would have been permitted. While the NPS's legislative mandate guarantees that no new mining claims will occur within the preserve, the Pleuss-Stauffer limestone claim may be a valid existing right. If so, it will be difficult for the NPS to halt it. For at least one local BLM staff member I spoke with, preventing this one large mine was the only good outcome from the park service takeover of the Mojave.

Ethos and Rhetoric

There are shared threads in the rhetoric of various opponents of the designation—the perceived victimization and valor of themselves as the little guy, elitism of environmentalists, and the need for continued access to public lands. But, over and over again, both sides to the debate tried to portray their opponents as selfish, parochial, and exclusionary—whether that was to describe wilderness advocates or off-road motorcyclists.

The two most economically significant interests in the debate were ranching and mining, yet each met vastly different outcomes in the designation. One of the primary differences between ranching and mining may be what images they conjure for the public. The lone cowboy out on the range, the homespun ranching family working together in the honest labor of putting meat on all of our tables, the foundational role of the idea of the yeoman farmer in the development of our nation—these are powerful and positive images. What does the mining industry have to compare? The lone miner, alienated from most of society and crazy for metals; the chaotic organization of early mining settlements; or more recently, the multinational corporation cashing in on antiquated U.S. mining laws to turn picturesque mountains into rubble—these are also powerful, but hardly favorable. Emotional claims may suffice for retaining grazing; for the less loved enterprise of mining, the arguments had to be economic and had to remind the listener of the importance of mining to our country. Emotional claims are far easier.[68]

CHAPTER 6

Alternative Visions,
Alternative Futures

With a world human population growing at a disastrous pace and the consequent need both for living space and for food, the deserts [of the world] are beginning to fill with people and livestock, to be stripped bare of fuel wood, of myriad resources. The deserts now sustain a sixth of the human population; in the next century, it may be half, and desert ecosystems—fragile for all their seeming fierceness—will suffer accordingly.

—GREGORY MCNAMMEE, *The Sierra Club Desert Reader*

It is all a matter of degree; we will never know an absolutely unsullied desert, and our traces are on every piece of desert we have seen—including some, like the surface of Mars, where no human foot has yet been set but where our vehicles have been junked. We need to learn to live with situations like that, to take pleasure and reward from the good we can extract from the results of our actions, as well as responsibility for our often unforeseeable consequences.

—P. REYNER BANHAM, *Scenes in America Deserta*

This chapter explores the narrative themes developed in the previous chapters by analyzing the frames the Mojave participants were using. Framing provides a technique for understanding the role of values and beliefs in a public conflict. It can help analysts, planners, and participants to find points of concurrence and possibilities for consensual outcomes. The frame analysis process pares down narrative complexity to look at the bare bones of the arguments, with both the strengths and weaknesses that simplification usually implies—it both clarifies the elements of the disagreement and removes the nuance that make the case unique. Because of this, it serves as accompaniment to the narrative analysis previously developed and does not replace it. Chapter 8 provides a more detailed theoretical argument for frame analysis.

Framing begins with the individual participant's worldviews, her or his set of ideas about the nature of the world, including the nature of human beings and their social processes and structures.[1] These create the foundation for and limit the possible range of an individual's beliefs and ethics.[2] Because worldviews are difficult to define, we begin analysis from the set of beliefs, the facts a group or individual accepts as true, because these are more readily discussed. Based on and interrelated with the individual's worldview and beliefs, the individual holds a set of moral values about what is right—their ethics. As a whole, worldviews, beliefs, and ethics prescribe a limited universe of ways the individual can view a situation and therefore are central to determining a set of possible consensual resolutions for any particular conflict.

Another significant influence on how an individual perceives a policy situation is the way that it affects her or his personal and economic position. We can call this threats to identity. Threats may be issues of straightforward economic interests, or they may also be challenges to the individual's core construct of self-in-relation-to-the-world.[3] Often these threats are complexly interwoven, such that attempting to clearly separate the economic and core-construct issues will reduce the correspondence between the frame analysis and the individual's experience. For instance, an issue that threatens to stop a person's source of income is likely to be opposed by that person both because it interferes with economics and because it threatens their experience of being a valued and productive member of society. Focusing only on the income issue by perhaps providing welfare payments would not solve the longer-term identity issue.

Each of these—worldviews, beliefs, ethics, and threats to identity—constrain and direct the individual's perception of the context of the issue of hand. That perception forms a policy frame, or a set of guideposts that suggest, out of a complex reality, what will be relevant for this particular policy issue. Problem definition follows from the policy frame, and what counts as a reasonable solution for the issue flows from the problem definition. A diagrammatic representation of this is shown in Figure 6.1.

Framing the Mojave

Beliefs

Let us apply this analytic process to the Mojave narratives and see if it helps understand that story. To begin, I will start with the basic beliefs the partici-

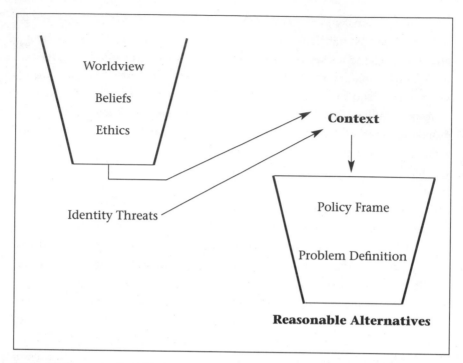

Figure 6.1: Frame Analysis Model

pants seem to express in their narratives. The primary narrative told about the preserve, and the story to which proponents and opponents returned time and time again, compares the Mojave to criteria set up by the park service for whether or not land belongs within its purview. The wording park proponents usually used was that the Mojave "merited" protection. The question is, what can have merit? Merit is a characteristic something contains within itself; when used as a verb, it is "to earn; deserve; warrant."[4] An item with no value in and of itself cannot merit anything; while a fork by virtue of good design might be said to have merit, to speak of a fork deserving (meriting) something would be odd indeed. Proponents then are arguing that the land by virtue of its intrinsic ecological qualities has earned and deserves protection—clearly it is in a different category than a fork.

When opponents phrased their rebuttal, it would typically be in terms of the land *not qualifying* as park service land. To qualify is "to describe by enumerating the characteristics or qualities of, to characterize."[5] In this case, opponents are comparing the characteristics of the land to something, whether that is the scenic quality of other national park units or the criteria of the park system for inclusion. In either case, the Mojave need not have intrinsic value because it is a comparison of the land's humanly defined characteristics to a set of humanly defined criteria. It appears that the two sides start out from very different belief sets. For proponents, the land itself has intrinsic value; for opponents, it has value only to the extent that it meets criteria.[6]

Related to this question of intrinsic value of the land is just what constitutes the land itself. For park proponents, the land is primarily its scenic and ecological functions. Human activity is a disruption to the appropriate condition of the landscape. Opponents instead view human interactions with the land as part of the reason for the land's existence in the first place. Human uses and effects from that, whether scenic or ecological, are a valid part of the landscape.[7]

One of the most fundamental ontological premises is the question of the relationship between the collective and the individual. Do we join in states or collectives to ensure that others do not encroach on our property and our person? Or do we begin from a collective and owe our duty to it, having our individual freedoms in response to our duties to the collective? Implicit here are the positions taken by Locke and Rousseau, with Locke arguing that property rights preceded the interests of the state and that an individual's labor on the land is what creates ownership, while Rousseau argued that it is only through our collective association that we achieve full humanity and so it is to the achievement of our collective goals that our first duty lies.[8] How we each answer this provides a very basic constraint on our understanding of social problems, and played a large role in the Mojave debate.

Viewed from a different perspective, we can see these arguments as expressing basic beliefs about human nature. Thomas Sowell examined visions of human nature and separated them into two basic categories, the constrained and the unconstrained. Constrained perspectives are suspicious of the motives and capabilities of people, either singularly or collectively, to achieve social good. Given that power is intensely corrupting, this view suggests that governments must be restrained to prevent abuses that follow from the normal limitations of men and women. Unconstrained visions believe that people have the power to better themselves and their society, and can exercise power justly and successfully. Governments are seen as the appropriate way for people to improve their situations, and to achieve social and economic justice.[9]

Park opponents such as the local mining company owners, ranchers Tony and Betty K., and homeowner Lydia H. clearly identified philosophical issues as the base of their opposition to the designation, and they begin from a constrained perspective. To them, the appropriate role of government was the protection of private property rights; when government acts to reduce those rights, it acted in ways that broke the social contract and thereby reduced the legitimacy of the entire social structure. Bigger government necessarily implied less freedom for individuals, which meant less justice and less opportunity for finding happiness. Under the Lockean philosophy, property rights develop not just through purchase of land, but through sweat invested in its improvement. Thus, although these folks may not have owned the land, their property rights were to them just as real as owners' because they had developed through a history of use and the investment of labor.

From the unconstrained perspective of park proponents, the appropriate role of government was to achieve those things we desire collectively but may not be able to accomplish on our own, such as control of rampant land development. Achievement of those collective goals superseded individual property rights or individual benefits altogether, because the individual began as part of the collective, rather than the other way around. They were not so naïve as to think that all government is good, and therefore believed in the importance of having groups watchdog the actions of governmental agencies. Nevertheless, there was a basic trust in the ability of right-thinking men and women joined together in a cooperative effort to accomplish more than they otherwise could individually.

Park opponents consciously traced their arguments to the Jeffersonian agrarian vision, in which a virtuous republic rests on the yeoman farmer and settler. Bringing in the park service limited access of these sacred settlers to the land from which their virtue springs. This perspective was particularly influential for local miners and ranchers. Park proponents, as urban folk, dismissed this as outmoded fantasy. For them, virtuous action occurred through the civic realm, and collective management of the federal lands was an important site for realizing that sort of virtue through proper (i.e., nonextractive) relationship with the land.[10]

Ethics

Like beliefs, ethics were important in creating a context for the problem. Again, by carefully examining the narratives the participants used in describing the situation in the Mojave, we can glimpse their ethical positions. At a very basic level, the premises regarding the role of the government that underlay the narratives suggest certain ethical positions. For park opponents, it was unethical for government to reduce property rights, unless it was to protect some clearly superior aspect of property rights such as health or safety. For example, if the United States went to war and needed exclusive federal use of the land to win the war and protect citizens and their property, I suspect few park opponents would argue. But there was no such clearly superior and pressing need for increases in the federal control over the local lands, in opponents' views. Therefore, for the federal government to interfere with peaceful enjoyment of their property (again whether it was actually theirs or they were simply accustomed to accessing it) was unethical.

For park proponents, to oppose the realization of collective goals when it does not cause undue individual harm was unethical. What qualifies as undue is, of course, tricky. In this case, their view was that the land was collectively owned in the first place and any perceived property rights resulted from an ill-advised government dispensation that allowed use of the federal land. Based on that, it was insupportable for individuals to claim an undue harm because they lost something that should not have been theirs in the first place.

Perspectives on who had standing in determining the future of the area were also influenced by this question of the appropriate role of the state. For proponents, the collective nature of the federal land suggested that nonlocals have standing equal to local residents in determining the future of that land. In their view, limiting decision making and benefits to only those who lived near the preserve wrongfully dispossessed the land's rightful owners. For opponents, with their belief in the priority of individual interests, local rights to self-determination carried more weight.[11] They believed that proponents' insistence on a national interest stripped away their most basic property right— the right to control the use of their land. Because of this divide, both sides could reasonably consider the other to be acting unethically.

The question of whether or not the land had intrinsic value brings a different ethical response. If something needs protection and has intrinsic value, to not provide that protection is unethical. This is one of the reasons people have such visceral reactions to any failure—by family, friends, or bureaucrats—to stop child abuse. The collective and the individual have a responsibility to ensure that what deserves protection, gets it. Thus, proponents felt a moral responsibility for protecting the Mojave. For opponents, treatment of the land was not an ethical question per se, except perhaps in terms of responsibilities to their descendants. Under this sort of instrumental view of the land, the proper object of ethical consideration was the humans who use the land, not the land itself. It was appropriate and desirable that the landscape included humans and their use-effects. Without an initial premise that humans have ethical duties to the land itself, actions to override individual rights in use of property become particularly incomprehensible, and unethical.

Threats to Identity

Threat to identity suggests the likely level of opposition to an action; the greater the threat, the stronger the opposition. Threats can come from a variety of sources. Working from the most personal to the more collective, threats may include loss of personal safety or health or the health and safety of one's family; loss of income or wealth; loss of standing and prestige in a community; devaluing of previous actions and positions, which would threaten the individual's sense of personal worth; more generalized threats to the value of one's history and the integrity of one's community and beliefs; threats to the well-being of the general world, and threats to the well-being of future generations.

What qualifies as a threat is conditioned on worldview, or ontological, commitments. As an example, let us imagine a person working for a corporation proposing a real estate development project. The site for that project contains a cave that is home to an endangered beetle.[12] One person believes that we are in community with the nonhuman world, and that causing extinction is not only unethical but dangerous for all life, given our existence in a web of interconnections. To him, the loss of the cave beetle constitutes a threat to the self-in-relation-to-the-world. Policies to protect the beetle are the only appropriate action, and failure to implement such policies appears to be flagrantly foolish and irresponsible. Now, imagine another person, one who instead believes that humans are fundamentally separate from the nonhuman world. For her, the beetle can have no intrinsic value and such a loss is problematic only to the extent that it threatens some aspect of human well-being. Halting a project with clear benefits to humans to save unattractive species such as the cave beetle is fundamentally illogical and foolish. Those who suggest such a move seem vaguely insane.

From either perspective, when a suggested policy creates sharp discord between what an individual views as ethical and the expected policy outcome, the result is a sense of a world gone mad, out of whack, lacking predictability and safety. This internal discord creates a threat to the individual's core identity, because that identity rests on the idea of a reasonable world. Thus, threats can be not just to the person, but can also result from conflict between our ethics and belief systems and proposed actions.

What we find in the Mojave is that for opponents, threats to identity were multiple and direct. For some, the threat was to their economic well-being and core identity as expressed in their choice of occupation and lifestyle—ranchers and miners. For others, it was their belief and participation in a reasoned and democratic decision-making process during the 1980 and later BLM planning processes, which the Mojave designation swept aside. For still others, the issue was personal freedom, which the increasing regulation that comes with the park service restricts. For BLM staff, the legislation was a direct negative review of their performance, thus threatening their sense of professional competence.

For many of the residents, one of the key issues at stake was their sense of themselves as responsible stewards of the land. All of those interviewed discussed particular ways in which they found the land unique, valuable, and important. Most residents talked of having received their land from their forebears and their hopes to bequeath the land to their children. Questioning their management of the land challenges the wisdom of their forebears and their care for their descendants. For people who identify themselves as in a close relationship to the land, calling them bad stewards of that land is a clear threat to their core identity.[13]

For most opponents, many of these threats were in play at the same time. This helps explain why opposition was so emotional and deep-seated; there was much that was at stake, including core identities of the individuals. This also explains in part why the local coalition to oppose the designation was an uneasy one. While all of those who joined had reasons to oppose the designation, the type of threat they experienced was often different, with the exception of the good steward issue noted above. For some, the threats were more directly to their selves, while for others the threats were more about their relations to the world. Nevertheless, all those in opposition seem to have shared the beliefs outlined above, including the priority of individuals over the collective, the priority of property rights, distrust of government, and an instrumental view of the land, along with the resulting ethical commitments. Taken together, these form a coherent view of the world, but one in direct opposition to the designation of their home as a national park. Despite varying reasons for opposing the designation, it threatened each of them and they could join in coalition, albeit an uneasy one.

Not surprisingly, for proponents the legislation actually supported their core identities. Proponents associated themselves with the future rather than the past, with new ideas rather than old, and the designation fit into that framework. Their identities were as urban, sophisticated, modern people; despite this, for a variety of individual reasons each felt deeply linked to the Mojave. Land that is under the jurisdiction of the Bureau of Land Management is, by definition, of low value, marginal—the opposite of a healthy sense of self. National Park Service designation, in contrast, is active management for recreation and preservation on what are now perceived as high-value lands. In subtle and less-than-subtle ways, the park service represents urban values.[14] Thus, in an interesting way, by bringing the park service there, the proponents brought the culture of the city to the Mojave. At the same time, they prevented the physical city from coming there, thereby achieving from their perspective the best of both worlds.

The conflict initially created fewer direct threats to park proponents' core identity than to opponents'. When proponents discussed threats it would be either a near-term threat to the land from current and planned uses, or a long-term threat from increasing development outside the preserve area. If one starts from the belief that the land has intrinsic value, to harm that land creates an ethical problem because it creates harm in the individual's community. At a more general level, in proponents' views the increasing urbanization and human population of the world is a threat in and of itself. The individual may not be able to directly address global population trends, but by protecting the Mojave and similar lands, at least some response to the threat is available. Over time, however, particularly for the Southern California activists, park designation became very central to their selves as they worked longer and became more invested in the outcome of the issue, and thus for these folks opposition to the designation came to be a very clear threat to their identities.

A key to these differences may be the sense of the land's vulnerability. To opponents, the land is fairly robust and able to accommodate and recover from human uses. To proponents, the land is fragile and easily harmed beyond fast recovery. Park proponents looked out across the increasingly urbanized world and saw the Mojave as highly vulnerable to the development that has paved over the desert to the west; if the land and its species have a moral claim to being protected, this is an intolerable thought. To opponents, a few changes, a few new houses, do not unduly stress the land; after all, it is here to assure human happiness.

Table 6.1 From Beliefs to Appropriate Responses

	Proponents	Opponents
Beliefs		
Items with inherent value	Includes the land	Humans only
Landscapes	Ecological and scenic	Include human use
Social contract	Collective	Individual
Ethics		
Moral community	Includes the land	Only to humans
Uses which interrupt ecology or scenic quality	Inappropriate	Appropriate
Priority on	Collective interest	Individual interest
Threats		
To core identity	Supports view of self	Opposes view of self
What is at risk	Integrity of the land	Way of life
Context of Problem		
Geographic scope	Southern California	Mojave area
Time	Very long frame	One or two generations
Moral responsibility	Includes the land	To local humans
Role of government	Achieve collective interest	Achieve individual interests
Problem Definition	Acheivement of collective good is threatened by current and possible future uses of that land	Achievement of the individual good is facilitated by minimizing governmental intervention
Appropriate Response	Increased protection	No increased protection

Perceived Context of Problem

The worldviews the various participants held, their beliefs, their ethics, and the threats to identity the legislation created worked together to suggest what that person would count as an appropriate context within which to view the legislation. Context suggests the problem definition, and likely solutions to the problem flow from the problem definition. Examining the narratives used by the various participants suggests the context held by the various sides, as shown below.

Geographical Perspective

The first element of participants' context of the problem is a question of exactly what constitutes the Mojave's region. Park proponents were deeply concerned by the increasing sprawl of Los Angeles and Las Vegas and believed that sprawl would eventually have an impact on the Mojave preserve area. Their view was of the Mojave in the context of the entire southwestern region, and even in the context of the global increase in population. Their community included the urban areas on either side of the Mojave. This was directly related to their identities as urban, sophisticated people, aware of the connections between the desert and the wider world.

Opponents, in contrast, viewed the Mojave in relative isolation from the rest of the region. They examined human activities within the area, saw that the land overall had changed little in their lifetimes, and perceived no problem. When they thought of their community, it was the desert community that stopped far short of the San Bernardino Mountains or the glitter of Las Vegas. To them, the relevant question was whether there was a problem with the land within the preserve; if not, there was no problem.

Time Perspective

This geographical perception difference is based in part on the second identifiable difference, a difference in time frame.[15] Opponents looked to the recent past as their guide for the future, and to them the lack of recent change in the landscape indicated there was no big change on the horizon. They spoke of inheriting the land from their forebears and passing it on to the next generation. Proponents instead thought in much longer time frames—fifty years, a hundred years—and spoke of keeping the land for future generations, plural. They seemed to reflect planner Bruce Tonn's[16] advice to think of five hundred years rather than ten when we try to plan for the future.

One rather odd thing about this difference is that with a longer time frame, proponents ought to see the land as less vulnerable because over time nature recovers from minor injuries. It seems likely that the explanation is the wider geographical perspective noted above, where the threats to the land are from development sprawl as much as local use. Paving is hard to undo and, given the fragility and slow processes of the desert, may be effectively irreversible. If one views suburban and second-home development as the real threat, assuming the human population continues to increase and the American habit of land-eating, low-density development continues, the land does indeed become increasingly vulnerable over time.

Moral Responsibility to the Land?

For almost all humans, central to our core identity is an idea of ourselves as moral actors. To act morally, proponents needed to support increased protection of the vulnerable members of their community. For park opponents, the moral question was the appropriateness of federal limitations on human use of the land; particular activities on the land were not of themselves ethical issues.

Government—Problem or Solution?

Similarly, the question of the appropriate ends of government provides a basic context of the problem. Government's role, in opponents' views, is to protect the individual's property rights. Thus, the context of the problem is the question of what actions will further the protection and enjoyment of individual property rights. For proponents, the government's role is to assure the provision of collective goods. Thus, the context of the problem includes whether the current management of the common lands was achieving appropriate goals.

Definition of Problem and Appropriate Responses

What does the previous analysis suggest about the way each side defined the problem of the Mojave? For proponents, we begin with a commitment to the achievement of collective good, which includes living in a moral society. The land is part of the community, and it is threatened by development within and particularly without its borders. The moral response is to do what is collectively possible to protect that land. For opponents, we begin with a commitment to the achievement of individual good. The land is there to serve that individual good, and historically through the good stewardship of those who own or use the land, it has done so. Little has changed in recent years, so there is no reason to think that the land is particularly threatened. Given that view, preventing the local residents from being able to achieve their individual interests is immoral. The appropriate response is to leave well enough alone. In this view, those who propose increasing protection fail to recognize either the appropriate relationship between government and individual and or the wise stewardship local residents have given the land over the years.

This chasm of difference suggests why the two sides were so far apart in how they understood the situation and its appropriate resolution. Their diametri-

cal opposition also suggests why there was so much bitterness and so little understanding between people who shared a deep relationship to the desert.

Reframing

The goal of reframing is to create a view of the situation to which multiple
sides in a debate can agree—probably not ecstatically, but at least in recognition that continued conflict does no one any favors. The reframing provides
participants with a potential way out of the policy dilemma. Reframing, to be
worthwhile, must acknowledge that there are clear and valid reasons why the
sides disagree. It is not simply a complaint of "can't we all just get along?" Reframing does not occur at the level of worldviews or even beliefs and ethics.
As has been widely noted, as moral actors in the world we cannot compromise
or change our most fundamental beliefs without great conflict to our core
identities. By making these beliefs more explicit, however, the process of discussion of frames and reframing may help participants acknowledge that the
other side is also a moral actor, just operating under different rules. This
should contribute to recognizing that the other is more "like self" than unlike,
because the other is not acting through evil intentions or being irrational—
they simply start from a different ontological position.

Reframing begins at the level of threats. A worthwhile reframing should, at
a minimum, reduce the threats to identity implied by the contested policy. An
ideal reframe might eliminate threats, but a reduction at least provides an improvement in the ability of the participants to move forward and is likely to
be more feasible. The reframing probably melds elements of the problem contexts of the various sides to the debate, and will likely be helped by a new description of the context. It clearly must develop a different definition of the
problem; without this, there is not much to go on. At its best, the new problem definition should create not just a problem, but a goal—an outcome of the
policy that the various sides can agree would be good, a vision they can share
and work toward realizing. Often, there are general goals to which very different people can agree, and then, as the phrase goes, the devil is in the details.
Creating shared goals does not remove the hard work of agreeing on methods
for accomplishing those goals when there are real differences between the participants, but it may make beginning a shared enterprise possible.

Issues of power need to be considered in the reframing, as further described
in Chapter 8. In the Mojave, Congress charged the park service with manag-

ing the area in accord with its twin congressional mandates of preservation and public recreation. The public's views may be important in planning the management of the area, but in the end it is the park service that holds the power. For a reframing to be implemented it must not contradict the particular goals and requirements of the park service. To be helpful, it should provide a bridge between the park service, the environmental community, and the residents who have worked to oppose the legislation. In the Mojave, this suggests that a helpful reframing should diminish the threats experienced by the opponents but largely fit the context described by proponents.

A Comment on Biases

Outlining the individual frames in use in a debate may be done with limited bias, particularly when the framer working toward that goal does not have strong emotional involvement in the outcomes and checks the analysis with the participants. Reframing, however, is mostly an act of creation, not analysis. The source of the reframing is the combination of knowledge of participants' narratives and policy frames and the professional expertise, knowledge, and creativity of the planner/policy analyst. Bias is central to creative processes—we imagine new and different things based on who we are and what we believe. The response to bias in reframing is not to try to eliminate it; instead, it is to acknowledge what the biases of the analyst are, and acknowledge them as both relevant and valuable to the process of imagining a new problem frame.

In light of this, I take a moment to be explicit about my own biases. My belief system matches closely with that outlined above for the park proponents. I am hopeful regarding the ability of people to work together to accomplish great and good things, and believe that we join together into collectives to achieve those things. One of the elements that make a good life and a good society is functioning ecosystems, and I believe property rights ought to be limited by that collective interest; the right to destroy land ought not be in the bundle of property rights. I believe it is important to preserve natural lands, and to do so for their own sake whether they are going to be of use to humans or not. This is so because other species are highly vulnerable to our actions, and we ought not harm that which is vulnerable to us.[17] The land and its constituent species, then, are morally considerable. Humans are rapidly increasing in population, and we need to take steps to assure that species other than Homo sapiens will also be around.

We will not be able to do this, however, unless we learn ways to balance protection and human communities, because there is less and less unpopulated land anywhere. If we wish to protect more land, we will need to improve our techniques of balancing local communities' needs and land protection, because the existing residents have a legitimate claim to remain where they have chosen to live and to make a living there. There is power in the local knowledge of a landscape, and most residents genuinely try to practice good land stewardship; such relationships between people and their landscape should be cherished and encouraged rather than severed. The central question is, how can we work to accommodate both resident communities and ecosystem preservation. This interest is what led me to the Mojave as a case study, and these beliefs influence my proposed reframing of the Mojave preserve planning, as will be clear below.

Reframing the Mojave

The place to begin the reframing is with the threats the legislation engendered. For opponents, one of the primary threats is to their identity as good stewards of the land; a reframing should be able to acknowledge this and support continued good stewardship by those who will live and work in the preserve. Another threat is to economic integrity. For many of the affected, the provisions in the legislation already have addressed this, and the objective is to not reawaken old fears. For some, such as Pleuss-Stauffer, the character of the preserve and their economic interest appear irreconcilable, and reframing will not be able to address this. The reality of the legislation is that uses that cause significant harm to the land will not be permissible under the legislated management mandate of the park service. Many opponents felt that the new legislation illegitimately overwhelmed a planning process they had contributed to; others felt that the new park service presence reduces their freedoms. A frame that includes extensive public participation in the preserve ought to be able to ameliorate these threats by making the individuals part of the process rather than victims of it.

For park proponents, a reframing must not create a new set of threats—it must not suggest that their hard-won battle for increased protection will be wasted in the preserve's implementation. It should create a vision of a satisfactory or even inspiring future, and engage the area in a regional perspective. And it should acknowledge that their view of the land as under siege and needing protection is appropriate. Without achieving these conditions, a reframing is unlikely to be accepted by these participants.

Based on this, I suggest the following:

1. Begin from a recognition that both sides to this debate care deeply about this land.
   - Park proponents worked long and hard volunteer hours not out of spite, but out of true concern for the future of the land and the good of future generations.
   - Park opponents and the previous BLM management are responsible for the current condition of the land, which must overall be good or it wouldn't become a national park unit. Opponents want to pass on to their descendants as beautiful a land as they now experience, and they want to provide those descendants with as many options as possible for living in place on the land.
   - The great majority of both park opponents and proponents do not want to see the area become either a suburban landscape or an enclave of wealthy retirees and city escapees. This does not serve existing residents' interests in retaining economic use of the land, nor environmentalist interests in land protection.
2. Take a long perspective, and connect to national and regional trends:
   - Development pressure on the desert for suburban, second-home, and miscellaneous undesirable uses is real.
   - Meanwhile the numbers of traditional desert residents, those who both live and work in the preserve area, are declining from lack of employment, among other factors.
3. Accept that, as defined by Congress, this is a working landscape where local residents are an integral part of the preserve.
4. Accept that, as defined by Congress, this is also a landscape where ecosystem protection will be a reality.
5. Realize that protection of the rural, undeveloped character of the land is in both local and environmental/pro-park interests, so long as future employment is sufficient to keep existing families in the area.

This context of the problem strongly suggests that opponents and proponents have shared interests. Where there are shared interests, there is the possibility of cooperation to achieve mutually satisfying conditions. What sort of

problem definition would fit the context, and provide the possibility of a mutually satisfying outcome? For this we need to stretch a bit, and work toward
a vision.

The vision I propose is of the Mojave preserve as an exemplar of land protection where both existing human and natural communities continue to
thrive. Developing such examples is a pressing need if we are to work out a
civil balance between those who promote land preservation and those who
live on that land. Perhaps we can call it a living landscape[18] or a working
ecosystem, where we protect an increasingly imperiled rural lifestyle and an
increasingly imperiled natural world. Or, following European examples, we
could call it a protected landscape.[19] To bring in a popular phrase, we might
even imagine the area as exemplar of a sustainable rural landscape.

Most of the early literature on sustainability focused on development policies and programs; more recently, there has been a turn toward sustainable
places and sustainable communities.[20] In the last decade, we have begun to see
the ideas of sustainability preliminarily applied at the landscape scale.[21] The
literature on sustainability is of course vast, but most authors agree that there
are three necessary conditions for sustainability—protection of environmental quality and improvement of social justice at an appropriate level of economic activity.[22] I would argue that when we apply sustainability to rural landscapes, the criteria for economic growth becomes one of assuring economic
opportunities such that existing residents can stay in place if they so choose.
For traditional resource users such as miners, ranchers, and farmers, these economic opportunities ought to include assistance in finding new ways to do
their existing business such that public ecological goals are combined with private economic goals, with only the level of regulation necessary to assure the
common good. If a traditional use seriously conflicts with ecological protection, then there needs to be generous transition time in phasing out that use
such that the residents can find alternative livelihoods and uses for their land,
and thereby be able to stay in place.

I arrived at this principle based on my personal concern for social justice
and my experiences in talking with rural people about their land. There is also
philosophical support for this principle from an exemplary green source—
Wendell Berry. In his writings as well as his life example, he demonstrates the
importance of staying in place, the recognition that local knowledge about the
land can be extensive, and that the relationship between people and the land
builds slowly and requires time.[23] Existing residents of rural areas often exem-

plify this, and to the extent that we agree on the importance of knowing a place, policy needs to move beyond philosophy and actually support those who do stay in place. Also, we hardly need be reminded that federal agencies, left without oversight, are not always optimal stewards of the land.[24] Sustaining the existing residents of rural areas provides a ready-made knowledgeable group with alternative perspectives to watchdog federal land management.[25] A truly sustainable rural landscape, then, will work with local knowledge about the land and its history, respecting the existing human community's relations with the land while finding ways to improve that relationship.

Robert Thayer (1994) defines a sustainable landscape as "a place where human communities, resource uses, and the carrying capacities of surrounding ecosystems can all be perpetually maintained."[26] Thayer suggests, and I paraphrase, some principles that sustainable landscapes will follow:

- Use primarily renewable energy sources at or below their replacement rates;
- Maximize the recycling of resources and byproducts and minimize production of unusable materials (waste);
- Preserve the stability and diversity of the ecosystem;
- Preserve and support the local human communities;
- Use technologies that reinforce these multiple goals.[27]

But, the question remains, what would a sustainable Mojave landscape look like? In this reframing I suggest some ideas as thought-pieces rather than as a to-do list; a proper plan should come out of consultation with the community and those who will be responsible for managing the area. The change as I imagine it begins with a community self-identification as an important test site, one that will show how rural areas can survive and thrive and lead the next century.

Specific ideas for the Mojave include:

- Begin by setting up a nonprofit community group and get foundation funding for studies of ways to implement sustainability while promoting current uses of the land, including ranching and mining.
- Develop niche marketing opportunities for local "green" products, providing business-entrepreneurship opportunities for local residents.
- Recognize that tourism provides a good additional, but not replace-

ment, source of economic activity. Encourage locally owned eco-tourism businesses.

- Look for ways to (gradually) combine existing resource-based industry with tourism to provide added income and assure greater economic security for the future.
- Continue existing mines, but provide for tourism to them (and earn revenues from it); educate the public about the value of mining, and prepare and show plans for reclamation.
- Continue existing ranching where the landscape can support it, but look for grants and incentives that can support actions that reduce the effects of grazing on the land. Consider ways to use tourism to increase profitability, employment, and ownership potential for future ranch generations. Provide ways for the public to learn about the value of ranching and the responsible nature of those who ranch.
- Encourage industry associations to provide funding or materials which will make the above less costly, in return for contributions to public relations.
- Consider a cooperative power-generation facility, using the local benefits of sun and wind to reduce the need to pay outsiders for energy. If this is inappropriate given the dispersed pattern of homes, find ways to promote solar and wind power use at residences.
- Consider a cooperative grocery store or shared purchasing, so that residents could have access to reasonable produce at reasonable prices without driving to Barstow or Las Vegas.
- Explore ways to grow produce in the area, reducing reliance on Barstow and Vegas for regular needs. This would, however, need to be a sort of xeriscape agriculture that acknowledges the desert nature of the area.
- Create a direct relationship between the community and the park service, to coordinate plans, encourage federal funding, and have a truly positive participatory process. This is contingent on local residents' realizing that the park service is here to stay, and working with them rather than fighting them. Having greater local input into preserve management should reduce the friction that has been hampering implementation of the preserve. With a positive resident-NPS relationship, the NPS would be in a position to provide advice and, potentially, incentives to residents interested in improving the connections

Table 6.2 Threats to Responses, Reframed

	Proponents	Opponents	Reframing
Threats			
To core identity	Supports view of self	Opposes view of self	Supports both
What is at risk	Integrity of the land	Way of life	Years of bickering
Context of Problem			
Geographic scope	Southern Califorina	Mojave Area	Southern California
Time	Very long frame	One or two generations	Very long frame
Moral responsibility	Includes the land	To local humans	Includes both the humans and the land
Role of government	Achieve collective interest	Achieve individual interest	Facilitate new approach
Problem Definition	Achievement of collective good is threatened by current and possible future uses of the land	Achievement of the individual good is facilitated by minimizing governmental intervention	Cooperation between residents and park service in creating an exemplar of a sustainable rural community
Appropriate Response	Increased protection	No increased protection	Cooperation in working toward shared goal

between their activities (whether economic or residences) and the desert ecology.

This reframing does not attempt to reconcile basic differences between the worldviews, beliefs, and ethics of the various participants in the Mojave National Preserve. Instead, it acknowledges those differences and understands that they provide the boundaries on the sorts of solutions that participants will find acceptable. Within those boundaries, the reframing begins with the threats to participants' identities the issue creates, redefines the context and definition of the problem, and suggests an alternative perspective on the issue.

Reframing—A Beginning, Not an End

This is my particular vision for the Mojave National Preserve. However desirable it may appear to me, that does not necessarily make it the appropriate vision for the area. The point of framing and reframing is to facilitate dialogue. The planner who is engaged in interpretive planning has the right, perhaps the duty, to use her or his expertise and creativity to develop a new vision that is based on the participants' stories of the area but adds the vision and knowledge available to a professional. That new vision, however, becomes just one more story of a possible future. It enters the public arena for discussion, dissection, revision, rejection, or acceptance in the same way that others' policy stories enter the debate. The final policy that gets implemented may bear little resemblance to the ideas the planner brought to the public arena. This sort of approach requires of the planner both the hubris to develop visions and the modesty to recognize that if a particular vision does not become owned by the people who will live with it, it will not be successful. The vision will and must change as it is developed by those affected.

CHAPTER 7

Policy Directions

The land does not give easily. The desert is like a boulder; you expect to
wait. You expect night to come. Morning. Winter to set in. But you expect sometime it will loosen into pieces to be examined.

When it doesn't, you weary. You are no longer afraid of its secrets,
cowed by its silence. You break away, angry, a little chagrined. You will
tell anyone the story: so much time spent for nothing. In the retelling
you sense another way inside; you return immediately to the desert. The
opening evaporates, like a vision through a picket railing.

You can't get at it this way. You must come with no intentions of discovery. You must overhear things, as though you'd come into a small and
desolate town and paused by an open window . . . You have to proceed
almost by accident.   —BARRY LOPEZ, *Desert Notes*

There is a war over nature in progress and nature itself is in the middle—
caught in a crossfire of competing interests. Such a contest is not over
empty prizes. Indeed, it is nothing less than the human struggle for access to reality. And for humans, access to something is what grants control . . . A contest over what is allowed to represent reality—and that is
what intelligible access is all about—is a struggle over that reality itself.
This is the heart of our age's modernism, the process by which we establish what '"counts"' as reality. Seen against this background, all our narratives—our many stories about nature and ourselves, whether '"scientific"'
or not—are striving for such representation.

—MICHAEL SOULÉ AND GARY LEASE,
Reinventing Nature? Responses to Postmodern Deconstruction

Patricia Limerick, in her wonderful book on the American deserts, describes
them as "paradise unedited," paradise that includes the attractive and the unattractive, comfort and discomfort, pleasantness and unpleasantness, and
even death as part of paradise.[1] More so than any other landscape, in their res-
olute inadaption to human needs, deserts force us to face nature's supreme in-

difference to human busyness. Limerick suggests three meanings of nature in American minds, and applies them to the American desert:

> Nature is on one count a reminder of the individual's own biological vulnerability; on another count, a source of commercially useful material; and on a third count, a satisfying visual phenomenon . . . These three categories provide some structure for American encounters with the deserts. In the first phase, beginning with the travels of American fur trappers in the 1820s and continuing on the overland trail, the desert was simply a threat to life, an ordeal to be endured. In the second phase, beginning by one count with the Nevada silver mines in 1859 and by the other with irrigated farming in Utah, Arizona, and elsewhere, the desert turned out to be valuable—a repository of minerals, a wasteland capable of becoming irrigated farmland. In the third phase, around the turn of the century, the desert began to qualify in some circles as beautiful and suitable for appreciation. The phases suggested here did not succeed each other in clear sequence: all three overlap and continue into the present.[2]

In the untamed Mojave, all these meanings are alive and well. The desert for some is a treasure box we should not lock, a resource for current and future human wealth production. For others, it is a space for human revitalization through aesthetic and spiritual experience and communion with nonhuman species. Even the desert as death remains active if less central, as environmentalists discuss wilderness in the desert and ask why we should feel the need to ensure that all who enter wilderness also leave it, while local residents worry about the naïveté of first-time desert visitors and local ability to provide for search-and-rescues as a result. A fourth meaning is clear in the Mojave debate. The desert is also a reminder of how we once lived, a bastion of American values and traditional lifestyles where Americans can go to reconnect with the traditions of self-reliance and daily interaction with the land—or at least take comfort in knowing that some still live that life.

Limerick notes: "It is perfectly possible for an individual or group to hold what appear to be contradictory attitudes [toward nature] simultaneously,"[3] and we see that for local residents, the desert is all of these things. As long as the desert is big, undeveloped, unpopulated, there is little conflict in believing in all of them. One could ranch one's bit of the desert, watch the sun set over it, and be filled with a sense of one's historic placement in the center of American cowboy myth, all in one day. These things come into conflict only when the desert becomes small, when uses collide, when population pressures reach even the desert. For most local residents, that conflict simply did not exist in the Mojave. There was no problem, because the desert remained big; recreation, ecology, mining, hunting, and ranching could easily coexist because there was room for all.

For the urbanites and the environmentalists, the world is a small and crowded place where people are threatening to overrun all of nature. They turned this vision onto the desert, and saw a landscape in need of salvation. Only one meaning of the desert is appropriate in this view, and that is its aesthetic/ecological values. This unitary position stands in direct contrast to the layered understanding of residents of the desert. Facing a unitary opponent, those who opposed the designation were in turn forced to simplify their positions, to serve as advocates for another, also unitary, vision of the value of the desert—the treasure-box meaning. They became caricatures, and were easily dismissed by the powerful urban interests. People resent being dismissed, resent having their complexity edited by others, and resent being forced to make themselves caricatures to respond to sound-bite wars. Anger that still lingers is the result.

Perhaps the most ironic part of the designation fight was the issue of control of the desert. As Limerick notes, "In American minds, the desert is the ultimate nonconformist landscape, a thing separate from the requirements of American materialism, the exemplar of freedom from control."[4] For environmentalists, traditional land uses conflicted with this meaning of the desert. For opponents to the designation, a stronger federal presence represented increased control of that which ought not be controlled, bringing with it a loss of personal freedom and a conformity to the needs and wishes of urban America. With the stricter regulation of visitors, even for the casual tourist the area will be more controlled. Almost by definition, the more crowded a place is, the more control is needed to prevent human conflicts. Again, we come back to crowded-world worldview.

The Meanings of the Desert

The arguments about the Mojave were constructed in a variety of ways. One of the most important was that it was an issue of access, of who has the right to benefit from these federal lands. Is it the local people who have been accustomed to having relatively unrestricted use of the land, with little commentary from outsiders? Is it the growing urban population with their demands for recreation, and the tourism-oriented business that serves them? Is it the nonhuman species who live in the Mojave and other Southern California deserts, who benefit from the increased habitat protection that the Mojave designation assures? This is the argument from rights, and it played a central role in the debate.

Another construction is one of politics and management. If we frame the sides in the debate as traditional resource users versus urban interests represented by environmentalists, we can view the debate as a microcosm of changes in political power. The BLM is generally aligned with a traditional-resource-user constituency; the park service with a tourism, recreation, and preservation constituency.[5] The combined political force of the resource-based industries and the BLM were not sufficient to overcome the desires of the largely urban environmental forces combined with tourism-related business interests. In this, we can see a mirror of the changes in economic and political power that have occurred in the country over the last fifty years or so, with the transition to a postindustrial, highly urbanized society.

Alternatively, we can understand this debate as an argument about the future of the area, in which both sides agree on the desired outcome—perpetuation of today's conditions—but because of different frames of reference underlying that desire, come to different policy prescriptions. The differences in frames include how far into the future the viewer's projections go, what land area is considered, and how it is related to the rest of the region, the country, and the world, and who is accorded central place in that vision—the land and its flora and fauna, or the people who make their living there.

When environmentalists discussed the future, they generally spoke of it in long time ranges, up to one hundred years in the future and sometimes in evolutionary time—millions of years. They begin with a picture of increasing development pressure, increasing urbanization surrounding the Mojave, and rapidly increasing global population. When they gaze out over the landscape, they see Los Angeles with its hoards of people looming. They project that the suburbanization that has occurred in areas like the San Bernardino Mountains and Central Valley will continue spreading. They see proposals for landfills, nuclear waste dumps, and open-pit mines threatening to fill up and destroy the landscape. This area, valued for its ability to provide solitude, becomes crowded. The future of the Mojave in their eyes is tied to the future of not just the desert region, but the future of the Southwest, the country, and the world. They see a landscape under siege, even if the foe is just barely visible on the horizon.

When the park opponents see the future, they begin with their families, their communities, their way of life. They are a special, chosen few who moved to the desert despite the hardship of conditions there, and have managed to wrest a living from the land. The land in return has endured very well because they have been good stewards of it. This is a landscape that begins in Barstow and ends at the Nevada state line, a contained landscape. When they look out across the desert, they see a landscape that is largely unaffected by human industry, with only small pockets of visible signs of use, and those pockets remind them of the dedication it has taken to remain there in the desert. But there are not many like them, willing to live in the harsh desert conditions and forgo the ease of a life closer to urbanized pleasures. They also perceive a landscape under siege. But it is a landscape largely composed of people and their communities, and the foe is modern life with its increasing bureaucratization and control, which seeks to cast out their traditional way of life.

Reconciling Stories: Directions for Land Protection

These meanings of the desert were all apparent at the time of the debate over the Mojave, and are based on how participants understood the issue—whether altogether consciously or not. Another way that the story can be constructed, however, and one of the most interesting, is largely a matter of reading history backward and seeing some unintended outcomes. In this view the Mojave was a tale of struggle to identify new ways of understanding land protection and the role of the National Park Service. When Congress enacted the legislation that created the Mojave National Preserve, they were acting in response to political pressures from all sides. The whole California Desert Protection Act and specifically the preserve status was a compromise that allowed the legislation to pass, and not a calmly considered new direction in land protection. As has been shown by historians, changes in social understandings of the world sometimes seep into legislation and political decisions quite indirectly, so that the individual participants are not even aware of the role they are playing.[6] I believe this was the case with the Mojave designation, and that Congress, perhaps unwittingly, may have created a relatively new purpose for the American national park system.[7]

The first part of this new purpose is the use of national parks as long-run growth control. The traditional purpose of parks was to secure sublime landscapes for future generations. Later, it was to provide for recreation and ecological protection. The Mojave case suggests that a new role has been added to designations: controlling the growth of megalopoli that will not control themselves. Whether this represents an unusual situation or the start of a new practice cannot at this point be determined. But we ought to be considering its appropriateness and its implications for management practices in such areas.

For planners, the irony is that growth management occurred on a scale that planners can usually only dream about, but this occurred in part because it was not cast as growth management at all. The situation in the Mojave, as agreed by virtually all parties to the debate, was not really going to experience significant development pressure for the next forty to a hundred years. Environmentalists could and did think in this time frame, but our public policy process generally does not. To justify reductions in property rights based on threats not likely to be visible for a generation is politically difficult, if not impossible. On the other hand, restricting property rights is equally as difficult once development pressures set in and property values begin to rise in response.[8] The environmental groups, as savvy political participants, recognized this and adjusted their rhetoric to match the rules of the public forum. Pointing to other issues of management, they created a sense of urgency that the growth-control scenario could not, and they achieved the most important of their goals.

The other irony, and one recognized by many participants in this debate, was that in some ways the solution created the problem. Development pressure in this part of the desert had been light prior to the CDPA. Since the designation of the Mojave area as a unit of the park service, development pressures have intensified. The sheer visibility resulting from becoming part of the park service brings many visitors, some of whom inevitably want to stay. Perhaps it accelerates development pressure that would have come to the area, or perhaps it redirects it from elsewhere. Either way, it is important to acknowledge that our desire to protect land often has this consequence.

A second outcome of the designation is also important. Typically, the purpose of national park units is environmental protection and visitor enjoyment. In the Mojave, Congress required the continuation of multiple use—hunting, ranching, and even some mining. The park service has been required to manage a working landscape. This is not the first time that has happened, but it is by far the largest such experiment in the continental United States. This creates a new model of what the relatively ill-defined term *preserve* means—a protected landscape that includes people in it, not just as visitors but as users of the land.

Reframing the National Preserves

This new use of the term *preserve* has the potential to lead to an important new direction for the park service—leadership in creating sustainable landscapes. These would include not just managing the area within park borders, but also working in partnership with the communities near the parks and the in-holding residents within the parks. This sort of leadership without necessarily having ownership is an idea the park service is already experimenting with in places like the Mississippi National River and Recreation Area, where the federal government is providing coordination and oversight in a corridor with many state and local parks and protected areas.[9] Working outside the borders of parks is also a topic the park service is deeply concerned with, due to recent threats from the peripheries of parks.[10]

We desperately need examples of sustainable rural landscapes, because it is only through place-specific implementation that we will find out what a sustainable landscape is. As Robert Thayer comments, "We must *make* sustainable landscapes to know *how* to make them, and we must make them in order to know *what* they really are."[11] Writing about the ideas is relatively easy; doing the implementation is the hard part. If that implementation is going to happen anywhere, it takes leadership, and the park service seems like a group that could provide exactly that. The dual mandates of the park service to provide for visitor enjoyment and for ecological protection, in combination with an understanding that the parks do not exist in a vacuum and instead are dependent on the lands around their borders for ecological health, seems well matched to the goals of sustainable landscapes.

For the National Park Service, this suggests a slightly different role than is their habit. The focus of the park personnel traditionally has been on managing the ecological resources and visitor experiences within their boundaries, with some necessary partnership with in-holders and residents of gateway communities. During the planning phase of managing parks, the park service typically aggressively recruits public comments on planning documents, but these deal with the unit's internal resources. The idea presented here has the NPS reaching out to do ecosystem planning in partnership with local residents as well as national interests, and considering economic benefits to the community as well as proactive consideration of the ecological effects of surrounding uses. This is the sort of role the NPS has increasingly taken on.[12] An example is the NPS's lead position in the Eastern and Northern Mojave Desert bioregion planning effort. While this deals primarily with federal lands, it also requires coordination with local governments' planning efforts.[13] Another example is the greenline parks described in Chapter 3, which require partnership with the local residents to manage the area.

This park service role includes working with residents to determine appropriate actions that both the park and the residents can take to move toward a sustainable landscape. The park service personnel would be technical advisors to the local area on sustainable design. They are already well placed to do this. NPS planners and specialists are often (although certainly not always) very knowledgeable about the ecology of the area, and that sort of knowledge is crucial to imagining place-appropriate solutions. Working with sustainability also is not new to the park service. The NPS publication *Guiding Principles of Sustainable Design* is an excellent primer on ecology-friendly design, and many park service personnel are very familiar with the goals of sustainability.[14]

One of the primary problems I see with this is the usual one—money. Providing leadership takes resources. It requires personnel who have been trained in sustainability criteria, who have been exposed to examples in other places, who know the land and the people of the community, and who are committed to and trained in community participation. That is not free. Over the long term, however, making parks work in partnership with local communities may be cheaper than the current structure. Creating situations in which local residents welcome the presence of the park service and creating relationships with elected representatives that encourage them to support the park service are likely outcomes of a NPS role in developing sustainable communities. And that would be good for appropriations.

This sort of vision seems particularly appropriate for the national preserves. Preserves, through the way they have been used, describe multiple-use areas that are not pristine and may not be scenic, but are ecologically important and deserving of protection. We could expand this definition, to rework a phrase from Joseph Sax, to make preserves into laboratories of innovation in sustainable landscapes.[15] These areas could lead the way in showing how humans and nature can not just coexist, but co-flourish. We can imagine that there might eventually be preserves for each of the many ecosystems in the United States, providing leadership and examples for rural life in that region, and providing learning laboratories for urban visitors to renew ties with their ecosystem.

Both the park service and the residents of gateway communities and park in-holders should be able to embrace this idea because it achieves each of their goals. For local residents, it would allow them to ensure jobs in the area for themselves and their children while reducing energy-consuming conflict with the park service. It will be important that these are not just tourism jobs, but also resource-industry jobs that still work toward the goals of sustainability.[16] For the park service, it achieves the goals of protection but reduces the frustrating work of coping with adversarial local residents. For the country as a whole, it is the chance to become an international leader in sustainable rural landscapes, which is absolutely necessary if we are to begin implementing sustainability as more than an academic goal. And for all, it represents a more just balance between the national or global good of land protection and the costs borne by local residents to achieve that.

This vision ought to be of great interest to the environmental community. The general American appetite for land protection seems undiminished, and the environmental community harbors grand and important ideas of increased protection for many lands. The most notable example of this is the Wildlands project, which forms the background to Earth First!'s agenda. This imagines that up to half the contiguous United States would become vast peopleless stretches of wilderness surrounding isolated "islands" of human civilization.[17] Other major proposals exist as well, from Frank and Deborah Popper's Buffalo Commons, which suggests that much of the rapidly depopulating rural Great Plains should be returned to buffalo, to calls for regional-scale protection of the newly regrown eastern forests.[18] If we can work out ways to create compromise so that resident humans can remain in these lightly populated areas while the lands recover and thrive, this would represent a way to potentially achieve these visions while still creating just, equitable outcomes. This builds from the idea of the greenline parks, an idea developed in part by the National Parks and Conservation Association.[19]

More pointedly, the intensity of local opposition to land protection is heating up, and becoming more effective. An example is the mid-1990s debate over wilderness in Utah, which ended with the quite unsatisfactory designation of a small portion of the desired wilderness as a national monument.[20] Under a different administration, even this would not have been achieved. So long as land protection means that local residents really are harmed, whether in their pocketbooks or in their identities and worldviews, these battles will be fierce. If those responsible for land protection can create models showing that protection is good for the local residents, future designations should be much less like declaring war. A beginning is to acknowledge the complexity of local relationships with the land, rather than dealing in caricature and dismissal. This would help dispel some of the subjective, personal trauma a designation proposal creates. Specifically addressing how a designation can sustain people in their chosen lifestyles is necessary in responding to the interests of the residents. Perhaps in the very long run, the U.S. population will be so completely urbanized that these issues will no longer be relevant. But until then, both justice and feasibility suggest that a different approach to land protection is in order, one that benefits and validates local residents while still achieving the good of the broader region, the nation, and the world.

CHAPTER 8

A Proposal for Interpretive Planning

> Imagine that you enter a parlor. You come late. When you arrive, others
> have long preceded you, and they are engaged in a heated discussion, a
> discussion too heated for them to pause and tell you exactly what it is
> about. In fact, the discussion had already begun long before any of them
> got there, so that no one present is qualified to retrace for you all the
> steps that had gone before. You listen for a while, until you decide that
> you have caught the tenor of the argument; then you put in your oar.
> Someone answers; you answer him; another comes to your defense; an-
> other aligns himself against you, to either the embarrassment or gratifica-
> tion of your opponent, depending on the quality of your ally's assistance.
> However, the discussion is interminable. The hour grows late, you must
> depart. And you do depart, with the discussion still vigorously in
> progress.   —KENNETH BURKE, *Philosophy of Literary Form*

The Interpretive Paradigm

Within the broad array of the social sciences, many authors have noted an
"interpretive turn," connected with a much larger scholarly turn away from
positivist approaches to those based on postmodernism, hermeneutics, and
critical theory. William Adams characterizes the interpretive turn as: "The con-
viction that collective life is in some fundamental way about those things its
members (elites and masses, peasants and kings) collectively think, imagine,
or believe . . . [It is] another stab at understanding how we humans mean
things, and where and how our meanings figure in the very concrete practices
and necessities that also compose our social lives."[1]

The essential elements of such a paradigm vary for different authors, but for
my purposes here an interpretive paradigm begins with the following premises:

1. Humans are storytellers. We all use stories all of the time to make sense of the world, to frame and highlight experience, and place an experience within what we judge to be an appropriate perspective. Stories are, in essence, how we think about the world and our place within it.[2] The way we tell those stories helps constitute both ourselves and our relationships to those with whom we talk.[3]

2. Values are not peripheral or suspect; instead, they are integral to the way we judge our lives and the way we construct our stories. What counts as a fact often depends on the perspective held by an individual. Values provide the frames we use to give shape and meaning to our stories; and facts, values, interests, and theories all are implicated in how we construct a problem.[4] Mythos and logos are, if not inseparable, at least mutually constructed.

3. Rather than a goal of pure rationality, the interpretive paradigm suggests a goal of reasonableness. People reach reasonable conclusions through a process of shared conversation and debate, as opposed to using individual logical deduction to achieve the goals of rationality.[5] Moral deliberation, aesthetic reasoning, passions, and webs of relationships are explicitly included rather than assumed irrelevant. This suggests that there can be multiple rationalities at work in any situation, and difficulties of communication between these multiple rationalities are not simple misperceptions, but the result of different worldviews.[6]

4. We are not solely individual actors, but are actors in communities. We tell stories to communicate to others, not just to explain things to ourselves. Our stories are rarely accepted verbatim by our listeners; instead, the listeners interpret our stories, judge them, select relevant bits, and often ignore the author's intention. These interpreted stories are often retold to others, or replies are made to the first author, involving us then in interpretive communities.[7]

5. Within these interpretive communities, rhetoric also serves to create group identity and solidify the social bonds of the individuals who share particular story lines. Stories are told not just to persuade outsiders, but to clarify "them" and "us." Small groups interact with other groups and share stories, and these individual stories become affiliated with stories from like-minded groups to form a network of narratives. Adhering to this general network creates and identifies coalitions; failing to adhere peripheralizes the individual or group.[8]

6. Our individual as well as group narratives are embedded in larger narratives, and are specific to a place and a time. The story of my life is enmeshed

in the story of the transition from the twentieth to the twenty-first century; the story of the Mojave is specific to that desert and those people in the 1990s. Our stories are also constrained by the narratives of others, so that we are only co-authors of our life stories.[9] In different words rephrased from Clifford Geertz, we exist in webs of significance spun in part by others, in part by ourselves, and in part by the interactions of other and self.[10]

7. Our individual and shared larger narratives are also structured and staged by institutional and cultural settings. In ways subtle and not so subtle, this text is influenced by the criteria that the publisher (a university press) sets for initial publication and that my profession (academics) sets for the bestowing of prestige and honors, including tenure and promotion. If I were employed by the National Park Service or this book needed to make a significant profit, it would be different—although in what ways and by how much is not particularly clear. The context of interpretive actions matters.[11]

Interpretive approaches are said to run the risk of a radical relativism—the idea that there are no facts at all, that because different things may be viewed as true by particular individuals, there is no way to judge or select between stories or even to communicate between discourse communities. There are two responses to this critique. First, we pragmatically know that there is a world out there and that the natural world has facts—trees need sunlight, nutrients, and water to grow, for instance. All things, then, cannot be true; trees do not grow without sufficient nutrients, no matter how good a story is told to the contrary. We can imagine "facts" as being either in a category of broadly accepted facts—trees need nutrients to grow—or in a category of contested claims—welfare is bad for recipients' morals. The interpretive paradigm brings attention to the social construction of facts, but does not deny that there are a group of claims that are so widely accepted as to effectively be facts. Using this, we can evaluate stories for goodness or badness—a task I take up later in the chapter. Second and relatedly, as noted by Thomas Harper and Stanley Stein (1996), while narratives differ, we share many of the basic conditions of being human and can converse across communities, finding commonalties as well as differences. Where there is a base of shared experience, as there is for most of us in just being human, there is the possibility of conversation; where there can be conversation, there can be intersubjectively developed reason, and thus conclusions about right and wrong, good and bad.

Within the field of planning, theorists have developed the implications of this general interpretive paradigm under the name of communicative theory and practice. Bob Beauregard describes the goals of communicative planning in the following way: "Simply put, rationalists hope to make the actions of planners rational and the outcomes of planning functional, while theorists of communicative practice hope to improve the quality and openness of the debate."[12] This work has largely focused on (1) deconstruction and interpretation of planning documents;[13] (2) the stories told by planners about their work;[14] and (3) the process roles of storytelling or communication in planning.[15] What I contribute to this ongoing conversation are concrete steps that can be used to apply the interpretive paradigm (a.k.a. communicative planning) to the planning process.[16]

The Interpretive Planning Model

To that end, I propose a general planning model with the following steps:

1. Gather data and analyze, including the traditional socioeconomic and other quantitative measures of planning and policy analysis, plus a political and administrative history and documents expressing the positions held by various participants to the land use debate.
2. Interview participants to the debate to determine their positions and their reasons for their positions (understood as their stories of what ought or ought not happen, and why).
3. Construct the narratives of the debate, based on both the textual and interview data gathered in the prior steps.
4. Analyze the frames at work in the debate, which include the values, ethics, and worldviews of the participants.
5. Create an alternative frame (reframe the debate) based on points of concurrence determined through the prior framing and the planner's vision, knowledge, and creativity.
6. Institutionalize dialogue, including public discussion of the narratives, frames, and reframing developed previously.
7. Prepare a plan or policy recommendation based on the consensual outcomes developed in the step above.

There is quite a bit packed into each of these steps, as explained more fully in the sections below.

Gather Data and Analyze

The model starts with traditional planning tasks—gathering of socioeconomic, geographic, and land use characteristics of the area in question, and analysis of these in ways that illuminate the issues at hand. To be effective, the planner needs to understand the situation.[17] What is slightly different in this model as opposed to the traditional models is how these facts are used. In rational planning, data and analysis are understood as essentially unproblematic, not political. The data can therefore suggest appropriate resolutions and reasonable recommendations.

However, in the real life of planning controversies, facts are marshaled like soldiers for each side; facts themselves become partisan. For the planner to step up in early stages and publicly present a summary of facts of the situation is likely to be political suicide, since the various disputants will evaluate the implications of the facts presented—which facts the planner buys into—and make a determination of "whose side the planner is on." The interpretive planner knows that she or he may need to be selective in which facts are publicly affirmed based on awareness of which points are generally accepted and which are contested. As a result, in the interpretive model data and analysis provide grounding for the planner in the situation of the community, allowing the planner to converse intelligently with the various participants about issues. This grounding creates an internal home base from which the planner can begin to privately make sense of the situation. Data and analysis will inform the reframing of the situation. But the interpretive planner knows that facts must also be understood in relation to the narratives of the debate, because, as Jim Throgmorton (1996) argued, the facts themselves become part of participants' rhetorical strategies.

This approach also calls for collection of additional materials beyond that usually included in planning analyses. For an issue to become a controversy implies that it has a history full of people acting for and against certain proposals. To begin to understand the emotions and reasons involved in such a dispute, the planner will need to become familiar with that history. This implies understanding the origins of the dispute, the way it has been institutionalized, the actions taken for and against it, and how individuals reacted to or created such actions—knowledge of the institutional and political history of the issue. In many situations in which the planner works for an institution that has long been active in the area and whose institution may even have been the genesis of the debate, this information will be ready at hand. The analysis of the data will result in a reasonable grasp of the local geographic, socioeconomic, and land use characteristics and a political/institutional history.[18] How formally arrayed these analyses are depends of course on the purpose and resources (not the least of which is time) of the planner.

Interview Participants

The planner also needs to be aware of the ways the issue has been publicly constructed and debated—the public stories of the issue. Initially, reading public testimonies, publicity memos, letters to the editor, and the like will provide familiarity with these public stories. However, knowing the publicly told stories of the issue will probably not be enough. People do not always mean what they say or say what they mean. As an issue enters the public domain, participants select those stories they feel will be most persuasive to the public, and these may or may not coincide with their personal motivations for undertaking support or opposition to the issue. Still, those private motivations are likely to weigh heavily in what someone will consider a reasonable resolution of an issue. As noted by Susan Carpenter and W. J. D. Kennedy: "Conflicts are rarely what they seem. Personalities, motives and relationships are as important as the substance of the issue . . . Adversarial positions, especially publicly stated ones, may result from a great variety of pressures and purposes that do not accurately reflect the actual needs of the contending parties."[19]

Because of this, working only with the public stories may mislead the planner when he or she evaluates what is at stake, and what resolutions are possible. To address this, the planner can meet with the individual participants themselves, asking about why an issue is controversial, why that person feels it is important, what points are critical to a positive outcome. As long as the interview respondent is speaking to a planner who will be acting in a public role, the respondent must be made aware of the possible public uses of the interview conversation. The result is that the stories told in the interviews have in reality a mixed public/private character. To the extent that the interview stories exactly match the publicly told stories, the analytic (although probably not the relationship-building) effectiveness of interviewing declines. Nevertheless, in the interviews respondents will stress some points above others, and which stories gain emphasis and which become secondary in interviews is an important indicator of the respondent's motivations and views of the situation.

Second, the interviewee's skill in consistently screening privately held positions to match public stories is likely to vary with her or his professionalism and emotional engagement in the issue. A professional lobbyist, for example, is unlikely to vary much between her public arguments and reasons given in an interview—she is a professional rhetorician, and her stake is less personal than, for instance, a local resident's. The local resident may be less likely to engage in the same level of rhetorical stratagems—he does not talk about the issue for a living, and is more personally involved. For those who are deeply engaged in an issue and are not professional speakers, the logic of passion may overwhelm the logic of reason, and private stories may slip through. If the individual's motivations were nefarious, we should not expect that this will be exposed in the interview. If, however, the respondent's motivations were reasonable but not persuasive in public, they may come through in an interview.[20] I will occasionally use the shorthand term of public and private stories to differentiate stories specifically expounded for public consumption versus those told in interviews, but at a very real level, even the interview narratives are public stories.

For the practicing interpretive planner, if my argument is correct and private stories are told in interviews that were not part of the public debate, an ethical question may arise. If the interview respondent lets slip a different narrative, a private story, should the planner make this public? Good judgment is required here. First, as further discussed below, the planner has the duty of presenting these narratives back to the respondents to test their accuracy; this also gives the respondent a chance to back off from a story and ask that the planner not use it. Second, the interpretive planner must, I believe, begin with a strong mandate of causing no harm. If there is any possibility that publicly discussing a private narrative could cause harm to the individual, her standing in her community, or to the process itself, the planner ought not do so.

This discussion presupposes that the persons the planner will interview are those who have been most active in the issue—the proponents and opponents, as well as those with organizational or political responsibility for the area. There is a significant problem with this. Those who are publicly active may not mirror the interests of the broader affected public, so interviewing only the activists may not represent the community's (or communities') interests particularly well—it may miss the views of the "silent majority." James Palmer and Richard Smardon (1989), following Lester Millbrath (1981), suggest that random sampling of the public is a more reliable indicator of public views than are hearings or meetings. This seems likely to be true, and including a public opinion survey appears desirable.

Similarly, those who are active in a debate may not include particular groups who are most directly affected by the issue, raising questions of justice and equity. While activity may not always equal power in an issue, identifying those who were most active is at least a place to begin. It may also be helpful during analysis and interviews to consider who is silent but still powerful (elected officials who have not publicly taken a stand, for instance) and attempt to determine the reasons for their silence and the implications of it (for instance, the legislation won't pass unless the local representatives both favor it). Beyond this, however, reaching out to underrepresented and minority populations, whether that underrepresentation is based on ethnicity, race, income, class, or simply stance on the topic at hand, will be an important criterion of a good interpretive planning process. Indeed, as I will present later, one of the exciting aspects of interpretive process is that it can assist in working toward a more level playing field among those of disparate power, education, and rhetorical levels.

One of the key aspects of interviewing is awareness that the process itself affects both the interviewer and the respondent. Done in the best way, it is a conversation about meaning-making, a way for both parties to investigate and together construct an account of a situation. Simply having a chance to speak directly to the planner, and to be taken seriously, may be of great significance to the debate participants and the resolution of the conflict. Interviewing is also relationship building, which can be central to the dispute resolution process as that phase of the project is entered. The process, then, has the potential to serve many goals. In the Appendix, I describe the particulars of how and who I interviewed, along with a brief review of some of the key theory behind this sort of qualitative data management.

Derive Narratives

At this point, the planner begins to analyze the public documents gathered in the first step and the interviews completed in the second. The analysis sorts out the stories, or narratives, that participants used to describe the issue. A narrative includes both plot elements—what happens to whom, when, why—and discourse—how the plot is communicated.[21] We identify narratives by their wholeness and integrity: they have beginnings, middles, and ends; they suggest purpose and agency; they foretell outcomes; and the pieces go together

coherently.[22] In working through the data, the planner looks for "those stories
. . . that are taken by one or more parties to the controversy as underwriting
[that is, establishing or certifying] and stabilizing [that is, fixing or making
steady] the assumptions for policymaking"—which is how Emery Roe defines
policy narratives.[23] As the analysis proceeds, some narratives will be shared by
multiple parties to the debate and will be central to the arguments of more
than one side. We can call these the major narratives. There may also be minor
narratives, told by only a few or one person, often not rebutted by the other
side. While major narratives generally set the terms of the debate, minor narratives can provide helpful insight into the issue and are important for representing the full spectrum of stories.[24] The overall narrative told by a respondent is likely to contain multiple arguments (we should do x because of y),
each of which individually may lack a time structure and causation. For analytic purposes, it is useful to break the narrative down into its particular arguments, thereby focusing the attention of the analyst and the audience on that
one aspect of the story. In planning and policy, narratives also have institutional or organizational placement, and consideration of this can shed light
on the purposes and meanings of the narrative.

It is essential to this process that the interpretive planner fairly describe the
debate's major and minor narratives, and the planning theory literature provides guidance for this. Interpretive planners need to meet at least two standards, according to Giovanni Ferraro: (1) the planner's interpretation must be
based on the "text" (participants' stories, in this case) itself, and use all of the
text's elements; and (2) the planner's interpretation must both make explicit
the prejudices (frames) existing in the starting texts and the prejudices
(frames) existing in the new, interpreted text. Both of these elements are designed to highlight that the new interpretation exists within a continuous
flow of texts and interpretations, and to "remind planners that every new interpretation and every new plan is a test of their intentions, knowledge, and
techniques."[25] In practice, we can test planners' interpretations according to
three criteria:

- Verisimilitude—Do the authors of the original stories agree that the
  planner's interpretation expresses the sense of the original story?
- Frame explicitness—Do the interpreted stories succeed in making the
  frames of reference implicit in the original stories more visible, and
  thus more available to discussion?

- Bias explicitness—Has the planner been explicit about his or her position in the situation, including institutional loyalties, individual beliefs, history in the debate, etc.? Can readers or listeners distinguish the interpreter from the interpreted?

The first and third points suggest that the planner must present the narratives back to the participants to assure that the planner's interpretation is correct or to suggest how it can be adjusted. A secondary goal of this stage is for the planner to demonstrate that he or she has recognized the speaker—recognized in the way that Forester uses the term, meaning conveying to others that we appreciate that their problems are real, their values understandable, their positions defendable.[26] This recognition allows movement beyond simple strategic actions. It also suggests the central place of frame-reflective discourse in this model. I return to both of these points.

In analyzing these narratives, the planner probably needs to make some judgments regarding the quality of these stories. At the most general level, the planner can test the narrative for the reasonableness of the story. As Walter Fisher suggests, as humans we test stories every day for their rationality. He identifies two basic principles upon which stories are tested: probability, which is whether a story hangs together, whether it is coherent; and fidelity, which means that the story is truthful, reliable, relevant, and consistent.[27] More specifically, policy claims are a kind of story, one that professionals or the public tell to justify changing or retaining a particular public policy. They therefore have some additional criteria. A good policy claim story must also be able to respond to the issues and counterarguments that appear in competing stories. For a policy claim, the stated need for the policy change and its outcome must be clearly related.[28]

These criteria suggest that for the interpretive planner, a good policy story must achieve the following general traits:

- Internal coherence—Is the story logical; are the actions of the characters believable given their particular situations; are the stated needs and outcomes fairly well related?
- External consistency—How well does the story respond to counterarguments and other stories? How well does it account for other stories or facts we believe to be true?

The complex relationship of passion and policy narratives is an issue to which the analyst will want to be sensitive. We use reason to persuade, Frederick Bailey argues, when we can find some value the other person accepts; we can then use logic to argue from a shared value. When the debate challenges sacrosanct values or when we fear that our argument has logical steps that will not survive scrutiny, we turn to the use of passion. Strong passion in a narrative may be a sign that reason is not sufficient to make a persuasive case—the narrative is a bad story, in the terms developed below. However, some passion is necessary in persuasive argument: "There can be no purposive activity without emotion, for purpose implies goal, and goal, in the end, entails passion . . . Reason has no power to move: without passion, one remains inert, unmoved oneself and unable to move others."[29] Passion may also imply that the speaker feels his core values are under attack. Many planners trust most in dispassionate, reasoned discourse, and view passion with suspicion. The interpretive planner needs to develop a more complex orientation to passion, welcoming it as a sign of sincere debate while maintaining some ironic distance in understanding its strategic use.[30]

At this point in the analysis, the planner is evaluating good stories versus bad. Emotional content does not necessarily imply a bad story, nor does rationality imply a good story. Instead, good stories pass the tests of internal coherence and external consistency, and bad ones fail them on one or more criteria. The purpose of the testing is to develop the planner's own understanding of the situation, not to go forward claiming definitive knowledge of the quality of the debate. What I found in the Mojave and expect others will find as well, is that the insight provided by bad stories is just as important as that from the good. While the literature is largely silent on how we explain bad stories and what we do with them, I will suggest some implications.

I begin from Fisher's argument noted above, that most individuals are able to, and in fact commonly do, apply narrative rationality criteria to their own and others' stories. We can therefore expect that people will have good, solid stories in initially defining and exploring their positions to themselves and to their group members, and again when presenting their positions to others. It seems likely that participants may end up telling bad stories for one of three reasons. One is that their initial stance is related more to passion (fear, pride) than to reason, and so they must construct stories to explain and rationalize their passionate response to others; since these stories are really covers rather than the fundamental reason for their position, they may be more likely to be bad stories.[31] A second and related situation may be where the participant is simply looking for ways to justify existing or desired economic or status advantages, but must develop some kind of story to justify (rationalize) them.[32] A third reason might be that the participant starts out with a perfectly good story that explains her or his position, but recognizes that this story is not going to be persuasive in a public forum and so switches to another, more rhetorically strategic story. Again, the result is more likely to be a story that does not fulfill the criteria of narrative rationality since the story told does not need to be fully explanatory to the individual storyteller or her group. The planner will have to listen closely and use some judgment to guess which of these appears to be relevant. In any case, being able to evaluate the stories will provide helpful insight into the actions and motivations of the participants as well as how the issue was itself constructed.

When the planner begins the public discussion of the narratives, what should he or she do with bad stories? I would suggest not labeling them as such, but, gently and without condescension, presenting them with their flaws intact and allowing others to make their own judgments. The planner can indicate the logical gaps, the characterological incoherence, the inability to respond to counterarguments; I do this within my commentary sections for the stories told about the Mojave. Exposing story problems can serve three important purposes. First, when the planner describes a problem with a story, participants may respond with a nuance or fact that the planner-as-interpreter has missed, suggesting that it is not the story that has problems, but the planner's reinterpretation of it. Second, as participants follow through the construction problems highlighted in the planner's analysis, the participants may become aware of new facts or perspectives on the situation. Third, identifying problems might allow those telling that story to back off of that particular claim, and acknowledge that it is not the central story in their position in the debate—thus moving the dialogue toward discussion of the stories that make up the real substance of the issue, rather than those constructed for rhetorical persuasiveness.[33]

Frame the Issue

Analysis of narratives gives the planner a rich understanding of the ways participants have constructed the issues at stake. This knowledge is essential in designing outcomes that might achieve consensus support. At the next

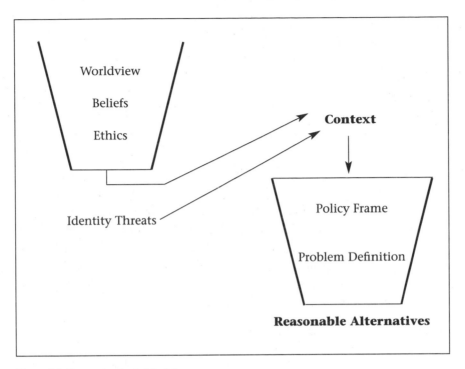

Figure 8.1: Frame Analysis Model

level of analysis, narratives can also suggest insights into the perspectives and values of the participants. Susan Hunter developed a conceptual model of how this sort of analysis could proceed, and I have modified it to better fit community policy-conflict situations.[34] The interpretive planning frame analysis model, previously shown in Chapter 6, is reproduced above for the reader's convenience. In it, I suggest that the level of policy analysis with which we should be concerned begins with worldviews, and that worldviews suggest appropriate sets of beliefs and ethics. These combine with individual identity and economic interests to encourage the particular policy frame an individual or group will use in a given situation. The way an individual or group frames a policy suggests the way the problem will be defined, and hence the alternatives that will be considered reasonable solutions.

Worldviews and Policy Frames

A worldview is, according to Robert Bush and Joseph Folger, "a framework composed of a set of beliefs about the nature of the world—including the nature of human beings and their social processes and structures . . . [It] provides the organized viewpoint from which one interprets the surrounding world. And individuals' viewpoints reflect generalized frameworks that operate within a culture or society." Worldviews do not spring up ungrounded, however. Worldviews come from an "intuition of value or purpose . . . an assumption made at the outset about the nature of the good, about what matters and is important"[35] —in other words, from ontologies. It is virtually impossible for individuals to describe their ontologies, however, because they are so deep-seated. For that reason it makes sense to begin planning or policy analysis with worldviews.

It is not common for people to describe their worldviews as coherent wholes.[36] They tend to be tacit, often unacknowledged; asking people to describe and discuss these in the abstract is unlikely to generate much insight. Instead, one can begin to see these worldviews in the stories people tell. Indeed, it is exactly the function of worldviews to explain and interpret the weltering mass of experience of the world, and the way general worldviews get applied to a particular issue is described by policy frames. Policy frames are the guidelines for organizing the complex reality surrounding a particular policy question. They suggest which facts should be selected as relevant and how those facts should be arrayed based on the individual's worldview. A major purpose of storytelling is to share our worldviews and policy frames. The process, as noted by Donald Schön and Martin Rein, is that "from a problematic situation that is vague, ambiguous, and indeterminate (or rich and complex, depending on one's frame of mind), each story selects and names different features and relations that become the 'things' of the story—what the story is about . . . Things are selected for attention and named in such a way as to fit the frame constructed for the situation . . . Through the process of naming and framing, the stories make the 'normative leap' from . . . 'is' to 'ought.'"[37]

By beginning with stories and narratives, the analyst allows people to explain an issue in ways that are comfortable and in terms that they select, which means they will be describing their policy frames and worldviews in a natural way. The job of the interpretive planner is to analyze those stories to understand how the applied policy frames both constrain some potential consensual outcomes and allow room for others.

Identities and Interests

Both identities and interests are significant in determining what policy frame a person will bring to bear on a situation. Identity, in Terrell Northrup's terms, encompasses the self-in-relation-to-the-world as well as the individual internal identity.[38] Economic interests can be defined as concern with maintaining or improving economic and social standing and related access to resources or power.[39] How significant an element this is will vary, of course, based how much economic impact participants believe the policy represents.

The effects of policy change on affected individuals can be quite complex, involving both their economic interests and their understanding of their place in the world. Even when a policy issue appears to be about economics, the story is likely to be more complicated. Imagine a farmer who is being offered a large cash settlement to sell his land to a town for use as a landfill. Part of the issue certainly is economic—will the payment be enough to live on? Does it equal fair market value? But part of it is likely to be about the farmer's sense of herself in the world; if she's not farming, who is she? If the land of her forebears becomes a garbage dump, is she a bad heir? Often the effect of a policy on economics and the individual's core construct of self-in-relation-to-the-world is complexly interwoven, and any attempt to manage the conflict needs to integrate these interrelations and layers of meaning to be effective.[40]

Part of self-in-relation-to-the-world is having a sense that the world is predictable, understandable. Policy changes can endanger this sense of a comprehensible world, and a more random or unpredictable world is a more threatening world. We can expect that different individuals or different organizations will have more or less ability to deal with threats to their core identity and relations to the world, depending on their ability to integrate change. As the severity of the threat to identity increases, the reaction against the threat will also escalate, moving the participant toward an increasingly rigid, defensive, and hostile position in opposition to the threat, and creating an increasingly intractable conflict. At a very advanced stage of conflict, the identities of the parties in the dispute becomes so defined by the dispute that all sides may collude to continue the conflict so as to retain their individual or organizational identities.[41]

The practical importance of policy frames is that they limit the ways the participant will define the issue. What counts as the facts of the situation—do we think about the last ten years or the last hundred years? do we worry more about the area's residents or the broader public?—depends in large part on how one frames the issue in the first place. From the policy frame flows the problem definition, and from the problem definition flows what might count as an acceptable resolution. Thus the set of possible solutions to a situation that will be acceptable to participants is constrained by their initial policy frames, and awareness of those frames allows the planner to make sense of what may work as a consensus outcome, and what is beyond the bounds of participants' sense of the possible.

Reframe

To resolve a particular conflict, the planner may choose to proactively reframe the issues, beginning by looking for points of concurrence in the frame analysis to suggest ways of understanding the situation that have not previously been available to the participants.[42] John Keltner suggests that "to change intractable struggles to viable ones [tractable] may require creative redescription [reframing] of the perceptions and the nature of the language surrounding the struggle situation. Changing or abandoning the metaphors of the conflict may be highly useful. Metaphors seem to play a significant role in escalation and changing them has relevance."[43]

An active reframing builds on the tradition of planners as visionaries, in which planners bring their creativity and knowledge to the resolution of community issues. It also acknowledges that even when working in the intermediary role, planners as public servants are not neutral parties, and instead bring their own agendas and ideas into the process.[44] Central to reframing, however, is listening—the active listening at the heart of the previous steps in the model.[45]

Lawrence Susskind and Jeffrey Cruikshank (1987) suggest that a reframing should not create conflicts with sacrosanct values. Mediation participants who negotiate away basic values will be greeted with suspicion by their constituents, who may disavow the commitment and seek new spokespersons. For the participants themselves, to trade on their basic ideologies is likely to create new identity threats, challenging their internal understandings of what it means to be moral. This suggests that a reframing should start at the level of threats to identity in the model presented above, and must include redefinitions of the policy frame, the problem definition, and likely options.

An important caveat here is that the reframing, the new story, created by the planner is not especially privileged. As noted by Fisher: "From the narrative perspective, the proper role of an expert in public moral argument is that of a counselor . . . not to pronounce a story that ends all storytelling. An expert assumes the role of public counselor whenever she or he crosses the boundary of technical knowledge into the territory of life as it ought to be lived. Once this invasion is made, the public, which then includes the expert, has its own criteria for determining whose story is most coherent and reliable as a guide to belief and action."[46] The planner's reframing must be persuasive to participants as a better view of the issue, one that is both reasonable to the facts and helpful to resolution, so that participants want to work within that frame.[47]

Enter the Fray and Institutionalize

Up until now, the planner has been acting as intellectual inquirer, trying to understand the situation, the participants, how their stories interact and frame the issue at hand, and a way to reframe the story. But planning is about action in the world, and so it is to that the process turns. The purpose and the promise of the frame analysis is its explicit recognition that multiple perspectives are engaged in the situation, and that recognizing this diversity is an important aspect of achieving effective outcomes. The frame analysis process assists in helping participants to feel acknowledged, and helping them to acknowledge others. As suggested by Schön and Rein: "It is plausible that when scientists or policy makers are caught up in frame conflict, their ability to reach agreement depends on their learning to understand one another's point of view . . . Reflecting on the frames of their adversaries, as well as on their own frames, they would try to reason their way to conflict resolution."[48]

The model suggested here applies the frame reflection process not just to experts, but to the citizens engaged in the issue, and proposes that the planner serve as facilitator of this dialogue. What the planner will be doing at this point is to design what John Bryson and Barbara Crosby define as a forum, a place to "link speakers and audiences through discussion, debate and deliberation in order to create and communicate meaning."[49] These forums achieve two main goals: to collectively establish a list of potential topics and decisions that can be debated and discussed, and then to transform those into a list of the actual topics and decisions that will be addressed, and those that will not. In other words, they have the power of the agenda.[50] This is a particularly appropriate and feasible role for planners. As noted by Bryson and Crosby, it is in their design of forums with open rules of access that planners often gain leverage, and it is in those forums that visions of a desirable collective future can arise. That shared vision can have "profound impact on subsequent decision making" in policy making and in the courts.[51]

The planner creates a forum that develops solutions through consensus building processes. Central to this process is the planner presenting his or her interpretation of the various positions and the planner's reframing. The planner's interpretation is incorporated into the sorts of collaborative processes, including role playing and scenario building, for which planners and mediation specialists are developing good techniques.[52] Such a process is, to quote Judith Innes and David Booher, "simply and foremost one of learning, which transforms participants' previously held convictions and helps them to develop new shared meanings, purposes, and innovative approaches to otherwise intractable issues."[53]

This sort of learning takes time. The situation will have developed over time, and it will take patience and effort to create a dialogue in which the framing and reframing can have an effect. Personal change rarely happens as great revelations; instead, it occurs through slow and gradual adjustments to new information. There must, then, be some institutionalization of the process of dialogue about the frames and reframing, about the issue as it has been understood and as it could be understood.[54]

During a process of shared deliberation, there will be both personal, internal learning and learning regarding the relationship between the process participants. The internal learning might allow a clearer or changed perspective on what the person or group thought was central to their interests. As Nigel Taylor notes, it is possible for people to be mistaken about what is actually in their interest, and people can "become better judges of their interests when they engage in considered reflection about their values in discussion with others."[55] The process of reflection may allow the participants the time and space to find outcomes they would not have expected to support, or did not previously imagine.

Other parts of learning may have more to do with the relationship between participants. The model I propose moves the process toward transforming the relationship of the participants, rather than merely settling the dispute. According to Northrup, settling a dispute implies leaving the relationship between the parties and the core identities of the parties intact and simply agreeing to change a condition of the situation. An example would be when long-time feuding neighbors agree to share the cost of a fence; no change is made in the central problem of the parties' identity engagement in the conflict itself (their emotional attachment to a troubled history), but the particular troublesome condition is addressed. Northrup argues that this sort of settlement will have little impact on the future of the relationship, because the reasons for the feuding, the conflict over core identities, continues. In communities, as for neighbors, future relationships matter.[56]

Transformation, in contrast, implies changes in the core identities of the participants in the conflict. Such a change will affect the entire system of the conflict, and result in a reinterpretation of the problem itself. Achieving this usually requires that for some reason the rigid separation between the parties, where each are divided into camps and define themselves largely in terms of opposition to the other, is altered so that "the individual sees that the other party is 'like-self' in some core ways."[57] Bush and Folger call this recognition "the evocation in individuals of acknowledgment and empathy for the situation and problems of others." A second condition is also required, according to those authors. The individuals engaged in the process must become empowered, meaning "the restoration to individuals of a sense of their own value and strength and their own capacity to handle life's problems."[58]

While transformation may remain a goal, it is wise to have modest expectations for transformation in real-world processes. As noted by David Harvey: "Knowledge and ideology do not change overnight. The concepts, categories, relationships, and images through which we interpret the world are, so to speak, the fixed capital of our intellectual world and are no more easily transformed than the physical infrastructure of the city itself."[59]

As a result, something less than transformation is more likely. This middle ground is what Northrup describes as changing the dynamics of a relationship, which lies somewhere between settling and transformation. This does not directly alter the core identities of the individuals, but over time the experience of working together and talking together can create a significantly changed relationship. When Mojave area ranchers became concerned with the threat of having the park service as land managers, they discovered an uneasy but real solidarity with miners and retirees. These were people with whom the ranchers would not previously have considered themselves in community, but as a conflict dies down, this kind of expediently developed community is likely to continue, as the identity of each of the participants has been slightly altered.

The purpose of the frame analysis and reframing is not just about facilitating a consensus-building process. These analyses allow the planner or analyst to understand what sorts of solutions are likely to be accepted by participants as possible consensual solutions, and which are out of bounds and why. Interpretive planning is a policy analysis tool. The reframing is a way of combining the insights of communicative theory with the history and hopes of planning as providing better solutions for people. Because it begins from the perspectives of constituents, it seems better placed to provide acceptable, politically supported outcomes than expert-based models of decision making, while still building on the policy expertise that the planner/analyst brings to the process.[60]

Interpretive Planning, Interests, and Power

While interpretive planning is primarily concerned with bringing world-views and policy frames into analytic consideration, a focus on values is not meant to suggest that planners should naïvely ignore the realities of power and interests. These will be implicit in interpretive planning processes, just as they are throughout all planning processes. Here I will address some of the steps in which power and interests are a particular concern: derivation of narratives, planners' interpretation of narratives, planners' reframing, and insti-tutionalizing dialogue. Previously I defined interests as concern with main-taining or improving economic and social standing and access to resources and power. Bent Flyvberg defines power as a "dense and dynamic net of om-nipresent relations," often exercised in subtle ways; it is the ability not just to prevent something from happening, but also to create desired outcomes.[61] We all have interests, but only some of us have the power to ensure that policy de-cisions reflect our interests.

In determining narratives, individual and group narratives will necessarily reflect not just their values, but also economic positions and futures—in other words, interests. To imagine people and institutions as bundles of values and worldviews without consideration of their interests is to make the same mistake as positivist researchers and practitioners who address only homo economi-cus—only in reverse. Instead, we must learn to manage people and processes that deal with both values and interests and the interplay between these.

Power influences both what participants say and who gets to talk in policy disputes. Flyvberg notes: "Not only is knowledge power, but, more important, power is knowledge. Power determines what counts as knowledge, what kind of interpretation attains authority as the dominant interpretation. Power pro-cures the knowledge which supports its purposes, while it ignores or sup-presses that knowledge which does not serve it." In other words, "power con-cerns itself with defining reality."[62] Powerful groups will work to make their particular story of an event the prominent, accepted one, and attempt to quell dissenting stories. Powerful groups work to first set the boundary of which nar-ratives will be broadly heard and thus available for public consideration, and then put resources and energy into promoting their favored narrative. There is some good news, however. As Flyvberg points out, power relations are constantly being produced and reproduced; they are constantly changing. There is, then, the ability to intervene in existing power relations.

Flyvberg's argument in many ways supports the importance of an interpretive approach to planning. An interpretive planner who chooses, to borrow John Forester's term, to speak truth to power[63] can use the interpretive platform to highlight how existing powerful interests have manipulated the policy conversation through their selection of facts. That planner could bring forward minor stories that otherwise might get lost, show that their worldviews are also reasonable, and encourage the participation of less powerful groups in the policy dialogue.

The planner may, realistically, have to make choices about which minor stories are worth the political capital to bring forward, and which are not worth the fight. If powerful interests set the boundaries of which narratives are acceptable, is the ethical planner required to solicit and support policy narratives that lie outside the boundaries? What about narratives that are outside the bounds of what the planner considers ethical or reasonable? In the Mojave, I was able to acknowledge the realities of participants holding a wide variety of positions and understand their sets of beliefs, even when I did not agree with them. An exception occurred, however, with the story that said the United Nations one-world army was behind the Mojave designation. To that, I could only bring disbelief. Would an interpretive planner be correct to encourage discussion of U.N. domination of federal lands just because some participants believe that is important? We can certainly say that all people deserve to be treated with respect, and that respect is the foundation of interpretation.[64] However, bringing forward some stories may backfire and reduce the credibility of a group. Prudence is part of a planner's role.

Planners and theorists may also be concerned about the power delegated to the interpretive planner/policy analyst. Flyvberg, discussing Nietzschean insights, argues that interpretation is itself a way of becoming the master of a situation, and becoming master of the situation always involves a new interpretation. By placing the planner in the center of the interpretive process, we place the planner in a position of power. Given that planners are humans and thus have biases and interests and work for institutions that also have particular interests and biases, this power will need to be carefully used. The planner must take care to correctly restate the stories of the various participants in the issue, and do so in ways the participants themselves actively agree represent their position. This reinforces the importance of ethics training in the education of planners and policy analysts. Generally, however, I doubt if the power of the interpretive planner is any more, or any less, than that of a traditional rational planner.

A final concern with power enters during the reframing process. If powerful interests are able to define what counts as reality and set boundaries on what qualifies as a feasible, implementable outcome, then we may need to acknowledge that in the process of reframing. The purpose of the frame analysis is to identify options that build on correlations and connections between policy frames. Some reframings might suit most participants, without suiting those with the most power. In that case, if the planner's main goal is to develop a readily implementable vision, there may be no point in suggesting a vision that contradicts the goals of those in power. In other situations, the planner/policy analysts may feel that the appropriate reframing is one that breaks the boundaries defined by those in power. Presenting this alternative reframing publicly and persuasively can be an important act of public service, of planning ethics, of doing good. But it needs to be done with awareness of the political and power realities. This is hardly different from other planning processes, however; political feasibility is usually a factor in choosing planning policy, even when the final choice is to buck the influence of power.[65]

Limitations

The interpretive planning process outlined above is very time consuming, which is one of its primary limitations. Added to the traditional tasks of quantitative data gathering and analysis are interviewing participants, transcribing the interviews, analyzing the interviews, framing, reframing, and engagement in the process of conflict transformation. This full-scale effort will likely only pay off in the worst sort of cases—situations in which there are strongly opposed sides who have long histories of antagonism toward each other, participants perceive that the stakes are high, basic values and worldviews conflict, and/or participants will need to work with each other during a future process.

In less intense, less complex cases or situations for which time and resources are more limited, a similar sort of analysis might use speedier methods. Administrative histories could be informal or shorter. The planner might conduct focus groups rather than individual interviews. The planner could skip full-scale transcription in favor of just taking notes during interviews. Analysis of policy frames might be done more quickly by using less rigorous treatment of the interview and written materials. No doubt if and as this method is more widely practiced, others will find ways to make the process quicker and more efficient. All processes evolve.

A second concern is with efficiency, and excessive attention to process as opposed to outcome. Participants are likely to be uninterested in expending effort and time in dialogue that does not have a clear outcome in the world; outcomes are usually understood to be the allocation of scarce resources. This suggests that the interpretive planning process needs to result in plans that will be implemented and the participants need to know that what happens in the dialogue will change what appears in the plan.

More generally, some readers may be distressed by the issue of planners' biases in working in this interpreter/mediator role. Prior to the reframing, the planner needs to be able to operate in a fairly neutral, information-gathering, analytic, and facilitative mode. I do not mean to suggest that planners are bias free and because of that have the right to be interpreters. No one who is human is bias free. I do believe, however, that in many situations the planner can hear, understand, and acknowledge a variety of conflicting stories, and this is essentially all that is required. As noted above, to test for biases the planner brings his or her story reconstructions back to the persons who were speaking in the first place, asking for correction of any perceived bias.

The reality of planners' institutional affiliations may also be an issue. As noted by Throgmorton, "planners do not enter community debates as objective observers. Rather, they work for an organization, are paid by that organization, and are influenced by that organization's legislative mandate and internal culture and history."[66] Interpretive planning is unlikely to be immune from the experience of rationality Flyvberg documents, whereby rationality becomes rationalization, and governmental units organize information and discussion to achieve their desired outcomes.[67] While this is a concern, it seems to me that it is no larger a concern for the interpretive planner than for rational planners, given that quantitative data can be selected and influenced for rhetorical purposes in the same ways as qualitative data. Still, based on either personal experience with that planner or general experience with the planning organization, in some situations some groups will see the planner as an untrustworthy interpreter. An active distrust of the planner or the related organization will make successful framing, reframing, and consensus building unlikely. In this case, an outsider who is acceptable to all parties should be chosen to manage the process.

If the planner chooses to reframe the debate, the planner naturally becomes a partisan for a particular view of the situation. That view, however, is not forced upon negotiating participants—evidence of the very limited nature of planners' power to force anything is abundant; instead, the planner's story must persuade, as does any other story. This approach may be susceptible to manipulation by badly intentioned and unethical planners; so are most other approaches. More generally, writers tend to agree that planners when working as mediators are not neutral anyway. They have the interests of their employers to consider, and their own visions of appropriate future actions.[68] As John Forester notes: "Public deliberation in participatory planning processes is a contingent, fragile, vulnerable possibility in a precarious democratic society; it depends not on some virtuous 'good planner' but on struggle and hard work, insight and imagination, moral sensitivity and political perception."[69]

There remain some significant problems with the rhetorical approach to planning that need to be admitted to this conversation. Of these, perhaps the most troubling is that noted by Peter Berkowitz, as follows:

> Hobbes shrewdly criticized democracy as, in effect, an aristocracy of orators. He meant that the public assemblies in which the people or their representatives gather to make decisions will inevitably come to be dominated by the most eloquent and persuasive speakers, those capable of inflaming people's passions and deflecting attention from what reason requires . . . The problem for democracies, where the people rule, is that not everyone reasons equally well . . . In practice, power is likely to flow to . . . all those who, by virtue of advanced education, quickness of thought and fluency of speech, can persuade others of their prowess in high deliberative arts.[70]

This is an issue central to communicative planning, which focuses on creating more and better forums for dialogue. If planning's proper role is to create unbiased forums for consensus building, we must deal very concretely with the reality that not all are equally situated to benefit from these processes.

The Promise of the Approach

Done in a suitable way, the planners' interpretations may serve to somewhat level the playing field of rhetorical abilities, and monetary and momentary circumstances. The interpretive planner takes the time to reflect on participants' stories and construct them in a form more resembling their ideal than speakers may manage under the heat and nervousness of public appearances.[71] The planner does not substantially change the elements of the stories, so a bad story will remain just that. In fact, construction problems are likely to be even more evident in the planner's interpretation since some passion is likely to be eliminated, passion that may have shielded story problems in first listenings. When the planner moves into the phase of suggesting an alternate story, one developed from her or his own sense of passion, justice, and efficiency, it will be up to the public to perform the same sort of analysis on the planner's story as the planner has done on theirs.

More generally, the model outlined here asks that planners explicitly recognize and manage conflict; this seems to be becoming a larger and more recognized part of the planner's role.[72] These conflicts appear to increasingly be over values. In 1983 James Creighton commented: "While the battles of the past may have been among those most immediately affected and concerned about economics and use, the battles of the present are a struggle among competing fundamental values about how the land should be used and the lifestyles associated with that use."[73] My sense at the start of the new century is that this continues to be true. This may explain in part why planning theory has become more and more concerned with communicative and collaborative processes—because these explicitly address competing values.

Land use planning occurs for the most part at the local level, and, outside of voting, land use planning is often the most direct involvement citizens have in democratic government. These grassroots, local issues are one of the few forums easily suited to participatory democracy, in that decision making is close to those whom it affects, affected publics are relatively easy to identify, and the topic tends to be one that people care about and can understand. Eliciting participation among busy people is one of the root problems of democracy. When conflict occurs, people become galvanized, so that one of the basic conditions for participatory democracy is already in hand. Conflict also creates the need for participatory democracy, as grassroots opposition to any plan is likely to doom it to failure.[74] While situations of conflict may not readily appear to be good laboratories for encouraging participatory democracy, I believe they are in fact the most promising opportunities we have.

Epilogue

Past and Future Stories

In the 1960s and 1970s, my family lived in an inner-ring suburb of Cleveland, not far from the Cuyahoga River and very near the steel plants for which the city was famous. My small town, Brooklyn Heights, cooperated with two other similar heavily industrialized suburbs to create one small but resource-rich school district. One of those other towns included a peculiar forgotten valley located directly alongside the polluted Cuyahoga River. It flooded regularly, so those who could afford to lived elsewhere. The result was what appeared to be a clean and green rural belt tucked inside the industrial city. My school friends who grew up there raised horses, belonged to 4H, and had only recently gotten plumbing—all literally within sight of the spire of Cleveland's Terminal Tower. These friends began to disappear from our school, for reasons that at age twelve I neither understood nor questioned.

As a doctoral student, I became interested in how we protect land, and how we work with the people who live on that protected land. During a visit back to the Cleveland area, I stopped by the relatively new Cuyahoga Valley National Recreation Area (CVNRA) and got a copy of their administrative history. Slowly, it dawned on me why these childhood friends had disappeared. The CVNRA was designated on the land that had been my friends' homes. The park service had used eminent domain to purchase homes in the area, tearing down structures to give the new park unit an appropriately "natural" feel. The river is much cleaner now, and the CVNRA provides a valuable oasis amidst the suburban sprawl of the metro area. But the unique community that dwelt in those forgotten bottomlands no longer exists. I don't know if those families found new places to live where there were both 4H clubs and factory jobs, but somehow I doubt it.

That was the early 1970s. In the 1990s, communities put up much more of a fight, as witnessed by the Mojave situation. Distrust of the National Park

Service runs deep, in large part because of ill-advised activities in places like the CVNRA. The fact is, in all but very exceptional cases the park service no longer has either the political will or the funding to do the big land purchases of the 1970s. Even if they did, the park service relies on public support and on its reputation as the best of government bureaus, and so needs to avoid blatant and unpopular exercises of power. Still, in areas where new units of the national park system are being proposed, history haunts. Institutions, like people, sometimes make bad choices, and payment can be long and dear.

In the fall of 1998 I drove west across Iowa to speak at a community land use forum in the Loess Hills. These unique glacial forms look like a red-brown giant's spine set inexplicably between the rolling farms of central Iowa and the rich alluvial soil leading to the Missouri River. In a state famous for plowing shelterbelt to shelterbelt, where neatness of fields is almost as important as farming profits, the Loess area has kept at least some remnant prairie. Citizens there had been actively thinking about land protection for some years, but in the late 1990s the topic began heating up. The *Des Moines Register*, the newspaper of note in these parts, began a campaign to get the Loess Hills designated as a national park. In 1999 Secretary Babbitt took a bicycle tour of the area, and by local accounts at least, was struck by the beauty of the prairie and the bluffs.

At the land use forum, local farmers, speakers from the Nature Conservancy, the Natural Heritage Foundation, the Iowa Department of Natural Resources, and others presented compelling arguments about why the Loess Hills were a significant resource and how local residents could take steps toward protecting the landscape. I described alternatives to full-scale national park designation of the sort I present in this text, alternatives that protect sensitive lands while also preserving existing local cultures. I had anticipated that, while the idea of the park service coming in would be exciting to some residents, it was likely to be frightening to even more. I was not mistaken, and I have since gone back to give similar talks.

Some Loess Hills residents have decided to take the initiative in land protection, not just fight it or respond to outside efforts. Together with some local institutions, residents formed the Loess Hills Alliance, a nonprofit group designed explicitly to find ways to protect the landscape and provide for increasing tourism to the area while supporting property rights and the existing farming and residents. The LHA does not have an official position on whether or not there should be a new Loess Hills national park unit, but it is clear that gaining their support requires a park unit that respects local residents. Other residents, of course, are talking about how to keep the park service out altogether. Park service personnel come to the meetings of the alliance, and are welcomed as partners rather than bosses or opponents, and park opponents are specifically invited to alliance meetings as well. The park service is studying the area, looking for ways to combine a federal presence with continued local power and private property.

There will be work to do in keeping the collaborative process going, finding a common vision for the area, and then designing ways to achieve that vision. But at least here at the start, environmentalists are in partnership with farmers and residents; researchers and extension agents from the land grant university are supporting local efforts; and the federal government is neither following nor leading, but instead is a participant in the search for good options. It is a good, and hopeful, moment.

Appendix: Applying Interpretive Planning in the Mojave

Qualitative Research

Interpretive planning as outlined in the previous chapters relies heavily on the skills of qualitative research, an area that is likely to be less familiar to planners and policy analysts than is the more traditional quantitative socioeconomic research. These two schools of research methodology are closely related to the two major paradigms in use today for research in the social sciences.[1] The first is the positivist paradigm, which, as described by George Noblit and Dwight Hare, is "optimistic about the prospects for general theories or laws and largely seeks to develop them . . . [P]ositivists quantify social events and assess the statistical relationships between variables in the service of constructing an abstract theory."[2] The second is an interpretivist paradigm, which seeks

> an explanation for social or cultural events based upon the perspectives and experiences of the people being studied . . . All interpretivist research is "grounded" in the everyday lives of people . . . Interpretivist studies usually rely on "thick description," the detailed reporting of social or cultural events that focuses on the "webs of significance" evident in the lives of the people being studied. Since these studies reveal that context affects the meaning of events, interpretivists are dubious about the prospects of developing natural-science-type theories or laws for social and cultural affairs.[3]

The goal of qualitative research, according to Noblit and Hare, is to enrich human discourse, and to understand the "sense of things, " leading not to prediction, but to something more emergent and less certain—we can call this anticipation. This book, and the proposed interpretive planning process more generally, fall squarely in the interpretivist tradition, seeking not to create models with which to predict the future, but simply to get a sense of one particular case study from which anticipations for that particular and other similar situations can be created.

Within the interpretivists paradigm, there are of course multiple approaches to research. This book uses two of the approaches—the ethnographic and the narrative. As described by Catherine Riessman, the ethnographic approach is "similar to other scientific descriptions in that it is intended as realistic description; it is the events, not the stories informants create about them, that are intended to command our attention; language is viewed as a transparent medium, unambiguously reflecting stable, singular meanings."[4]

In Chapter 3, I use a limited kind of ethnography, relying on my informants' descriptions of events to create a reasonably full description of the process of designation for the Mojave National Preserve, without reflecting too carefully upon their language choices or questioning the shared meanings of their words. In Chapter 4, I follow the narrative approach, which Riessman describes as a skepticism about a correspondence theory of truth. In Chapter 5, I make some effort to test the quality of the stories to the facts of the natural world, as best I can determine them. By Chapter 6, however, language is understood as deeply constitutive of reality, not simply a technical device for establishing meaning. Informants' stories do not mirror a world "out there"; instead, they are constructed and creatively authored; they are rhetorical, replete with assumptions, and interpretive.[5] Note that this does not mean that the world does not exist outside our constructions. Instead, it implies that the way we understand those facts is through language, which is constitutive of our view of reality.

The general research goal of interpretive planning and this text is to meet the stringent criteria for interpretivist research indicated by Spicer (1976):

> In the study there should be use of the emic approach, that is, the gathering of data on attitudes and values orientations and social relations directly from people engaged in the making of a given policy and those on whom the policy impinges. It should be holistic, that is, include placement of the policy decision in the context of the competing or cooperating interests, with their value orientations, out of which the policy formulation emerged; this requires relating it to the economic, political, and other contexts identifiable as relevant in the sociocultural system. It should include historical study, that is, some diachronic acquaintance with the policy and policies giving rise to it. Finally, it should include considera-

tion of conceivable alternatives and of how other varieties of this class of policy have been applied with what results, in short, comparative understanding.[6]

The heart of this research approach is in interviewing, because through direct conversation a researcher can hear people's stories, as well as their reflections on their experience. Irving Seidman describes the experience of being interviewed from the interview respondents' perspective, and the goals of the interview: "It is this process of selecting constitutive details of experience, reflecting on them, giving them order, and thereby making sense of them that makes telling stories a meaning-making experience . . . [A]t root, interviewing is not about testing hypotheses, getting answers to questions, or evaluating; it is understanding the experience of other people and the meaning they make of that experience."[7]

While acknowledging his point, I used the interviews to achieve two goals—to get answers to questions so that I could improve my understanding of the situation in the Mojave, and to understand the experience of my respondents and the meanings they made of that process. To have not done so would have dismissed the intimate knowledge of the situation held by my respondents and weakened this resulting text. I imagine that most planners, who are obliged to act in the world, would do the same.

One of the major advantages to the interpretivist, emic approach is that it does not require that data be tested to pre-set hypotheses, with an outcome of null or a fit. Instead, the data are allowed to suggest the outcome, and theory that supports the findings is then brought in.[8] Seidman argues that it is best not to have too much theory in mind prior to the interviewing, because the interviews should shape the theory that is developed from them, and not the other way around, so that theories from other contexts are not force-fit to the case study. Seidman goes as far as to argue that extensive reading prior to the research is inappropriate, as it may "contaminate" the view and understanding of the researcher.[9] I chose to take a middle road on this, doing some reading on the situation in the Mojave to facilitate the interviews—appearing perfectly "cold" in them would, it seems to me, to have been unwise. This is supported by Foddy, who indicates that appearing informed is important in creating a sense of rapport and trust and discouraging inaccurate responses, particularly when the topic is difficult or potentially politically explosive for the respondent.[10]

My approach to the data changed greatly from how I initially imagined it. In my preliminary research plan, I anticipated using various quantitative measures, such as counting word usage or numbers of times an issue was mentioned. As the writing process progressed, it became clear that this would not aid the interpretation of the data, and given that each respondent had a peculiar interest in and knowledge of the designation, it would reflect nothing more than my choice of interview respondents. The theoretical underpinnings for the text changed in response to data analysis changes, focusing instead on rhetorical analysis; my increasing certainty that that was the appropriate choice also influenced my treatment of the interview data. The results of the interviews, then, greatly influenced their analysis—an appropriate outcome in this approach.

Research Method

Interview Respondent Selection and Outcome

I interviewed participants to the debate in Washington, D.C., Sacramento, California, and in the area of the Mojave. I identified a first sample of potential interview respondents from mentions or quotations in articles about the designation debate. Following the snowball technique for finding interview respondents, during this first and each subsequent round of interviews I asked each respondent whom else they felt I should talk to, and from those suggestions I generated an extended list of potential respondents. By the last series of interviews, most of the names that were mentioned were people I had already contacted, indicating that I had achieved a pretty good census of the important figures or at least representatives of important organizations and important roles in the debate.

Finding appropriate persons in Washington-based lobbying organizations proved generally quite easy, as the people there constitute an organized set of lobbying organizations, most of whom know each other and know which organizations are active in lobbying. Finding the individuals responsible for working on the CDPA within the Department of the Interior proved much more difficult; the NPS and BLM in Washington were remarkably anonymous, and the lobbyists either did not provide suggestions on who would be an appropriate contact in those organizations, or the persons they suggested denied involvement. My sample of Washington-based DOI persons is therefore limited; in response to this, I interviewed California-based DOI people extensively, providing a more balanced interview set. A second frustration was that no one at Senator Feinstein's office agreed to speak with me on the record. Thus, her views are underrepresented in the interview data base. The senator, naturally, said a good many things officially about the CDPA, and I have relied on those public comments to make up for deficit.

My initial list of contacts for the California-based research came from suggestions from the Washington community, as well as a list of names of people who had been interviewed by the popular press. Once in California, I asked local respondents to recommend other contacts, and thereby created an extended list. From this list, I prioritized those individuals who lived in the preserve area or nearby, and attempted to arrange in-person meetings with those individuals. I conducted telephone interviews with key respondents who lived far from the preserve, and left uninterviewed non-key respondents who lived far from the preserve. Key respondents were considered to be those who several other respondents had mentioned as important.

I was fairly successful at finding names of local individuals who had opposed the bill—they were very eager to talk. My list of local proponents was shorter; this seems to be representative of the breakdown of local sentiment about the preserve, with more people in public opposition than were publicly supportive. Most of the California interview respondents were involved in the debate through some organized group; for many of these local residents, however, their interview responses were based on their personal views and feelings, rather than representing the official view of an organization. This is very different from the Washington interviews and the DOI individuals in California, who largely responded in ways intended to represent their organization.

One of the most difficult tasks in this sort of research is knowing when to stop—how many interviews are enough? Seidman suggests three criteria for deciding that enough interviews have been conducted. The first regards the sufficiency of information—has the number of participants been broad enough to fairly represent the range of views that make up the population? The second is the saturation of information—has the interviewer stopped hearing anything new? The third is when the process of interviewing becomes laborious rather than pleasurable for the interviewer.[11] I worked from two basic propositions. When multiple respondents provided the same name as an important contact, I tried to meet with them. When respondents began struggling to identify names of people I had not met with, I assumed I had spoken with the key decision makers or spokespersons. The second was, have I spoken with at least one or two other people who share this sort of view, this sort of interest or role? If the answer was affirmative, I found that I was not likely to get any new information, so the interview was not necessary. In effect, I stopped when diminishing returns set in with a vengeance—when I knew what the respondent was likely to say.

Eleven Washington-based individuals were interviewed in May and August of 1995; two other individuals, an environmental lobbyist and a park service retired director, were interviewed at other times, but are included in the Washington counts. I interviewed twenty-nine California-based participants to the debate in May and June of 1996. Specific statistics of the interviews are presented below.

Interview Technique

There is a great deal of dispute among methodology scholars about the best way to conduct interviews. The approach I selected was to be very nondirective in my interviewing, allowing the respondents to tell their stories as they saw fit, and thereby letting them determine what areas were important— which determination was one of the primary goals of the interviews. The first step in the interview process, introduction of the interviewer and purpose of the interview, is crucial to the reliability of interviews. Foddy describes why the setting of the initial understanding is so important: "Social actors in any social situation are constantly negotiating a shared definition of the situations; taking one another's viewpoints into account; and interpreting one another's behavior as they imaginatively construct possible lines of interaction before selecting lines of action for implementation."[12]

The significance of this for the interview is, among other issues, that if the researcher does not clearly indicate the purpose of the questions, the respondents will try to guess, so that they can provide the right information. The problem is that each respondent is likely to guess differently, and the outcome will be a different answer to the same question. If there is clear and consistent insight into the goals of the interview and the reasons for it, the answers become more comparable.

The other goal of the initial few moments of the interview is to create a rapport between the respondent and the interviewer. Because, particularly at the local level, this was such a bitter and emotional issue, many local respondents—particularly the opponents—would try to get a sense of my position on

Table A.1 *Interview Statistics*

Interviews	Washington	California	Total
Total formal interviews[a] (no. persons)	13 (13)	25 (29)	38 (42)
Of interviews, no. in-person and taped	10	19 (23)	29 (33)
Of formal interviews, untaped phone interviews	1	4	5
Of in-person interviews, no. not taped	2	2	4
Interviews lasting less than 30 minutes	1	4	5
Interviews lasting 30 to 60 minutes	1	6	7
Interviews lasting 1 to 2 hours	11	9	20
Interviews lasting 2 to 3 hours	0	6 (10)	6 (10)
Estimated average interview length	1.5 hrs.	1.5 hrs.	1.5 hrs.
Respondents residing within preserve area[b]	0	8 (11)	8 (11)
Respondents who reside outside preserve, but within area influenced by CDPA[c]	0	12	12
Respondents who reside elsewhere	13	5 (6)	18 (19)
Respondents in support of the CDPA	5	7 (9)[d]	12 (14)
Respondents with a moderate stance on CDPA	1	4	5
Respondents in opposition to the CDPA	7	14 (16)[e]	21 (23)
Respondents with federal or state government land management agency affiliations	2	8	10
Respondents working in official local government or Congressional staff capacity	2	5	7
Respondents working in lobbyist-type positions	9	1	10
Respondents commenting largely from personal views (including business owners)	0	11 (15)	11 (15)
Gender of respondents: % Female	15%	34%	28%
Race of Respondents: % Caucasian[f]	100%	100%	100%

[a] Two Mojave National Preserve employees were actually interviewed twice; each of these are treated as one interview for these statistics.
[b] Including Needles, Baker, Nipton, and nontown areas within the preserve.
[c] Including Barstow, Victorville, Lucerne Valley, Twentynine Palms.
[d] Includes 3 NPS employees
[e] Includes 4 DOI or State of California employees.
[f] As reported in Chapter 2, about 19 percent of area residents are Hispanic and 6 percent are black. Unfortunately, I did not locate any members of these groups for interviews.

the designation prior to speaking with me. Why this was an issue for opponents in particular became clear when one respondent remarked something to the effect that, since I was an academic studying the issue, I was probably a rabid environmentalist. Based on other similar comments, I assume that this sort of supposition was fairly common. Creating a sense of trust was therefore most critical with the local opponents to the debate, although it was also an issue with the local environmentalists. The more professional the respondent's role in the designation, the less a problem it was—no doubt because for them the issue was intellectual and professional rather than emotional and personal.

My introduction, then, had to accomplish the dual and often conflicting goals of being a consistent introduction of the research goals and creating a sense of trustworthiness and moderateness. I would introduce myself by giving my role (department and university affiliation), indicating the specific topic (the Mojave designation), and describing the research as identifying the issues and procedures of the designation. I would indicate that I am interested in how we plan in areas in which there are conflicting values and that my interest in the issue comes from a sense that it is a situation of conflicting values. Among local residents in particular this last part would generally draw nods of approval. With a respondent who was particularly skittish I might then talk about how I was interested in land protection that keeps residents in place; this seemed to satisfy opponents that I was open-minded on the issue without, I think, introducing unwarranted bias.

The shared body of the interviews consisted of a simple set of questions. These usually included:

- What is your background?
- How did you come to be involved in the designation?
- What was your position on the designation of the Mojave?
- Why did you think that?
- Did this change over time?
- What actions did you take during the debate over the designation?
- What do you see as issues for the future?

Beyond this were many other questions designed to elicit information about whatever it was the respondents knew best; examples include the legislative give and take, the situation of ranchers in the area, the NPS's position on mining, and protection of the desert tortoise.

For the people who were involved from an organizational position—lobbyists and activists—I would ask what arguments they used to persuade others of their position. If answers were not flowing, I would describe certain claims made by their opposition and ask how they would respond. I also asked what organizations they worked with during the debate and what organizations they saw as the opposition. For the local people, I would ask them about their sense of the land itself. Usually the phrasing of that would be something like, "The one thing that all sides to this agree on is that the land is really special. What is it about this land?"

The interviews tended to last about one and one-half hours—the length of time I asked interviewees to allow and the length recommended by Seidman. This length proved beneficial, allowing sufficient time for exploration of the issues without unduly tiring the patience of either the respondent or the interviewer. Several interviews were significantly longer. These were conducted in the respondents' homes with more than one respondent—situations that were more casual.

One of the issues of the interview method is that of imperfect memory. Foddy indicates that people's memory for salient events has been found to be satisfactory for up to one year.[13] My Washington series of interviews fell just on or over that time limit, given that main activities I was inquiring about occurred between the start of the 103rd Congress in 1992 and when the bill was passed on October 31, 1994, whereas my interviews were conducted in the summer of 1995. Because we were essentially discussing highlights of the bill's movement through Congress, most respondents seemed to have more than adequate recall of the events and their positions. The California interviews were conducted a year later. Local respondents by then were much more interested in how the park service had begun its administration than in local activities during the designation. My information on local activities is therefore somewhat sketchy. I was, however, able to obtain a good idea of the planning issues and feelings in the community both after and during the debate, so I believe that not too much salience was lost and perhaps some perspective was gained.

One of the unanticipated issues that arose, particularly with the local interviews, was that many of the respondents had been interviewed about the Mojave debate many times before by the popular press. One respondent even referred me to his other interviews when I asked about a particular dimension of the debate. In several instances the initial part of the interview was clearly "canned"—they had on previous occasions thought through their points and structured what they felt was the best way to present them. By the middle or end of the interview my sense of the talk was that it was less rehearsed. Additionally, several felt that they had been poorly treated by the press and were concerned about control of what they were quoted as saying. It does not appear to me that this biases the outcome of the research, but for those respondents, it added another level of interpretation between the events and my hearing about them.[14]

Transcription Process and Selection of Quotations

Shortly after completing the interviews I transcribed the interview tapes. For most of the interviews the transcription was word for word. For those few which were very extended and for which the respondent tended to repeat him or herself or to digress, some parts of the interview were not recorded word for word; instead, notes were made about the topic of discussion at that point. After the transcription was completed, a profile was made of the respondent. These profiles contained the following sections, which correspond roughly to the book's chapters:

- Background and description of the respondent
- Events described in the interview
- Organizational cooperation and opposition (where relevant)
- Narratives described in the interview—arguments about why the designation was needed or unwarranted
- Metaphors used in the interview
- Issues for future planning

Analysis then proceeded from the profiles, with reference to the full interviews when required. This follows the general method described by Seidman.

Selection of quotations followed two separate paths. For the chapters that focused on actions (Chapter 3), I reviewed the events described by the respondents and organized those into coherent explanations of the steps of the designation. For chapters that describe narratives (Chapters 4 and 5), I scrutinized the profiles for thematic connections within and among them, and selected quotations that best represented the discernible themes. In either approach, the story elements were corroborated by at least two sources, and these corroborated story elements are the ones I have included here. Where only one respondent commented on something that appears controversial, I have indicated that in the body of the chapter. Where more than one source made similar comments (which is all potentially controversial elements unless otherwise noted), I chose the interview segment which was most representative and clear.

Validity of Research

The challenge of assuring the validity of qualitative research is probably the primary reason why many researchers are uncomfortable with qualitative research. At the most general level, as suggested by Riessman, testing the resulting analysis for the trustworthiness of the interpretation rather than the truth of it is the true test of qualitative research. Jerome Kirk and Marc Miller (1986) describe the goal of qualitative research as reporting the research in such a way that the system of hypotheses can be tested and exposed to falsification. The truth of an interpretation is bounded both by the tolerance of empirical reality and by the consensus of the scholarly community.

Moving into a more specific realm, Riessman suggests that that there are four basic tests of validity for qualitative research:

- Persuasiveness: is the interpretation reasonable and convincing? Persuasiveness is greatest when theoretical claims are supported with evidence from informants' accounts and when alternative interpretations of the data are considered.
- Correspondence: have informants had the opportunity to view and comment on the findings?
- Coherence: does the research achieve the overall goals the narrator set out to accomplish? Are the events coherently related to each other? Do the interview abstracts presented in the text explain the particular themes of the narrative?
- Pragmatic use: to what extent does that particular study becomes the basis for others' work? This is future oriented and collective, and assumes the socially constructed nature of science.[15]

The correspondence criterion has been met by having interview respondents review draft chapters, as is further discussed below. Other than that, these guidelines are largely addressed to the reader of the research; do you, the reader, find the research persuasive and of pragmatic usefulness? While these goals can help direct the research, authors cannot be assured of achieving them just by virtue of good methodology.

An approach more addressed to the design of the research is suggested by Kirk and Miller, who indicate that for ethnographers investigating complex questions such as understanding people's values the following issues should be addressed:

- Creating extensive, explicit, and perceptive field notes
- Self-analytical reporting of research procedures and research contexts
- Documentation of sources
- Documentation of bases for inference
- Documentation of the ethnographer's theories of society and biases.[16]

Because this is not a true work of ethnography the requirement for extensive field notes is less. This section seeks to answer the second point above by providing full and searching reporting of procedures and contexts. Within the book, sources are documented and bases for inference are supplied. I have tried to be explicit about my biases.

Robert Yin (1989) borrows from positivist approaches to develop a guide for evaluating the validity of qualitative case-study research. Following his approach, I adapted the following set of tactics for assuring validity, as shown in Table A.2.

An important step in the assurance of validity and reliability was to have respondents review relevant parts of the draft text. This has two goals—assuring that the account is accurate in its facts and that it accurately reflects the comments of the respondents who are most quoted. This sort of recognition of respondents' roles in creating and reviewing the research is supported by the philosophical positions inherent in interpretivist approaches.[17] I sent out copies of a draft version of the chapter to respondents on the basis of whether they had extensive familiarity with the Mojave issue and/or were extensively quoted in this text—and in some case because they requested the opportunity to review the findings. I included letters saying on exactly which pages of the draft manuscript they were quoted.

Most of the comments received back were corrections of minor facts or spelling. Several comments indicated bias in my choice of words in explaining the debate, and when I agreed that the wording was indeed biased, I corrected it. When I felt the original wording was accurate or balanced, I footnoted the objection. One respondent felt that in the draft I had overstated his role in the debate, and I corrected this. Other than that there were no issues with my presentation of quotations or selection of quotations, with facts or interpretation.

Table A.2 Case Study Validity Tactics

Design Tests	Case-study Tactic	Response in This Work	Phase of Research
Construct validity	Use multiple sources of evidence	Use both interviews and documentation	Data collection and composition
	Establish chain of evidence (allows an external observer to follow the derivation of any evidence from initial research question to conclusions)	Through citations in work, logic checks, following the research protocol, and keeping data base which can be referred back to	Data collection and composition
	Have key informants review draft case study report	Either have a few key informants review whole work, or have informants from important organizations read sections relevant to them	Composition
Internal validity	Do explanation building	Within chapters	Data analysis
External validity	Replication logic—test to other cases	In literature review, both of other cases and of history	Composition
Reliability	Use case study protocol (i.e., specific plan) throughout data collection	Protocol developed prior to interviews and referred to periodically during interview data collection	Data collection
	Develop case study data base	Electronic and paper files of interview transcripts and org. literature	Data collection

Community Presentation

Another important aspect of the validity of the research, one central to interpretive planning, is presenting the analysis back to the community. Because I am not the planner for the Mojave, my ability to implement this part of my proposed interpretive planning process was limited. I did do a community presentation; as described in Chapter 6, the presentation and resulting conversation brought out stories of which I had previously been unaware. This confirms the importance of bringing the analysis back to the participants.

The presentation was held at the Desert Studies Center, which is located on the west side of the preserve, neither particularly inconvenient or convenient for local residents (the reserve lacks an appropriate venue in a central location). I invited all the California-based participants I had interviewed to that presentation, about forty people, by mail with an initial note and then a follow-up reminder. Flyers were also sent to the local community center in Baker, inviting the general public. Attendance was light, and unbalanced.[18] Seven community members, three National Park Service personnel, and the Desert Studies station manager attended; of the community members, two actually lived within the preserve; I had only interviewed three of the people. All community members were ones who had strongly opposed the designation. It is unclear why no park proponents attended, but the folks who did attend suggested it was because the proponents "had already won."

I had anticipated that I would talk for about an hour, and then we would discuss for perhaps another hour. In the end, I spoke for perhaps half an hour, but the participants talked much more than I had anticipated—for about three hours. In the presentation, I discussed the six major narratives of the debate. Because participants had great familiarity with the narratives, having in part created them themselves, I focused on describing some of the underlying values as determined in the analysis discussed previously. At several points I suggested (or questioned whether it would be feasible) to start a community dialogue including both opponents and proponents regarding possibilities for creating sustainable industry. The results were not encouraging. The problem seemed to be finding someone on the proponents' side who was a reasonable person in these folks' view; when I suggested one name, they in effect hissed. Clearly, beginning a real dialogue among residents of various stripes and park personnel would not be easy. Still, the eagerness of the group to talk to me, talk among themselves, and talk with the park service personnel suggests that the potential remains.

The presentation was a one-time event, and does not represent a full-scale institutionalization of dialogue as recommended for the full interpretive process. This work, then, outlines how an interpretive planner might proceed in a similar case rather than serving as a full demonstration of the method's efficacy. Such field testing and refinement of the approach is important, but remains a task for another day.

Notes

Introduction

1. Bornemeier (1996).
2. See, for instance, Abbott, Adler, and Abbott (1997).
3. Sax (1980).

ONE: A Solitary—but Not Lonely—Place

1. In Arizona, the Mojave desert is spelled Mohave, but they are one and the same.
2. McKinney and Rae (1994), pp. 73–74.
3. McNammee (1995), p. xv.
4. Burk (1994b), p. 3. Note that the Sonoran desert in this part of the country is often called the Colorado desert, because it is bounded by that river.
5. Schad (1988).
6. McKinney and Rae (1994), pp. 73–74.
7. Austin (1987, 1909), pp. 9–11.
8. The 250,000 visitor statistic comes from U.S. National Park Service. The language of the MNP's designatory act gives the preserve approximately 1,419,800 acres. The NPS's final management plan (p. 209) indicates that after mapping and including Lanfair Valley, the correct acreage is 1,589,165 acres.
9. Burk provides the following statistics for species in the MNP: over 700 species of vascular plants including 25 that have been listed as rare or endangered; 300 species of wildlife including 47 species of mammals and 36 species of reptiles; and 206 species of birds, plus occasional migratory species. Burk (1994b), pp. 7–9.
10. Based on Burk (1994b) and McKinney and Rae (1994), my experience, and conversations with local residents.
11. Austin (1987, 1909), p. 13.
12. Burk (1994b).
13. Adapted from McKinney and Rae (1994), pp. 126–183.
14. Clarke (2000).
15. See Casebier (1983); Casebier and Friends of the Mojave Road (1987).
16. Mark (1984).
17. Schad (1988), p. 17; McKinney and Rae (1994), pp. 99–100.
18. McKinney and Rae (1994), p. 22.
19. Limerick (1985), p. 20.
20. Limerick (1985), p. 19.
21. Burk (1994b), p. 4.

22. Ibid.

23. Schad (1988), p. 23.

24. Burk (1994b), p. 5.

25. U.S. Bureau of Land Management (1980), p. 4.

26. Casebier (2002).

27. U.S. National Park Service (1987).

28. The preserve boundaries do not match census tracts, zip codes, or any other geographical boundary; the BLM did not analyze the question; and the NPS has not had time to do so at the time of my research. Burk (1993) did his estimate by counting by name the residents whom he and others knew of estimated the 71 residents, which is clearly a low estimate. By counting residents at various settlement areas within the preserve, he estimated a population of 189. The BLM in their *1988 Plan* for the Scenic Area estimated the permanent population at 500 residents within or adjacent to the boundaries of the Scenic Area, but since they provide no basis for the estimate, it seems likely to have been a guess. The NPS in their General Management Plan (p. 212) give the preserve's permanent population as fifty.

29. As reported in Burk (1993). The original source is State of California, *Indemnity Selection and Low-Level Radioactive Waste Facility: Final Environmental Impact Report/Statement,* SCH: 80052308.

30. A Needles city planner indicated that the preserve was not a significant source of employment, revenue, or even recreation for area residents. Barstow, on the other hand, historically has been one of the main stopping points for travelers from Los Angeles into the desert or on to Las Vegas, and, according to a Chamber of Commerce representative, it hopes to capitalize on increased tourism revenues from the designation.

31. These zip codes are for the towns or unincorporated areas of Essex, Kelso, and Nipton, which lie primarily in the preserve, and the town of Baker, which is mostly outside the preserve but serves as its gateway community. The table includes the 250 male prisoners living at the minimum-security facility in Baker. The 2000 zip-code census data was not yet available at the time of this writing.

32. The "traditional economic base" is based on perceptions of interview respondents, who usually discussed this as mining, ranching, and transportation.

33. NPS General Management Plan, p. 212.

34. The state lands include 5,900 acres in the Providence Mountains State Recreation Area, 2,280 in University of California's Granite Mountains Reserve, and 140 acres deeded to the Department of Fish and Wildlife—all uses compatible with MNP management. The rest of the state lands, 49,900 acres originally established to provide for state teachers' retirement funds, are scattered throughout the preserve. U.S. Bureau of Land Management (1988), p. 106, and Mark (1984), p. 112.

35. Burk (1993), pp. 6–7.

36. Viceroy Gold owns twenty-two parcels totaling 191 acres. Viceroy has a large gold mine just outside the preserve boundaries. The lack of syndicate or corporate ownership suggests that at that time the area was not under significant resort or home development pressure. Brown, Philips, et al. (1981), pp. 131–44.

37. This comment is based on two things. First, Burk does not live in the preserve area and never has, and I doubt if much social mixing occurs. Second, his list of preserve residents in another publication did not include several families that I, in my relatively

brief acquaintance with the area, know of. His research has been very valuable, nonetheless, because it presents some of the only data specific to the preserve area along with documentation of his methods in reaching those conclusions.

38. U.S. National Park Service (1993a). The $266 price is an average for parcels between 5 and 200 acres located in Lanfair Valley that sold between 1989 and 1994. The $305 price is an average for 150,000 acres of Catellus Development Corporation land, as valued by the BLM in 1993; Catellus concurred with that value. Obviously, some parcels are worth more and some worth less over the large area of the Mojave.

39. NPS (2000), p. 212.

40. Mark (1984)

41. The act clearly gives the secretary authority to purchase lands within the preserve boundary from a willing seller, but is silent on authority to purchase lands not in the preserve. 108 Stat. 4494-95.

42. Clifford (1998).

43. Population numbers are from David Moore, Community Planner for the Mojave National Preserve, under the National Park Service, and are based on local data; density of population is from U.S. Census Bureau (1993). Fulton (1991) reported that by the late 1980s "some of L.A.'s biggest home builders [were] banking land in Rosamond," which is about a hundred miles from the western border of the preserve. Based on personal inspection and reports of interview respondents, Victorville, lying about sixty miles from the western edge of the preserve, is currently becoming suburbanized. There is significant development to the east much closer than suburban Las Vegas—casinos at the Nevada state line. These currently are just splotches of neon with little surrounding development, and whether they will become more than that is uncertain.

44. The Ivanpah Airport land transfer was legislated in P.L. 106–362, signed by President Clinton on October 27, 2000.

45. Clifford (1998).

46. Clarke (2000).

47. Luke, Karl, et al. (1991), pp. x and xi. A big problem with trash sites in the desert is that they attract ravens, who find immature desert tortoise to be a delectable dish. Some authors think that the raven is the biggest addressable cause of tortoise population declines. Probably the overall largest factor in tortoise populations declines is upper respiratory disease syndrome, which is like a fatal cold. Captive tortoises are infected by humans and then infect their wild counterparts if returned to the desert. Because prevention requires stopping the actions of the many people who temporarily bring a tortoise home, halting spread of the disease is difficult.

48. Noble (1996); Schine (1996). The dump(XE "dump") site is located above the water table of the Colorado River, which supplies most of Southern California. Controversy regarding the safety of that and the financial health and management abilities of proposed site-developer U.S. Ecology have halted the project, perhaps permanently.

49. Abbott, Adler, and Abbott (1997), p. 6.

50. White (1991), pp. 212–235, chap. 19. See also Worster (1992), "New West {XE "new west"}, True West," in which he describes two primary ecological modes of white occupation. The first is the pastoral cowboy/sheepherder mode, which describes much of the rural culture. The second is a hydraulic mode, developed by water engineers and irrigators, which both supports and requires dense urban growth.

51. Mark (1984).

52. U.S. National Park Service (1993a).

53. U.S. NPS General Management Plan, p. 256.

54. Outdoor Recreation and Wilderness Assessment Group (1991).

55. Based on reported sample numbers in Outdoor Recreation and Wilderness Assessment Group (1991), Table 19, p. 32.

56. Most hunters stayed from three to seven days. Outdoor Recreation and Wilderness Assessment Group, p. 28. An average stay might be five days, which suggests that removing hunting would have prevented 1,500 visits to the preserve. Most hunters visited between two and four times a year; averaging again would suggest three visits per year, which suggests that only 500 people would be impacted each year by preventing hunting. There are so many estimates built into this calculation that it is obviously incorrect, but it probably is reasonable to the magnitude of effects.

57. U.S. National Park Service (1993a).

58. Ibid.

59. Ibid., p. 5.

60. Ibid.

61. U.S. Census Bureau (1992).

62. Bradsher (1997) reports that the stereotype of anti-park sentiment in the west is inappropriate, and that many local residents are now or always were in support of the National Park Service. While data are only anecdotal, the paper reports that newer arrivals to the area tend to be more sympathetic to the NPS than long-time residents.

63. Howe, McMahon, et al. (1997), pp. 1–3.

64. Stephen Graham and Simon Marvin suggest two likely scenarios for the effect of telecommunications on the generic urban form. In the first, the better availability of high-quality telecommunications encourages the centrality of the city. In the second, widespread and equal internet access encourage footloose industry and home work. Graham and Marvin (1996); see esp. chap. 8. Obviously, which of these proves most prescient will be important to the Mojave and to gateway communities generally.

TWO: Parks, Preserves, and Land Management Bureaus

1. Runte (1987), p. 32.

2. Runte (1987), pp. 30–32.

3. Runte (1987), p. 48.

4. The emphasis on recreation at national park areas was formalized in the Parks, Parkway, and Recreation Act of 1936. This new focus did not supersede the NPS's original legislated goals of managing for preservation of the environment and for visitor enjoyment; those were set by the park service's enabling legislation (39 Stat. 535), commonly known as the Organic Act, and continue to be legally binding. Instead, it seems to have been in response to Mission 66, a parks infrastructure project which created much of the physical plant of parks as we know them today—roads, cabins, visitors centers, treatment facilities. Many at the park service and elsewhere felt that Mission 66 placed excessive priority on creating infrastructure for recreation and sacrificed areas that ought not to have been developed. Foresta (1984).

5. Foresta (1984), p. 97.

6. The initial push for increased focus on biotic conditions came from a commission

chaired by A. Starker Leopold, which stated that the appropriate goal of park management was the re-creation of the "conditions which prevailed when the area was first visited by the white man." Hartzog (1988), p. 88. See also Bratton (1985).

7. Conservation Foundation (1972), p. 105.

8. Foresta (1984), p. 112.

9. Wikle (1991), pp. 56–57.

10. Ibid.

11. Lowry (1998), p. 56. See also Frome (1992); Lowry (1994).

12. U.S. Department of the Interior (1999), p. 7.

13. Carls (1985), p. 50.

14. One of the newer additions to the national park system is also a preserve, Tall Grass Prairie National Preserve in Kansas. For forty years, proponents tried to get this part of the tall grass prairie protected, while local farmers and other residents and their elected representatives strongly opposed such a designation. Finally, in 1996 Congress approved the preserve based on an unusual ownership structure. First, the National Park Trust (NPT), a private, nonprofit conservation trust associated with the National Parks and Conservation Association bought the area that would become a preserve—11,000 acres including historic ranch buildings and important remnant prairie. The NPT donated the central piece of the preserve, 180 acres including the ranch buildings, to the federal government, and it continues to own the remaining approximately 10,820 acres that make up the preserve. The NPS and the NPT will cooperatively manage the whole area. Since the area has been a ranch for many years, some level of grazing appears likely to continue there. See Estes (1995); National Park Service (1999); Hamin (2001b).

15. Bratton (1985), p. 121.

16. Carls (1985), p. 50.

17. The term used for greenway parks is similar, but the ideas are quite different. Greenways are linear in nature, often following rivers, streams, or abandoned railways, and generally have as their goals environmental protection and recreation. They are usually urban in nature, and by virtue of being narrow, do not cover many acres. Little (1990).

18. Corbett and Batcher (1983), p. xii.

19. IUCN Commission on National Parks and Protected Areas (1994); Hamin (2001a).

20. In fact, the 1986 creation of the Columbia River Gorge National Scenic Area can be viewed as an intellectual heir to the BLM's 1980 plans for the East Mojave National Scenic Area. There is one major difference between the BLM's 1980 plan and the plan for the Columbia River Gorge National Scenic Area and other greenline parks, however. The BLM plan dealt strictly with federal lands, and lacked any component of regional planning including local and state governmental units; this was a central part of the goals for the Columbia River Gorge National Scenic Area. Abbott, Adler, and Abbott (1997).

21. U.S. National Park Service (1987).

22. In the final section of the report on the Mojave, management options are considered. One of these is making the area a national park; another is continued management by the BLM; a third is the designation of the area as part of the park system, but as a national recreation area or "some sort of hybrid unit." U.S. National Park Service (1987), p. 8. A final option is to legislatively establish the East Mojave National Scenic Area, allowing Congress to set specific goals and land controls while continuing BLM

management of the area. No conclusions are drawn as to which of these options is preferable. U.S. National Park Service (1987), p. 8.

23. U.S. Bureau of Land Management (1980), p. 4.

24. The Federal Lands Policy and Management Act of 1976, known as FLPMA, is P.L. 94–579, 90 Stat. 2743.

25. Hastey (1996).

26. Section 601 of P.L. 94–579, 90 Stat. 2783.

27. U.S. Bureau of Land Management (1980), p. 5. The first definition of multiple use included in the section is "management of the public lands and their various resource values so that they are utilized in the combination that will best meet the present and future needs of the American people." Other phrases in the definition include: "making the most judicious use of the land," "the use of some land for less than all of the resources," "coordinated management of the various resources without permanent impairment of the productivity of the land and the quality of the environment." Sustained yield is set out as a goal, and defined as "the achievement and maintenance in perpetuity of a high-level annual . . . output of various renewable resources." Section 103 of P.L. 94–579, 90 Stat. 2745–46.

28. The 1980 plan document itself claims no authors. According to Ed Hastey, who was responsible for the plan, Perloff was the one who recommended the inclusion of an official amendment process so that the plan could change as conditions changed. Ironically, the amendment decisions became the scenic area's undoing, as these angered environmentalists.

29. U.S. Bureau of Land Management (1980), p. 6.

30. Ibid.

31. U.S. Bureau of Land Management (19800, pp. 162–63). The 1980 Plan does not go into much detail regarding the East Mojave. The East Mojave is identified as one of many "special areas," and the plan indicates that the secretary of the interior had designated the region as a national scenic area (NSA). The reason for this designation was "to judiciously identify the area, yet not threaten the values through overuse." Ibid., p. 128.

32. Amendments are listed in the first pages of the 6/26/90 edition of the 1980 Plan, and were legislatively enacted through H-1617.1, *Resource Management Plan Amendments for the California Desert Conservation Area Plan.* Changes in the multiple-use classification guidelines include these examples: allowing communication sites into Class L areas; allowing sale of public land only in Class M or Class I areas, but "lands in Classes C, L, and I can only be sold after first changing their classification"; prohibiting agricultural use except grazing in Class M and I land; and prohibiting disposal of hazardous or nonhazardous waste on Class M and I lands, not including mining wastes such as tailings or chemicals used in producing the ore.

33. Amendments that reduced the class of an area, reduced the size of an area, or eliminated an area were considered to weaken the environmental protections of the plan; grazing amendments that would increase allotments or increase the number of months an allotment could be grazed were also considered to weaken the protections. Where the implication of a change was not clear, it was not included in these counts. Note that these are amendments for the whole California Desert Conservation Area, not just the East Mojave portion of it.

34. See Darlington (1996), pp. 248–312.

35. According to one environmentalist source, the creation of the NSA was a com-

promise brokered by the National Parks and Conservation Association (NPCA), a park service watchdog group, between the BLM and those who were already advocating NPS designation for the area. The NPCA did not support NPS designation because it would further stretch already insufficient NPS funding, and the California desert was already overrepresented in the park service system. Other sources describe it as an effort by the BLM to pre-empt national park designation after the BLM's own 1979 finding that the area merited inclusion in the national park system.

36. U.S. Bureau of Land Management (1980), p. 128.

37. My BLM interview respondents were remarkably cynical about the 1988 Plan, suggesting that the BLM wrote it just to fulfill bureaucratic requirements and to quiet environmentalists rather than to direct management of the area. It appears to have entirely lacked the support of those who had to implement it. This helps explain why it took so long for the plan to be produced. When people interviewed for this study discuss "the BLM plan," they almost always mean the 1980 Plan, again suggesting that the 1988 Plan was not a significant tool in actual decision making.

38. U.S. Bureau of Land Management (1988), p. 3.

39. Ibid., p. ix.

40. P.L. 103–433, page 108 Stat. 4471. The bill also created the New Orleans Jazz National Historical Park, to guarantee the support of the powerful Senator Bennet Johnston (D-LA). See Chapter 3 for a discussion of the complex politics behind the passage of the bill.

41. Clinton (1994).

42. U.S. National Park Service (2000).

43. The secretary of interior was directed to prepare a study of the validity of all existing claims, determine the environmental consequences of the mineral extraction at valid claim sites, make recommendations on which if any claims ought to be purchased by the United States, and only then issue plans of operation which would include the environmental regulations allowed under the Mining in the Parks Act.

44. See U.S. Congress, *An Act to Establish a National Wilderness Preservation System for the Permanent Good of the Whole People, and For Other Purposes,* 1964 (78 Stat. 890), as reprinted in Dilsaver (1994), pp. 278–83.

45. 108 Stat. 4494-95. The advisors are supposed to represent the variety of interests in the preserve, including ranchers, miners, environmentalists, residents, and local government representatives. This council was reportedly designed by Representative Jerry Lewis to be "a fly in the ointment" for the NPS (statement by Aaron H., activist). The council is only required to meet twice a year, and how significant a role it would play was uncertain at the time of my writing.

46. Destry (1982), pp. 153–62.

47. U.S. National Park Service (2001).

48. See press release available at U.S. National Park Service (2000).

49. U.S. National Park Service (2001), p. 164; modification in final GMP.

50. Ibid.

51. See press release available at U.S. National Park Service (2000).

52. Ibid.

53. (California Desert Managers Group) (1991). State signatory agencies are the following: the Resources Agency, the Department of Fish and Game, the Department of Forestry and Fire Protection, the Department of Parks and Recreation, the State Lands Commission, the Department of Conservation, the Department of Water Resources, the

Department of Food and Agriculture, the Association of Resource Conservation Districts, the Energy Commission, the Coastal Commission. Federal signatory agencies are the following: Bureau of Land Management, Forest Service, Fish and Wildlife Service, National Park Service, Department of Agriculture Soil Conservation Service, Bureau of Reclamation, Environmental Protection Agency, Department of Transportation, Geological Survey, Bureau of Mines, and National Biological Service. California Counties, an association of regional councils of government, signed an attached "Statement of Intent to Support the Agreement on Biological Diversity."

54. (California Desert Managers Group) (1991), p. 2.

55. (California Desert Managers Group) (1994). Federal signatory agencies were Bureau of Land Management, California; Western Region of the National Park Service; Fish and Wildlife Service. California state signatory agencies were the Resources Agency; Department of Fish and Game; Department of Parks and Recreation. Signatures are dated December 7, 8, and 9, 1994.

56. Notable in this regard is the (California Desert Managers Group) (1991). In this popularly oriented document, the BLM indicates a commitment to protecting the ecological sustainability of its lands based on ecosystem management. Management efforts and resources are now to go to conserving and restoring habitat, rather than focusing on resource production of the land. This is balanced with continued acknowledgment of the agency's multiple-use mandate, but the essence of the statement is much more environmentally oriented than past BLM approaches. Interagency cooperation and ecosystem management approaches are central to this newly defined mission.

57. (California Desert Managers Group) (n.d.).

58. This pressing interest comes because in the military's view, to achieve their mission of training for national protection, they need to be able to utilize their bases in ways that are often harmful to vegetation and wildlife (driving multi-ton tanks across fragile desert soil, for instance). At the same time, increasing development of private lands and protective legislation for endangered species have made the military in some cases a preserve of last resort for species, creating a difficult situation on some bases. The military's motivation in getting involved with the DMG is to assure that they will be able to continue to use their bases in ways they view as necessary to achieving their basic mission—which means that the species living on the bases need to be protected elsewhere or in particular spots on the bases themselves. My source was interview respondent John J., DOI liaison to DOD.

59. The first bioregion to experience significant planning effort was the Western Mojave Desert, which has a great deal of private land, including the towns of Barstow and the Los Angeles-influenced developing areas of Antelope Valley. Planning there has been rocky at best, with several false starts and regroupings. These plans need to have some support from the local governments of the areas involved, and that has been the source of trouble for the Western Mojave planning effort. The MNP's region does not have the same level of development, private lands, or mineral values to manage, so the process had the potential, at least, to be less controversial.

60. *NEMO: Northern and Eastern Mojave Planning Effort*, 2001.

THREE: Legislating and Designating the Preserve

1. See Rorty (1979).

2. The Rockefeller family both originated the idea and made it possible through their donations of land and funding such parks as Acadia, Great Smokey Mountains, Virgin Islands, and Grand Teton. The Mellon family helped significantly with Cape Hatteras National Seashore and gave the land for Cumberland Island. Catherine Filene Shouse (as in Filene's Department Stores) gave the land and funding for Wolf Trap Farm National Performing Arts Park. Hartzog (1988). This elite support was waning by the 1960s and 1970s, as new leadership at NPS did not effect ties to business or government leaders. Foresta (1984).

3. Freemuth (1989), pp. 278–86.

4. Corbett and Batcher (1983).

5. Wikle suggests this may not be such as new phenomena. He reports that in 1936 the NPS had more than two hundred projects to investigate, many initiated by senators and representatives who were under pressure from their constituents to assist in local economic development. Wikle (1991). While Wikle finds that this began in the 1930s, Foresta (1984) and Runte (1987) date it to the 1960s; see also Soden (1991).

6. Foresta (1984) found several reasons for this increased politicization of the process. These included weakening party discipline, an increased interest in outdoor recreation, the environmental unpopularity of other large public works such as dams, and the increased power of environmental groups. I would add the increased economic importance of tourism, and the attractiveness of federal provision of local open space through the urban national parks. See also Hartzog (1988).

7. Lowry (1998).

8. Based on my reading of multiple cases of park designation.

9. See Lowry (1998), chap. 3. In the Mojave, for instance, the National Parks and Conservation Association did not originally support the Mojave's inclusion in the NPS.

10. See Hartzog (1988) for an example of opponents to the Ozark National Scenic Riverways legislation in 1964.

11. An example is the negotiations over park designation in Alaska; local interests were highly anti-park. Zaslowsky and the Wilderness Society (1986). Another example is Canyonlands National Park, where "one can conclude that if local interests had their way politically, they would first support resource development. If this was not obtainable, they would then support parks and recreation areas if public access was provided." Freemuth (1991), #489, p. 46.

12. An example is the Cuyahoga Valley National Recreation Area (CVNRA), where the economy is not dependent on locally extracted resources; most local interest was pro-park. Cockrell and National Park Service (1992).

13. At both Biscayne National Park and the CVNRA, local pro-park interest developed largely as a result of unwanted proposals for the development of the land. At Biscayne, the proposal was for a massive petrochemical plant and shipping facility. American Land Forum (1982). At CVNRA, it was repeated efforts to run high-voltage power lines through the valley, as well as a proposal for a massive subdivision. Cockrell and National Park Service (1992).

14. In the Alaskan park land battle, for instance, home state senators and representatives were unanimously and vociferously opposed to park interests, as were most of their constituents. Runte (1987).

15. The NPS and the Interior Department were dead set against the CVNRA, but it passed anyway. Cockrell and National Park Service (1992)

16. See Lowry (1994) or Frome (1992) for more discussion of the internal workings of the park service.

17. Because of the split between creating new park units and appropriating funds for park management, by the 1980s there was a backlog of over a billion dollars in unfunded but planned acquisitions. Foresta (1984).

18. The exception is the rare instance when a majority of the members of the House sign a petition to discharge the committee from further consideration of the bill. Hartzog (1988).

19. In 1976, for instance, Representative Joseph McDade amended the 1978 appropriations bill to include $28 million for establishment of the Steamtown National Historic Site in Scranton, Pennsylvania. The Senate and House passed the appropriations bill, and the park came into existence completely bypassing the normal NPS planning procedure and the Interior and Insular Affairs Committee. Hartzog (1988).

20. Burk (1994a), pp. 1–9.

21. For discussion of the Wise Use Movement, see Echeverria and Eby (1995); Jacobs (1996); Rowell (1996).

22. Burk (1994a).

23. To mobilize support, Cranston went so far as to hike most of the length of California in a publicity campaign.

24. U.S. National Park Service (1987).

25. Robert P. described this as a very conscious strategic decision, which he calls the "Flagship Theory." By focusing contention on the Mojave, all the wilderness and the other national park upgrades and expansions would sail through behind the Mojave flagship.

26. The most successful occurred in 1991, when park opponents succeeded in the attachment of an amendment to the then-current CDPA bill which would have allowed hunting in the Mojave National Monument.

27. Staffperson for Representative Lewis, in comments on a draft of this chapter.

28. The association of park rangers publicly opposed the Mojave designation, because there was already not enough funding to pay for existing parks.

29. Hastey denied lobbying against the bill, indicating that the role of his office was to provide information, which he did, but that lobbying as such would be an inappropriate activity for someone in his position.

30. There were fewer than ten ranching families with allotments in the Mojave preserve area. See Chapter 5 for a discussion of ranching in the area, environmental effects of grazing, and the narratives regarding the issue.

31. Note that while the number of cattle was few because each animal needs hundreds of acres to graze, the vast majority of land within the Preserve area was grazed.

32. The LaRocco amendment, sponsored by Congressman Larry LaRocco in the Resources Committee.

33. The CDPA came up at the same time as appropriations bills, and this made progress very slow, as appropriations always take precedence.

34. Burk (1994a).

35. According to Jack T., while all those involved knew that the NRA was very active on the issues, they were also very quiet about it, so that proponents of the CDPA felt like they were fighting shadows. Besides the NRA, the most powerful lobbying group in the debate in the House was the Congressional Sportsmen's Caucus. Both pro- and anti-park

lobbyists mentioned this power. The caucus in 1989 was just a group of House members who liked to hunt. There are about 240 members now, over half of the total members of Congress, from both the House and the Senate. The Caucus has monthly breakfast meetings at which around twenty-five members will show up to hear a presentation, and it holds a $500 per plate annual fundraising banquet for the related Congressional Sportsmen's Foundation.

The head of the caucus is not officially allowed to lobby. What the caucus head provides, according to some insiders, is access to representatives. From the caucus many "Dear Colleague" letters were sent, indicating that the caucus supported national preserve designation, and would appreciate it if its members also did so. That a large percentage of caucus members did vote with the caucus position is clear, in that only about twenty-five Caucus members did not fall into line.

36. P.L. 103-433, page 108 Stat. 4471. The bill also created the New Orleans Jazz National Historical Park, to guarantee the support of the powerful Senator Bennett Johnston (D-La).

37. Clifford (1995c); (1995b); (1995a).

38. Clinton (1996). In the final omnibus budget bill, which included the DOI budget, the Mojave was given $1.1 million for operations from October 1, 1995 to September 30, 1996. Approximately $812,000 of that was reprogrammed from other NPS units and the rest was made up from money that had already been budgeted for various special projects and regular cyclical funding.

39. Little (1990).

40. Regarding the Adirondack State Park, see for example Lewis (1976). Regarding the Utah wilderness fight, see Egan (1995); Freedman (1995); Freedman (1996a); Freedman (1996b); Kenworthy (1996).

41. See, regarding the Sagebrush Rebellion, Herndl and Brown (1996); Rowell (1996).

42. The designation of the urban recreation areas of the 1970s and the Presidio now, with their strong local support, show that this first class of designation is far from finished.

FOUR: Narratives of the Preserve Debate: My Way or the Highway

1. Maines and Bridger (1992).

2. A theme is similar to an argument; the particular story told by a participant about an issue will usually include several arguments, each of which may not have the time trajectory and causation implicit in stories. See Chapter 8 for a detailed explanation of story, narrative, and theme.

3. U.S. Bureau of Land Management (1979); U.S. National Park Service (1987). As indicated in Chapter 2, the NPS report was ambiguous about whether the area merited inclusion, but it was accompanied by a cover letter from Howard Chapman, Western Regional Director, indicating that it did.

4. Two pro-park lobbyists stressed this as the first argument they would use in presenting the Mojave's case to congressional representatives, discussing the beauty and ecological uniqueness of the area.

5. Individuals within the NPS do not take official positions on the designation of units; as noted in Chapter 3, that determination is made on the highest levels.

6. Reminders of the history of our industry are often commemorated at designated

national historic sites, which are also managed by the park service. Two examples include an iron forge in Chester County, Pennsylvania, and the town of Lowell, Massachusetts, managed for its historic role in the transition to modern manufacturing techniques.

7. (Sierra Club) (1994).

8. Statements by two BLM staffers; see also Darlington (1996).

9. Wording to this effect was used by Renata W., a mining company representative, Doug P., a BLM employee, and Howard G., a retired BLM manager.

10. The plan amendments that aroused the most anger included the BLM 's decisions to reinstate the Barstow-to-Vegas motorcycle race, delete the northern 10 percent of the scenic area, and withdraw some 300,000 acres of wilderness study area from recommendation for wilderness designation. Burk (1994a), pp. 16–17. According to Howard G., a former BLM manager, the decision to reinstate the motorcycle race was made in response to lawsuits from the motorcycle user groups, and the new race was run under very careful management rules designed to limit environmental impact. In the park proponents' eyes, that race was a potent symbol of what was wrong with BLM management. It was finally halted in the early 1990s. While the race was an important issue for the overall CDPA, very little of the course ran through the MNP area, so discussion of it for the MNP was more about persuasive rhetoric than fact. See also Darlington (1996).

11. Public land grazing critics would point out that this new wealth comes from conversion of a public resource—grasses—to private wealth—cattle. (Rob Fulton, in comments on a draft of this chapter).

12. White (1991), p. 634.

13. As pointed out by Rob Fulton, draft chapter comments.

14. When I received these maps from a local activist, they had no attribution of authorship and it is unclear if they were attached to any report. I suspect that they were just used for talking points, but by the time I got them, how they were used or what their source was had become uncertain.

15. While a visual review suggests these maps are reasonably accurate portrayals of the changing boundaries of protected lands in the desert region, I make no claim for their full accuracy. Instead they should be understood as part of the park opponents' rhetorical arguments.

16. Given that the BLM 's budget was likely to be cut by the amount they reported they spent on the EMNSA when it transferred and that they did not have a separate office for managing the EMNSA, there was both reasonable motive and opportunity for understatement.

17. U.S. National Park Service 2000, p. 23.

18. The idea that landscapes can or should be frozen in time is not realistic, of course. See Marcucci (2000).

19. Rob Fulton in reviewing the draft of this chapter noted that characterizations of the area as in good shape were not part of park proponents' original arguments. He writes: "In the early years this was expressly *not* the opinion of proponents; they constantly spoke of the degradation taking place that needed reversal. This 'things are good now' view was only adopted in response to opponents contention that it wasn't suitable for park status."

20. Note that he was not applying this to the Mojave in particular, simply discussing the general role of national parks in this country.

21. Statements by Dr. Roger Raufer (Philadelphia, June 30, 1996) and Dr. Alex Farrell (Philadelphia, June 28, 1996), both specialists in energy at the University of Pennsylvania. See Wilkinson (1992) regarding the role of water and water rights in western development.

22. This sort of subtext appears as well in views expressed by other Sierra Club activists, a local ecotourism-oriented business owner, and other proponents.

23. Jane J. pointed out that the ideology of the Reagan/Watt years was important in encouraging the Sierra Club efforts to get the CDPA lands a higher level of protection.

24. And Forest Service lands; which is more vulnerable is certainly debatable.

25. Ann Strong gets credit for this apt turn of phrase.

26. Fulton, comments on draft of the chapter.

27. Babbitt (1994).

28. This was discussed by Babbitt at the Golden Hammer Award, presented by Babbitt on behalf of the vice president to the desert area ecosystem managers group (the Mojave Desert Initiative Team) at Fort Irwin on May 21, 1996.

29. It probably is not a particularly good indicator species, however. The tortoise takes a very long time to reach breeding maturity and has a very long lifespan; population changes resulting from a change in habitat take many years to become visible. Because the tortoise requires a large amount of non-mountainous habitat, protecting its habitat theoretically provides protection for many desert species. However, as noted by biologist Rob Fulton, "most species richness, and specifically those with narrow ecological requirements, are in upslope and mountainous habitats"—not tortoise territory.

30. Literature written to generate political support for the bill addresses this reason less directly, indicating for instance, "the Clinton administration supports the national park status for the Mojave." Sierra Club, Wilderness Society, et al. (various dates).

31. Senator Barbara Boxer, the other California senator in the 103rd Congress, has never been reported as visiting the preserve area. Representative Lewis has family who own property in the Lanfair exclusion; whether or not he regularly visits is unclear, but he certainly knows the area fairly well.

32. Rob Fulton, in comments on a draft of the chapter.

33. Rob Fulton notes that this is a significant change from how opponents felt before the CDPA. "Most hated the BLM, but NPS/CDPA was considered worse. BLM and opponents became very strange bedfellows indeed." (Draft chapter comments).

34. My thanks to Randall Jones for his observation of this local-level narrative.

35. For discussion of what makes a plot, see Chapter 8.

FIVE: Of Miners, Cowboys, and the NRA

1. For parks where deer populations and lack of natural predators require herd thinning, annually hunters may be deputized as NPS employees and allowed to hunt, but under highly controlled conditions and with a primary goal of ecological management rather than one of hunting per se.

2. U.S. Bureau of Land Management (1988).

3. Luke, Karl, et al. (1991), chap. 4, p. 61.

4. Hastey (1996).

5. U.S. Bureau of Land Management (1988), p. 122.

6. Fulton, comments on a draft of this chapter.

7. This comes from a lobbyist for the Wilderness Society, but was quoted by most proponents as well as rebutted by most opponents.

8. Barstow Mayor Mal Wessel and his wife; Rob Fulton, manager for the California Desert Studies Center; and Ed Rothfus, Sacramento-based former regional Fish and Wildlife director. That represents 100 percent of the people of whom I thought to ask the question.

9. There are desert-area residents who are active volunteers in big-horn habitat improvement efforts, and who are largely supportive of big horn hunting. I did not locate any within a two-hour drive of the Mojave, however, and so did not do in-person interviews with them. I did do a fairly long telephone interview with a representative of the Society for the Conservation of Big Horn Sheep, a pro-hunting group which services and builds guzzlers for the sheep as well as doing population counts and other volunteer activities. At the time we talked, which was after hunting in the preserve was assured, his main concerns were with access and other nonhunting issues.

10. U.S. Bureau of Land Management (1988).

11. Calculated as 1,225,343 acres divided by 3,500 cows, as reported in the EMNSA Plan, which equals 350 cow units per acre. Statements by Henry M., Sierra Club lobbyist, Washington, May 24, 1995, and other interview respondents put the figure at one cow unit per 600 acres.

12. Russell (1994).

13. Some families' cattle graze on multiple allotments (there are a total of eleven allotments). Just how many families ranch depends in part on how a family is counted (since multigenerational ranches are common) and who is doing the counting.

14. U.S. Bureau of Land Management (1988). The preserve provides forage for 35,503 active animal unit months (AUMs, the amount of forage consumed by one cow and one calf each month). U.S. Bureau of Land Management (1988).

15. U.S. National Park Service (1987).

16. U.S. Bureau of Land Management (1988), p. 126.

17. In conversation with Luke, she indicated that the final report varied little from the draft; personal interview, Granite Mountain Research Station, June 8, 1996. Their report was prepared for the City of Ridgecrest, California, and the American Motorcycle Association to review the U.S. Fish and Wildlife Service's emergency listing of the desert tortoise; much of the report deals with the broader ecosystem issues of the Mojave. Because of the extent of the literature review in the Luke report, I rely on it in the following discussion.

18. Luke, Karl, et al. (1991), chap. 4, p. 35.

19. Ibid., chap. 4, p. 33.

20. Ibid., chap. 4, pp. 33–41.

21. Ibid., chap. 4, p. 38.

22. As noted by Fritz Steiner in a personal communication, at the time of publication of that book, Leshy was a professor at Arizona State University. He became Secretary Babbitt's solicitor general for the Department of the Interior soon after, and was in that position during the debate over the CDPA. His name was never mentioned by interview respondents as significant in the debate, but he may have had a behind-the-scenes role in the Department of the Interior's ultimate support for the change of management.

23. Leshy (1987), p. 26.

24. As of 1975, which is the last time a major study attempted to determine the

amount of land withdrawn, about 26 million acres of land had been withdrawn to protect wildlife, 5.2 million acres for Department of Energy activities and shale oil development, 1 million acres to protect water supply, and 2.4 million acres for assorted public purposes such as prisons and airports. Leshy (1987), p. 33.

25. Buono et al. (1990), p. 18. $2.50 is for placer claims, $5.00 is for lode claims. According to the American Heritage Dictionary (1978), a placer claim is for materials mined through washing or dredging of sand or gravel which contains eroded particles of valuable minerals. A lode mineral is a vein of mineral ore located between clearly demarcated, nonmetallic layers of rock.

26. U.S. National Park Service (1993). The $266 price is an average for parcels between 5 and 200 acres located in Lanfair Valley and sold between 1989 and 1994. The $305 price is an average for 150,000 acres of Catellus Development Corporation land, as valued by the BLM in 1993; Catellus concurred with that value. Obviously, some parcels are worth more and some worth less over the large area of the Mojave. No figures of value for proven-mineralized land were available, although this would be the more appropriate comparison and presumably a much higher number.

27. This is a relatively new rule, implemented around 1993. Prior to that, the prospector had to perform $100 worth of improvements or labor on the claim each year (Leshy [1987], p. 18). This rule change had significant implications for the Mojave, as the total claims dropped from around 10,000 to between 2,000 (according to Bill F. of the NPS) and 5,000 (according to Doug P. of the BLM). I will use the 2,000 number because Bill F. dealt more recently with mineral claims in the Mojave than Doug P. did, but the uncertainty about the number should be recognized.

28. The claimant also has the right to establish a mill site for processing the minerals, usually of no more than five acres.

29. Leshy (1987).

30. Buono et al. (1990).

31. Leshy (1987), p. 31.

32. Buono et al. (1990).

33. Leshy (1987).

34. Leshy (1987), p. 319.

35. According to anonymous NPS sources.

36. Buono et al. (1990).

37. FLPMA is *Statutes at Large,* vol. 90, pp. 2745–46; *United States Code,* vol. 43, section 1701(c).

38. Leshy (1987), p. 31.

39. Within the scenic area, the BLM had excluded the extraction of sand, gravel, and cinders for nongovernmental purposes, in recognition of the wide availability of those materials in the rest of the desert.

40. U.S. Bureau of Land Management (1988).

41. U.S. Bureau of Land Management and Division of Mineral Resources (1991).

42. Miller and Miller (1992).

43. Based on personal observation and discussions with Rob Fulton, California Desert Studies Center station manager, and other residents of the area. One of the ironies of the old mines is that, once abandoned, these mine shafts often become good bat roosting and nesting habitat, such that filling them in or closing the entrance completely can create a negative ecological impact.

44. Viceroy Gold Mine and Castle Mountain Gold Mine, both of which were bound-aried out of the MNP.

45. In addition, the Castle Mountain Mine and the Viceroy Mine were subject to ex-tensive hearings and reviews, which resulted in state-of-the-art-defining environmental protection and remediation. In fact, Robert P. wanted the Viceroy Mine within Park boundaries, because he felt the mine was so environmentally sound.

46. The limestone site is in the Caruthers Canyon drainage area. Draft chapter com-ments by Rob Fulton. Fulton goes on to comment, "It is important to save as much lime-stone habitat as possible because it usually harbors species endemic *only* to calciferous soils, and is where [one] finds many of the Mojave's rare and endangered plants."

47. The dollar value is from a conversation with a Pleuss-Stauffer Corporation em-ployee. I mentioned this number in conversation with an NPS employee, who indicated that determining an extremely high claim value could be a strategic decision for Pleuss-Stauffer in case the NPS does not permit the mine, and Pleuss-Stauffer sues for lost prop-erty value.

48. Rare earths are exotic materials such as sericite and cerium and others that are found in relatively trace amounts and are important in such new technologies as super-conducting ceramics. For some of these rare earths, the Mojave is the only U.S. location where the metals have currently been identified.

49. U.S. Bureau of Land Management and Division of Mineral Resources (1991). The full mineralization study is U.S. Bureau of Mines (1990).

50. See discussion of socioeconomics of the area in Chapter 1.

51. Wilshire and U.S.G.S. (1992), p. 119. U.S.G.S. is the United States Geological Sur-vey. No citation to the exact study is provided, but context indicates it is the 1991 BLM report previously cited here. Wilshire summed up his view of the mineralization statis-tics with a favorite quote from fiction author Douglas Addams (*The Restaurant at the End of the Universe*): "Many stories are told of Zaphod Beeblebrox's journey to the Frog Star. Ten percent of them are 95% true, 14% of them are 65% true, 35% of them are only 5% true and all the rest of them are told by Zaphod Beeblebrox."

52. U.S. National Park Service (1993).

53. That this was my sample is largely a result of my source for local mining contact names, who was one of the local organizers of park opposition and thus was very moti-vated to present a negative image of the CDPA's effects and local feelings. I attempted to contact representatives of some of the mines that were boundaried out, but was not suc-cessful in finding any appropriate persons willing to talk with me. Two of the interviews conducted with local mine manger/owners were done by telephone without speaker-phone, so no tapes were made of the interviews; as a result, only paraphrases are available.

54. Mark (1984), p. 134.

55. Personal, subjective opinion of this author after having various car parts literally fall off on roads that maps present as reasonable. The ever-present, if rare, risk of sheet-flooding makes the "unwise" statement particularly true.

56. Luke, Karl, et al. (1991), chap. 4, pp. 26–27.

57. Ibid.

58. Given the wildness of the cattle, this is an impressive feat, but I saw burros scare cows away from watering holes during my visit there.

59. Mark (1984), p. 133.

60. U.S. Bureau of Land Management (1980).

61. U.S. Bureau of Land Management (1988).

62. Luke, Andre, et al. (1992).

63. U.S. Bureau of Land Management (1988).

64. Rob Fulton, comments on a draft of the chapter.

65. Wilshire and U.S.G.S. (1992).

66. Examples include the tenure of private property holders—local or absentee? How long had they owned their parcels, and with what intentions? What is the actual annual production of minerals in the EMNSA/MNP political boundaries? How many people come to tour in the Mojave, and how many of those are local, regional, state, national, and international?

67. This assumes that the current ecological community is relatively stable with current levels of grazing. Scientific evidence on this point is inconclusive; the ecology could also be on a gradual downward slide, as response to grazing pressures takes decades or centuries to reverberate through the ecological system. Because the primary environmental determinant of the desert is rainfall, and that varies significantly year by year, determining trends in the desert ecosystem is particularly frustrating and prone to dispute.

68. Ann Strong pointed out this difference in ethos.

six: Alternative Visions, Alternative Futures

1. See Bush and Folger (1994).

2. See Hunter (1989).

3. See Northrup (1989).

4. Morris (1978), p. 822.

5. Ibid., p. 1067.

6. Original sources on environmental ethics are many, but Rolston (1988) and Callicott (1989) together provide a good introduction to the field. In planning, see Beatley (1994a); Jacobs (1995).

7. The literature on the relationship of humans to landscape is of course vast. Some notable sources include Marx (1963); Jackson (1980); Oelschlaeger (1981); Schama (1995).

8. See Rousseau (1927); Locke (1952, 1690). For a more contemporary discussion, see chapter 4 by Hilda Blanco for communitarian perspectives on planning and Chapter 1 by Thomas Harper and Stanley Stein for a liberal/libertarian perspective, both in Hendler (1995).

9. Sowell (1987).

10. See Hess (1992), for one perspective on landscape visions, including the environmental perspective on the federal lands. See Sagoff (1988) for further discussion of virtuous action in the civic realm, and why not all political issues are functions of economics.

11. This issue of standing was pointed out by Dan Marcucci in comments on a draft of the manuscript.

12. This is a situation I was in during the 1980s when working for a real estate developer. The cave beetle was an endangered species, and its cave was in the parking lot for our proposed regional mall in Austin, Texas. The situation was resolved by fencing off the beetle's cave and protecting it in perpetuity. I do not know whether the beetle population has actually thrived in its protected, isolated cave or not, but the mall did fine.

13. Of course, most of the five hundred or so preserve-area residents did not get actively involved in the debate. Perhaps this explains why—not only were they not threatened in their economic interests, but they may have less connection to the land and less of themselves invested in the idea of being good stewards for the land.

14. This is not meant to imply that rural residents don't recreate—of course they do, and often do so on public lands. But as is widely true, when something is freely available it is unproblematic; for urbanites for whom open land is a scarce resource, open land for recreation is an issue in a way it cannot be when land for recreation is readily at hand.

15. It is interesting to note, for instance, the difference in grammatical tense with which the respondents constructed the future—proponents looked to preserve the current situation ("keep it the way it is"), while opponents looked to preserve the past ("keep it the way it was"). This difference does not merit too much weight, as it is only two cases and particulars of the conversational context may have influenced the selection of tense structure, but it does provide more evidence of differing time frames, differing temporal reference points, between opponents and proponents.

16. Tonn (1986).

17. See Goodin (1985).

18. This lovely term was suggested by Fritz Steiner.

19. Hamin (2002).

20. For place-oriented sustainability, see Van der Ryn and Calthorpe (1986); Haughton and Hunter (1994); A. Platt et al. (1994); Beatley and Manning (1997); Roseland (1998); Barton (2000).

21. For example, the 1988 Council of Educators in Landscape Architecture issued a call for papers on Sustainable Landscapes (Department of Landscape Architecture, California Polytechnic State University, Pomona, Calif.); see also Thayer (1989); Grumbine (1995).

22. Campbell (1996). The vagueness of these three goals, of course, leaves plenty of room for discussion: What is the appropriate level of growth—zero? How do we balance achieving social justice with achieving environmental protection if these come into conflict? Fortunately, in this text I need not resolve these conflicts except to say that, just as in the rest of life, it all depends on the place and the time.

23. Berry (1977); Berry (1981).

24. See, for example, Ferguson (1983), for one account of the BLM 's poor stewardship of its grazing lands.

25. See Hess (1992), for vivid descriptions of local frustrations with poor federal agency stewardship of the land. While I strongly disagree with his conclusion that shares in the public lands ought to be distributed to the whole American public, his comments on the need for multiple visions of appropriate landscape use are insightful.

26. Thayer (1994), p. 100.

27. Ibid., p. 243.

SEVEN: Policy Directions

1. Limerick (1985).

2. Ibid., pp. 6–7. There is a vast literature on the meanings of wilderness for humans. Notable historic reviews are Nash (1982), Oelschlaeger (1981), and Merchant (1980).

Those with more postmodern tastes can see Evernden (1992), McKibben (1989), or Soule and Lease (1995).

3. Limerick (1985), p. 6.

4. Ibid., p. 158.

5. Outdoor recreation and tourism are resource-based industries—the resource is the natural area, some of which ends up sacrificed to meet mass tourism needs. Saying that mining and grazing are resource based and tourism is not is therefore somewhat deceiving. It is also the traditional construction, and I use it to facilitate communication—but this caveat should be kept in mind.

6. Burke (1990).

7. One could argue that the Alaskan parks that allow indigenous people to continue traditional activities including hunting are of a similar vein, and these precede the Mojave. However, Alaska is so far from the contiguous states, and the indigenous people are so far from most contiguous state people's image of themselves, that I don't believe the Alaskan parks create much of a popular example.

8. Strong (1975).

9. Hamin (2001).

10. Frome (1992).

11. Thayer (1994), p. 324.

12. See, for instance, recent approaches to the whole ecosystem of Yellowstone described in either Keiter and Boyce (1991) or Reese (1991).

13. See Chapter 2 regarding the bioregional planning efforts and the NPS's leadership in those.

14. U.S. National Park Service (1993b).

15. Sax (1980).

16. I don't pretend to know exactly how this would work, but I have faith that the knowledge of how it could be is out there somewhere among experts and local people involved in the various industries.

17. Foreman and Earth First! (1986/1987). *Wild Earth* periodically reports on the status of efforts toward realizing the Wildlands project.

18. Popper and Popper (1987); Mathews (1992); McKibben (1995).

19. Corbett and Batcher (1983).

20. Egan (1995); Kenworthy (1996).

EIGHT: A Proposal for Interpretive Planning

1. Adams (1986), p. 548.

2. Fisher (1987), p. 5.

3. MacIntyre (1981), pp. 216–17; Mandelbaum (2000).

4. Rein and Schon (1993), pp. 145–46.

5. See Healey (1997). Authors such as Healey and Northrup use the term *rational* while I use the term *reasonable*. This choice stems from my sense that it is better to bring new words into the conversation than to confuse issues by recycling the old words.

6. Northrup (1989); Healey (1996).

7. See Mandlebaum (1991); Mandelbaum (1996); MacIntyre (1981).

8. Maines and Bridger (1992); Brown and Herndl (1996).

9. MacIntyre (1981), esp. p. 221.

10. Geertz's famous statement is that "man is an animal suspended in webs of significance he himself has spun." Geertz (1975), p. 5.

11. John Forester suggested this specifically, as did Jim Throgmorton more generally.

12. Beauregard (1996), p. 108.

13. Mandelbaum (1990); Tett and Wolfe (1991); Healey (1993); Hillier (1996); Malkawi (1996).

14. Healey (1992); Forester (1993); Hoch (1996); Sandercock (1998); Forester (1999).

15. Forester (1987); Innes (1992); Innes (1993); Sager (1994); Healey (1996); Throgmorton (1996); Taylor (1998); Forester (1999); Mandelbaum (2000).

16. Forester (1989); Forester (1999) presents process recommendations for practicing planners. Healey (1997) also present a process argument, as does Sandercock (1998). These authors focus on the roles of stake-holders in designing acceptable outcomes. If the work of these authors and my proposed interpretive planning process model become commonly used, it will represent the partial completion of Alexander's three-stage framework for discerning when a paradigm has become sufficiently developed to claim center stage in the planning profession. His components are:

- A meta-theoretical framework that commands respect as a true account of social and individual relationships and interactions in the process of transforming ideas into reality;
- Derived from this framework, a set of contingencies identified and described in such a manner that they will be useful for exploration and prescription;
- For each of these contingencies, a normative decision-making model that would be sufficiently concrete for it to be made operational and used in real-life problem-solving and decision-making situations, yet abstract enough to be applicable over a range of substantive contexts. Alexander (1984), p. 67.

Writing in 1984, he did not see an emergent paradigm ready to fulfill these requirements. Now, it seems apparent that the communicative or narrative approach to planning has emerged as the successor to the long-embattled but still robust rational approach.

17. This will be particularly important where many members of that community, by virtue of engagement with the area's issues and long residency, themselves have a good grasp of the facts of the situation; otherwise in interviews the planner risks looking either naïve or foolish. For a discussion of the role of prior knowledge in interviews, see the Appendix.

18. Marcucci argues that a deep history of human interactions with the landscape is necessary for good planning; this suggests other needed data as well. See Marcucci (2000).

19. Carpenter and Kennedy (1988), p. 35.

20. Ibid.

21. Chatman (1979), pp. 19–23.

22. For the classic discussion of what makes a story, see Aristotle (1991). For more recent work, see Fisher (1987) or Mandelbaum (1991), or in policy analysis see Roe (1994), Hajer (1993), or Kaplan (1993).

23. Roe (1994), p. 3. Note that Roe indicates that stories are not the only kind of narrative; there are nonstories and counterstories, which do not have all of the characteristics of a story (a beginning, middle, and end), or which are designed to respond to a dominant policy narrative. This concern is not particularly relevant in the approach set out here.

24. Roe (1994) uses the terms *dominant* and *minority narratives*. I am uncomfortable with the connotations of pairing the terms *dominant* and *minority*, and prefer to borrow from music the metaphor of major and minor (chords), both of which are necessary and valued. There is also a connotation of more numbers adhering to the major narrative and less for the minor, which is appropriate for this use.

25. Ferraro (1996), p. 320.

26. Forester (1999), see esp. p. 40.

27. Within Fisher's probability criterion, there are three considerations. These are the story's argumentative or structural coherence; its material coherence, whether it makes sense in context of other stories we know to be true; and its characterological coherence. The importance of this last element, characterological coherence, "cannot be overestimated. Determining a character's motives is prerequisite to trust, and trust is the foundation of belief." Fisher (1987), p. 47.

28. Mandlebaum (1990); Fisher (1987), esp. pp. 71–73; Dunn (1993). See also Kaplan (1986), esp. pp. 772–74.

29. Bailey (1984), p. 24.

30. See Baum (1996); Forester (1996); Hoch (1996). In addition, public or private use of passionate argument is likely to be culturally specific, and may be gender implicated as well. Study of this awaits another day and perhaps another scholar. In general, however, these considerations point to the importance of training planners to have more skill in rhetoric.

31. See Bailey (1984).

32. Flyvbjerg (1998), chaps. 4 and 20.

33. Narrative analysis is demonstrated in Chapter 4. In that chapter, however, I avoid the use of the term *argument* in favor of the use *theme*. *Argument* implies logical, unimpassioned actors rationally expounding truths derived from universals, while a major point of interpretive planning is learning to deal with people in all their messiness, including anger, passion, ideals, and reason. ' seems to avoid creating unrealistic characters. Chapter 5 also provides narrative analysis of the debate surrounding the particular uses of the Mojave. In that chapter, however, I used a modified interpretive method that combined some background on the facts of the situation as best I judged them, and the narratives expressed by the various user groups and environmental protection proponents. In this way readers can see both a fairly "pure" narrative analysis, and one that is more conventional because in it the planner acts as judge of which facts are relevant for the situation.

34. Hunter (1989). Her focus is on environmental risk-taking.

35. Bush and Folger (1994), p. 236.

36. We can understand psychotherapy, for instance, as a process of making visible the individual frames the patient uses to understand and structure his or her world. The energy required to successfully do this in therapy suggests that being able to consciously view our own frames is, while certainly not impossible, difficult.

37. Schön and Rein (1994), p. 26.

38. Northrup (1989), p. 55.

39. My definition of interests centers on economic concerns. Other writers such as Taylor (1998) define interests more broadly as whatever will further an individual or group's well-being in comparison with their current situation.

40. Northrup (1989).

41. Ibid., pp. 68–76. See also Marris (1996); Susskind, McKearnan, et al. (1999).

42. This active stance in the reframing is different from the role of reframing antici-pated by Schön and Rein, who view the reframing as an outcome of changes in the en-vironment or changes in participants' views through the process of frame reflective di-alogue.

43. Keltner (1994), p. 172.

44. Susskind (1995).

45. On the importance of listening and strategies for doing so, see Forester (1999).

46. Fisher (1987), p. 73.

47. Roe (1994) suggests that the outcome of narrative analysis should be a metanar-rative, which would "recast the issue in such a ways as to make it more amenable to de-cision-making . . . [with] . . . conventional policy analysis tools" (p. 4). The planner's ability to implement the sort of top-down decisions this suggests is limited, and the logic of the metanarrative keeps the expert in a central place of power. The goal of reframing is more modest—to suggest a feasible alternative perspective on the situation, which may or may not persuade participants.

48. Schön and Rein (1994), p. 45.

49. Bryson and Crosby (1996), p. 472.

50. Regarding the planner's power of agenda, see Forester (1989).

51. Bryson and Crosby (1996), p. 477.

52. This literature is of course large. In planning, see particularly Healey (1997); Lowry, Adler, et al. (1997); Innes and Booher (1999); and for cases studies in collabora-tive land preservation, see Beatley (1994b). In the public policy mediation field, I par-ticularly like Carpenter and Kennedy (1988); Crawfoot and Wondolleck (1990).

53. Innes and Booher (1999), p. 9.

54. Forester (1999), chaps. 5 and 6.

55. Taylor (1998), p. 72.

56. Northrup (1989), p. 80.

57. Ibid., p. 78.

58. Bush and Folger (1994), p. 2.

59. Harvey (1996), p. 188.

60. See Healey (1997).

61. Flyvbjerg (1998), p. 5.

62. Flyvbjerg (1998), pp. 226–27.

63. Forester (1989).

64. Even respect, however, has limitations. While much of the interpretive process lies in creating community and shared respect, there are some positions with which eth-ical people can and must refuse to be in community with or to accord respect. Being in-cluded in a collaborative interpretive process accords a certain amount of recognition of a particular position and power in creating outcomes. There are groups for whom most would agree that this would be an unfortunate outcome—proponents of genocide and the Ku Klux Klan come to mind. An interpretive approach in situations of true evil would obviously be wrong.

65. The relationships between planning and power constitute some of the most im-portant avenues for theoretical inquiry—and therefore the literature is very broad. Along with Flyvbjerg (1998), one could begin with the work of Benveniste (1977); Fried-mann (1987); Hoch (1996).

66. Personal communication, James Throgmorton.

67. Flyvbjerg (1998).

68. Forester (1987); Forester (1992).

69. Forester (1999), p. 246.

70. Berkowitz (1996), p. 39. Ian McHarg offered a pithy statement of this: "Bullshit baffles brains." Personal communication, Fritz Steiner.

71. See Baum (1996).

72. See, for example, Dotson, Godschalk, et al. (1989); Susskind (1995).

73. Creighton (1983), p. 146.

74. See, for instance, the lessons from the case studies in Lake (1986).

APPENDIX: Applying Interpretive Planning in the Mojave

1. Guba and Lincoln (1994) find that there are four paradigms in action—positivist, postpositivist, critical theory, and constructivism. Viewed this way, the positivist rubric would enfold both positivism and postpositivism, while interpretivist would include critical theory and constructivism. Generally, see also Denzin and Lincoln (2000).

2. Noblit and Hare (1988), p. 12.

3. Ibid.

4. Riessman (1993), p. 4.

5. Ibid., pp. 4–5

6. As quoted in Noblit and Hare (1988), p. 17.

7. Seidman (1991), pp. 1–3.

8. Yin (1989).

9. Seidman (1991), pp. 28–29, based on propositions developed by Glaser and Strauss (1967).

10. Foddy (1993), p. 122. He also recommends stressing the importance of the respondents having their side of the story told accurately as a way of encouraging them to talk, and talk accurately. This desire to be accurately represented was probably the primary motivating factor in respondents' decisions to speak with me.

11. Seidman (1991).

12. Foddy (1993), p. 20.

13. Ibid., p. 93.

14. Regarding levels of interpretation, see Foddy (1993); Riessman (1993).

15. Riessman (1993), pp. 65–68.

16. Kirk and Miller (1986).

17. Schwandt (1994).

18. One reason for the light attendance no doubt was the lack of an obvious outcome for those who came. Everyone knew I was a researcher and thus not in a position to change the situation, so respondents had to be so passionate about the topic that curiosity was motivation enough to give up a Saturday afternoon. I expect that where there is a real anticipation of participation changing the outcome, attendance would be greater.

Bibliography

(1995). Inland Empire City Report: Riverside and San Bernardino Counties, California. April.

(1995a). Clinton Stands up for the Wilderness. *Los Angeles Times*, December 22, 1995, B8.

(1995b). Environmental Amnesia. *Los Angeles Times*, October 25, 1995, B8.

(1995c). Money for Mojave Park Draws Veto Threat. *New York Times*, November 1, 1995, A20.

Abbey, E. (1988). *Desert Solitaire*. Tucson : University of Arizona Press.

Abbott, C., S. Adler, et al. (1997). *Planning a New West: The Columbia River Gorge National Scenic Area*. Corvallis: Oregon University Press.

Adams, W. (1986). Politics and the Archeology of Meaning. *Western Political Quarterly* (September): 548–63.

Alexander, E. (1984). After Rationality, What? A Review of Responses to Paradigm Breakdown. *Journal of American Planning Association* 50(1): 62–69.

American Land Forum (1982). *Alternatives for Land Protection: A Review of Case Studies in Eight National Parks*. Bethesda, Md.: American Land Forum.

Aristotle (1991). *On Rhetoric: A Theory of Civic Discourse*. Oxford: Oxford University Press.

Austin, M. H. (1926, 1903). *Land of Little Rain*. New York: Allen and Unwin.

—— (1987, 1909). *Stories from the Country of Lost Borders*. New Brunswick, N.J.: Rutgers University Press.

Bailey, F. G. (1984). *The Tactical Uses of Passion*. Ithaca, N.Y.: Cornell University Press.

Balzac, H., and J. Arnosky (1983, 1896). *A Passion in the Desert*. Mankato, Minn.: Creative Education.

Banham, R. (1982). *Scenes in America Deserta*. Salt Lake City, Utah: Gibbs M. Smith Inc.

Barton, H., ed. (2000). *Sustainable Communities*. London: Earthscan.

Baum, H. S. (1996). Practicing Planning Theory in a Political World. In *Explorations in Planning Theory, ed*. S. J. Mandelbaum, L. Mazzo, and R. Burchell. New Brunswick, N.J.: Center for Urban Policy Research: 365–82.

Beatley, T. (1994a). *Ethical Land Use: Principles of Policy and Planning*. Baltimore, Md.: Johns Hopkins University Press.

—— (1994b). *Habitat Conservation Planning: Endangered Species and Urban Growth*. Austin: University of Texas Press.

Beatley, T., and K. Manning (1997). *The Ecology of Place: Planning for Environment, Economy, and Community*. Washington, D.C.: Island Press.

Beauregard, R. A. (1996). Advocating Preeminence: Anthologies as Politics. In *Explorations in Planning Theory, ed*. S. J. Mandelbaum, L. Mazzo, and R. Burchell. New Brunswick, N.J.: Center for Urban Policy Research: 105–12.

Benveniste, G. (1977). *The Politics of Expertise*. 2d ed. San Francisco: Boyd and Frasier.

Berkowitz, P. (1996). The Debating Society: Review of Amy Gutman and Dennis Thompson, *Democracy and Disagreement. New Republic* (November 25): 36–42.

Berry, W. (1977). *The Unsettling of America: Culture and Agriculture.* San Francisco: Sierra Club Books.

———— (1981). *The Gift of Good Land: Further Essays, Cultural and Agricultural.* San Francisco: North Point Press.

Bornemeier, J. (1996). In Desert War, Feinstein: 1, Lewis: 0. *Los Angeles Times,* April 26, A3 and A25.

Bradsher, K. (1997). Federal Encroachment or New Opportunity? *New York Times,* January 7, A10.

Bratton, S. (1985). National Parks Management and Values. *Environmental Ethics* 7: 117–33.

Brown, H. J., R. S. Philips, et al. (1981). Land Markets at the Urban Fringe. *Journal of American Planning Association* 47(2): 131–44.

Brown, R., and C. Herndl. (1996). Beyond the Realm of Reason. In *Green Culture: Environmental Rhetoric in Contemporary America.* C. Herndl and S. Brown, eds. Madison: University of Wisconsin Press: 3–20.

Bryson, J. M., and B. C. Crosby (1996). Planning and the Design and Use of Forums, Arenas, and Courts. In *Explorations in Planning Theory, ed.* S. J. Mandelbaum, L. Mazzo, and R. Burchell. New Brunswick, N.J.: Center for Urban Policy Research: 462–82.

Buono, F., et al. (1990). Mining Laws and Regulations and the National Park System. In *Managing National Park System Resources, ed.* M. Mantell. Washington, D.C.: The Conservation Foundation: 125–44.

Burke, K. (1957). *Philosophy of Literary Form.* Rev. ed. New York: Vintage Books.

Burke, P. (1990). *The French Historical Revolution: The Annales School, 1929–89.* Stanford, Calif.: Stanford University Press.

Burk, P. (1993). *The Facts about Private Land in the East Mojave National Scenic Area.* Barstow, Calif.: Published by the author.

———— (1994a). *The Making of Mojave National Preserve.* Barstow, Calif.: Citizens for Mojave National Park.

———— (1994b). *Mojave National Park: Gem of the California Desert.* Barstow, Calif.: Published by the author.

Bush, R. A. B., and J. P. Folger (1994). *The Promise of Mediation: Responding to Conflict through Empowerment and Recognition.* San Francisco: Jossey-Bass.

(California Desert Managers Group). (1991). Memorandum of Understanding: California's Coordinated Regional Strategy to Conserve Biological Diversity.

———— (1994). Statement of Intent by State and Federal Agencies to Participate in the Implementation of the California Desert Protection Act.

———— (n.d.). California Desert Innovative Management Laboratory.

Callicott, J. B. (1989). *In Defense of the Land Ethic: Essays in Environmental Philosophy.* Albany: State University of New York Press.

Campbell, S. (1996). Green Cities, Growing Cities, Just Cities? *Journal of the American Planning Association* 62(3): 296–312.

Carls, E. G. (1985). Some Approaches to Natural Protection in the United States. *Environments* 17(3): 50.

Carpenter, S., and W. J. D. Kennedy (1988). *Managing Public Disputes: A Practical Guide to Handling Conflict and Reaching Agreement.* San Francisco: Jossey Bass.

Casebier, D. (1983). *Reopening the Mojave Road: A Personal Narrative.* Norco, Calif.: Tales of the Mojave Road Publishing Co.

Casebier, D. G. (2002). *Lanfair Valley: A Black Homesteading Experience.* U.S. National Park Service. Available: http:www.nps.gov/moja/home.htm [3/27/02].

Casebier, D., and Friends of the Mojave Road (1987). *Guide to the East Mojave Heritage Trail.* Norco, Calif.: Tales of the Mojave Road Publishing Co.

Chatman, S. (1979). *Story and Discourse: Narrative Structure in Fiction and Film.* Ithaca, N.Y.: Cornell University Press.

Clarke, W. M. (2000). Defending the Desert. *National Parks* 74(1–2): 28–31.

Clifford, F. (1996). Firm Threatens to Mine, Build in Mojave Preserve. *Los Angeles Times,* October 31, A2 and A22.

——— (1997). U.S. Pursues Major Land Swap in Mojave. *Los Angeles Times,* May 21, A17.

——— (1998). Mojave Park Feels Pressure of Growth. *Los Angeles Times,* June 23, A3–A17.

Clinton, U. S. P. W. J. (1994). Statement by President William J. Clinton upon Signing S. 21. *Weekly Compilation of Presidential Documents 2210.* Vol. 30. November 7.

——— (1996). Memorandum to the Secretary of the Interior. *Subject: Suspension of Subsection 119(a) of the Department of Interior and Related Agencies Appropriations Act.* Washington, D.C.

Cockrell, R., and National Park Service (1992). *A Green Shrouded Miracle: The Administrative History of Cuyahoga Valley National Recreation Area.* Omaha, Neb.: National Park Reserve Service.

Conservation Foundation (1972). *National Parks for the Future: An Appraisal of the National Park System as They Begin Their Second Century in a Changing America.* Washington, D.C.: Conservation Foundation.

Corbett, M. R., and M. S. Batcher (1983). *Greenline Parks: Land Conservation Trends for the Eighties and Beyond.* Washington, D.C.: National Parks and Conservation Association.

Crawfoot, J., and J. Wondolleck, eds. (1990). *Environmental Disputes: Community Involvement in Conflict Resolution.* Washington, D.C.: Island Press.

Creighton, J. (1983). The Use of Values: Public Participation in the Planning Process. In *Public Involvement and Social Impact Assessment, ed.* M. Daneke, M. Garcia, and J. D. Priscoli. Boulder: Westview Press: 143–60.

Darlington, D. (1996). *The Mojave: A Portrait of the Definitive American Desert.* New York: Henry Holt.

Denzin, N. K., and Y. S. Lincoln, eds. (2000). *Handbook of Qualitative Research.* 2d ed. Thousand Oaks, Calif.: Sage Publications.

Destry, J. (1982). How to Help Plan Parks. In E. H. Connally and National Parks and Conservation Association, eds., *National Parks in Crisis*: 153–62.

Dilsaver, L., ed. (1994). *America's National Park System: The Critical Documents.* Lanham, Md.: Rowman and Littlefield.

Dotson, A. B., D. Godschalk, et al. (1989). *The Planner as Dispute Resolver: Concepts and Teaching Materials.* Washington, D.C.: National Institute for Dispute Resolution.

Dunn, W. (1993). Policy Reforms as Arguments. In *The Argumentative Turn in Policy Analysis and Planning, ed.* F. Fischer and J. Forester. Durham, N.C.: Duke University Press: 254–90.

Echeverria, J., and R. B. Eby, eds. (1995). *Let the People Judge: Wise Use and the Property Rights Movement.* Washington, D.C.: Island Press.

Egan, T. (1995). In Utah, a Pitched Battle over Public Lands. *New York Times*, November 13, A1.

Estes, C. (1995). Sea of Grass. *National Parks*. March/April 1995: 38–45.

Evernden, N. (1992). *The Social Creation of Nature*. Baltimore, Md.: Johns Hopkins University Press.

Ferguson, D. A. N. (1983). *Sacred Cows at the Public Trough*. Bend, Oreg.: Maverick Publications.

Ferraro, G. (1996). Planning as Creative Interpretation. In *Explorations in Planning Theory*, ed. S. J. Mandelbaum, L. Mazzo, and R. Burchell. New Brunswick, N.J.: Center for Urban Policy Research: 312–27.

Fisher, W. R. (1987). *Human Communication as Narration*. Columbia: University of South Carolina Press.

Flyvbjerg, B. (1998). *Rationality and Power: Democracy in Practice*. Chicago: University of Chicago Press.

Foddy, W. (1993). *Constructing Questions for Interviews and Questionnaires: Theory and Practice in Social Research*. Cambridge: Cambridge University Press.

Foreman, D., and Earth First! (1986/1987). A Modest Proposal for a Wilderness Preserve System. *Whole Earth Review* 53(Winter): 42–45.

Foresta, R. (1984). *America's National Parks and Their Keepers*. Washington, D.C.: Resources for the Future.

Forester, J. (1987). Planning in the Face of Conflict: Negotiation and Mediation Strategies in Local Land Use Regulation. *Journal of American Planning Association* 53(3): 303–14.

——— (1989). *Planning in the Face of Power*. Berkeley: University of California Press.

——— (1992). Envisioning the Politics of Public-Sector Dispute Resolution. In *Studies in Law, Politics, and Society*, ed. S. Sibley and Austin Sarat. Greenwich, CT: JAI Press. Vol. 12, Part B, pp. 247–86.

——— (1993). Learning from Practice Stories. In *The Argumentative Turn in Policy Analysis and Planning*, ed. F. Fischer and J. Forester. Durham, N.C.: Duke University Press: 186–209.

——— (1996). The Rationality of Listening, Emotional Sensitivity, and Moral Vision. In *Explorations in Planning Theory*, ed. S. J. Mandelbaum, L. Mazzo, and R. Burchell. New Brunswick, N.J.: Center for Urban Policy Research: 204–224.

——— (1999). *The Deliberative Practitioner*. Cambridge, Mass: MIT Press.

Freedmann, A. (1995). Amid Criticism, Panel Approves Utah Wilderness Legislation. *Congressional Quarterly* 53(December 9): 3737.

——— (1996a). Dole Pulls Omnibus Measure after Democrat's Action. *Congressional Quarterly* 55(March 30): 876–77.

——— (1996b). With Utah Provision Gone, Senate Ok's Parks Bill. *Congressional Quarterly* 55(May 4): 1220.

Freemuth, J. (1989). The National Parks: Political vs. Professional Determinants of Policy. *Public Administration Review* 49(3): 278–86.

——— (1991). *Island under Siege: National Parks and the Politics of External Threats*. Lawrence: University Press of Kansas.

Friedmann, J. (1987). *Knowledge and Action: Mapping the Planning Theory Domain*. Princeton, N.J.: Princeton University Press.

Frome, M. (1992). *Regreening the National Parks*. Tucson: University of Arizona Press.

Fulton, W. (1991). The Trouble with Slow-Growth Politics. In *Balanced Growth, ed.* J. De-Grove and P. Metzger. Washington, D.C.: International City/County Management Association: 151–60.

Geertz, C. (1975). *The Interpretation of Cultures: Selected Essays.* London: Hutchinson.

Goodin, R. (1985). *Protecting the Vulnerable.* Chicago: University of Chicago Press.

Graham, S., and S. Marvin (1996). *Telecommunications and the City: Electronic Spaces, Urban Places.* New York: Routledge.

Grumbine, E. R. (1995). Wise and Sustainable Uses: Revisioning Wilderness. In *Wild Ideas, ed.* D. Rothenberg. Minneapolis: University of Minnesota Press: 3–26.

Guba, E., and Y. Lincoln (1994). Competing Paradigms in Qualitative Research. In *Handbook of Qualitative Research, ed.* N. Denzin and Y. Lincoln. Thousand Oaks, Calif.: Sage Publications: 105–17.

Hajer, M. (1993). Discourse Coalitions and the Institutionalization of Practice: The Case of Acid Rain in Great Britain. In *The Argumentative Turn in Policy Analysis and Planning, ed.* F. Fischer and J. Forester. Durham, N.C.: Duke University Press: 43–76.

Hamin, E. M. (2002). Western European Approaches to Landscape Protection: A Review of the Literature. *Journal of Planning Literature* 16(3): 339–58.

——— (2001). The U.S. National Park System's Partnership Parks: Collaborative Responses to Middle Landscapes. *Land Use Policy* 18: 123–35.

Harper, T. L., and S. M. Stein (1996). Postmodernist Planning Theory: The Incommensurability Premise. In *Explorations in Planning Theory, ed.* S. J. Mandelbaum, L. Mazzo, and R. Burchell. New Brunswick, N.J.: Center for Urban Policy Research: 414–29.

Hartzog, G. B. J. (1988). *Battling for the National Parks.* Mt. Kisco, N.Y.: Moyer Bell Ltd.

Harvey, D. (1996). On Planning the Ideology of Planning. In *Readings in Planning Theory, ed.* S. Campbell and S. S. Fainstein. Malden, Mass.: Blackwell Publishers: 176–97.

Haughton, G., and C. Hunter (1994). *Sustainable Cities.* London: J. Kingsley Publishers; Regional Studies Association.

Healey, P. (1992). A Planner's Day. *Journal of American Planning Association* 58: 9–20.

——— (1993). The Communicative Work of Development Plans. *Environment and Planning B: Planning and Design* 20: 83–104.

——— (1996). Planning through Debate: The Communicative Turn in Planning Theory. In *Readings in Planning Theory, ed.* S. Campbell and S. Fainstein. Malden, Mass: Blackwell Publishers: 234–57.

——— (1997). *Collaborative Planning: Shaping Places in Fragmented Societies.* Vancouver: UBC Press.

Hendler, S. (1995). *Planning Ethics: A Reader in Planning Theory, Practice, and Education.* New Brunswick, N.J.: Center for Urban Policy Research.

Herndl, C., and R. Brown (1996). *Green Culture: Environment Rhetoric in Contemporary America.* Madison: University of Wisconsin Press.

Hess, K. (1992). *Visions upon the Land: Man and Nature on the Western Range.* Washington, D.C.: Island Press.

Hillier, J. (1996). Deconstructing the Discourse of Planning. In *Explorations in Planning Theory, ed.* S. J. Mandelbaum, L. Mazzo, and R. Burchell. New Brunswick, N.J.: Center for Urban Policy Research: 289–98.

Hoch, C. (1994). *What Do Planners Do?* Chicago: American Planning Association Press.

———. (1996). What Do Planners Do? In *Explorations in Planning Theory, ed.* S. J. Mandelbaum, L. Mazzo, and R. Burchell. New Brunswick, N.J.: Center for Urban Policy Research: 225–40.

Howe, J., E. McMahon, et al. (1997). *Balancing Nature and Commerce in Gateway Communities*. Washington, D.C.: Island Press.

Hunter, S. (1989). Conflict in the Tahoe Basin. In *Intractable Conflicts and Their Transformation, ed.* L. Kriesberg, T. Northrup, and S. Thorson. Syracuse, N.Y.: Syracuse University Press: 28–39.

Innes, J. (1993). "Planning through Consensus Building: A New Perspective on the Comprehensive Planning Ideal." *Journal of the American Planning Association* 62(4): 460–72.

Innes, J., and D. Booher (1999). Consensus Building as Role Playing and Bricolage: Toward a Theory of Collaborative Planning. *Journal of the American Planning Association* 65(1): 9–26.

Innes, J. E. (1992). Group Processes and the Social Construction of Growth Management: Florida, Vermont, and New Jersey. *Journal of the American Planning Association* 58(4): 440–53.

IUCN Commission on National Parks and Protected Areas (1994). *Parks for Life: Action for Protected Areas in Europe*. Gland, Switzerland: IUCN—The World Conservation Union.

Jackson, J. B. (1980). *The Necessity for Ruins and Other Topics*. Amherst: University of Massachusetts Press.

Jacobs, H. (1995). Contemporary Environmental Philosophy and Its Challenge to Planning Theory. In *Planning Ethics: A Reader in Planning Theory, Practice, and Education, ed.* S. Hendler. New Brunswick, N.J.: Rutgers University Press: 83–103.

——— (1996). Whose Rights, Whose Regulations? Land Theory, Land Policy, and the Ambiguous Future of the New Private Property Rights Movement in the U.S. *Environmental Planning Theory* 13(3): 3–18.

Johnson, R. F. (1992). Human Uses and Impacts. In *Proceedings of the East Mojave Desert Symposium, ed.* C. Luke, J. Andre, and M. Herring. Los Angeles: Natural History Museum of Los Angeles: 107–13.

Kaplan, T. (1986). The Narrative Structure of Policy Analysis. *Journal of Policy Analysis and Management* 5 (4): 761–78.

———. (1993). Reading Policy Narratives: Beginnings, Middles, Ends. In *The Argumentative Turn in Policy Analysis and Planning, ed.* F. Fischer and J. Forester. Durham, N.C.: Duke University Press: 167–85.

Keiter, R. B., and M. S. Boyce (1991). *The Greater Yellowstone Ecosystem: Redefining America's Wilderness Heritage*. New Haven, Conn.: Yale University Press.

Keltner, J. W. (1994). *The Management of Struggle: Elements of Dispute Resolution through Negotiation, Mediation, and Arbitration*. Cresskill, N.J.: Hampton Press.

Kenworthy, T. (1996). Ah, Wilderness!—but Not Right Here. *Washington Post National Weekly Edition*, December 31, 9–15.

Kirk, J., and M. L. Miller (1986). *Reliability and Validity in Qualitative Research*. Beverly Hills, Calif.: Sage Publications.

Lake, R. (1986). *Resolving Locational Conflict*. New Brunswick, N.J.: Center for Urban Policy Research.

Leshy, J. D. (1987). *The Mining Law: A Study in Perpetual Motion*. Washington, D.C.: Resources for the Future.

Lewis, S. (1976). New York's Adirondacks: Tug of War in Wilderness Development. *Planning* 42: 9–15.

Limerick, P. N. (1985). *Desert Passages: Encounters with the American Deserts*. Albuquerque: University of New Mexico Press.

Little, C. E. (1990). *Greenways for America*. Baltimore, Md.: Johns Hopkins University Press.

Locke, J. (1952, 1690). *The Second Treatise of Government*. New York: Liberal Arts Press.

Lopez, B. H. (1976). *Desert Notes: Reflections in the Eye of a Raven*. New York: Avon Books.

Lowry, K., P. Adler, et al. (1997). Participating the Public: Group Process, Politics, and Planning. *Journal of Planning Education and Research* 16(3): 177–87.

Lowry, W. R. (1994). *The Capacity for Wonder*. Washington, D.C.: Brookings Institution.

——— (1998). *Preserving Public Lands for the Future: The Politics of Intergenerational Goods*. Washington, D.C.: Georgetown University Press.

Luke, C., J. Andre, et al., eds. (1992). *Proceedings of the East Mojave Desert Symposium*. Los Angeles: Natural History Museum of Los Angeles.

Luke, C., A. Karl, et al. (1991). *A Review of the Emergency Listing of the Desert Tortoise Gopherus Agassizi*. Tiburne, Calif.: Prepared for the City of Ridgecrest, California.

MacIntyre, A. C. (1984). *After Virtue: A Study in Moral Theory*. (2d ed.). Notre Dame, Ind.: University of Notre Dame Press.

Maines, D. R., and J. C. Bridger (1992). Narratives, Community, and Land Use Decisions. *Social Science Journal* 29(4): 363–80.

Malkawi, F. (1996). *Hidden Structures: An Ethnographic Account of the Planning of Greater Amman*. Ph.D. dissertation, University of Pennsylvania.

Mandelbaum, S. (1996). Open Moral Communities. In *Explorations in Planning Theory*, ed. S. J. Mandelbaum, L. Mazzo, and R. Burchel. New Brunswick, N.J.: Center for Urban Policy Research: 83–104.

——— (2000). *Open Moral Communities*. Cambridge, Mass: MIT Press.

Mandlebaum, S. J. (1990). Reading Plans. *Journal of American Planning Association* 56: 350–56.

——— (1991). Telling Stories. *Journal of Planning Education and Research* 10: 209–14.

Marcucci, D. J. (2000). Landscape History as a Planning Tool. *Landscape and Urban Planning* 49: 67–81.

Mark, S. R. (1984). Wilderness Review in the East Mojave National Scenic Area, California. Master's thesis, Southern Oregon State College.

Marris, P. (1996). *The Politics of Uncertainty: Attachment in Private and Public Life*. London: Routledge.

Marx, L. (1963). *The Machine in the Garden*. New York: Oxford University Press.

Mathews, A. (1992). *Where the Buffalo Roam*. New York: Grove Press.

McHarg, I. L. (1996). *A Quest for Life: An Autobiography*. New York: John Wiley.

McKibben, B. (1995). An Explosion of Green. *Atlantic Monthly*, April 1995, 61–83.

McKibben, W. (1989). *The End of Nature*. New York: Random House.

McKinney, J., and C. Rae (1994). *Walking the East Mojave*. New York: Harper Collins West.

McNammee, G., ed. (1995). *The Sierra Club Desert Reader*. San Francisco: Sierra Club Publishers.

Merchant, C. (1980). *The Death of Nature*. San Francisco: Harper and Row.

Millbrath, L. (1981). Citizen Surveys as Citizen Participation Mechanisms. *Journal of Applied Behavioral Research* 17: 478–96.

Miller, R., and P. Miller (1992). *Mines of the Mojave.* Glendale, Calif.: La Siesta.

Misrach, R., and R. Banham (1987). *Desert Cantos.* Albuquerque: University of New Mexico Press.

Morris, W., ed. (1978). *The American Heritage Dictionary of the English Language.* Boston: Houghton Mifflin.

Moynihan, R., S. Armitage, et al., eds. (1990). *So Much to Be Done: Women Settlers on the Mining and Ranching Frontier.* Lincoln: University of Nebraska Press.

Nash, R. (1982). *Wilderness and the American Mind.* New Haven: Yale University Press.

National Park Service (1999). Mississippi National River and Recreation Area, National Park Service.http://www.nps.gov/miss/1999.

NEMO: Northern and Eastern Mojave Planning Effort (2001). 222 E. Main St., Suite 202, Barstow, Calif., 92311. Available: http:www.nps.gov/moja/nemo.htm [3/27/02]

Noble, K. (1996). U.S. Delays Opening Site for Dumping Atomic Waste. *New York Times,* February 16, A16.

Noblit, G. W., and R. D. Hare (1988). *Meta-Ethnography: Synthesizing Qualitative Studies.* Beverly Hills, Calif.: Sage Publications.

Northrup, T. (1989). The Dynamics of Identity in Personal and Social Conflict. In *Intractable Conflicts and Their Transformation,* ed. L. Kriesberg, T. Northrup, and S. Thorson. Syracuse, N.Y.: Syracuse University Press: 55–82.

Oelschlaeger, M. (1981). *The Idea of Wilderness.* New Haven, Conn.: Yale University Press.

Palmer, J., and R. Smardon (1989). Measuring Human Values Associated with Wetlands. In *Intractable Conflicts and Their Transformation,* ed. L. Kriesberg, T. Northrup, and S. Thorson. Syracuse, N.Y.: Syracuse University Press: 156–79.

Platt, R. H., R. Rowentree, et al. (1994). *The Ecological City: Preserving and Restoring Urban Biodiversity.* Amherst: University of Massachusetts Press.

Popper, D. E., and F. J. Popper (1987). The Great Plains: From Dust to Dust. *Planning* 53(12): 12–18.

Reese, R. (1991). *Greater Yellowstone: The National Park and Adjacent Wildlands.* Helena, Mont.: Montana Magazine: American and World Geographic Pub.

Rein, M., and D. Schon (1993). Reframing Policy Discourse. In F. Fischer and J. Forester, eds., *The Argumentative Turn in Policy Analysis and Planning.* Durham, N.C.: Duke University Press: 145–66.

Riessman, C. K. (1993). *Narrative Analysis.* Beverly Hills, Calif.: Sage.

Roe, E. (1994). *Narrative Policy Analysis: Theory and Practice.* Durham, N.C.: Duke University Press.

Rolston, H. I. (1988). *Environmental Ethics: Duties to and Values in the Natural World.* Philadelphia, Penn.: Temple University Press.

Rorty, R. (1979). *Philosophy and the Mirror of Nature.* Princeton, N.J.: Princeton University Press.

Roseland, M. (1998). *Toward Sustainable Communities.* Gabriola Island, B.C.: New Society Publishers.

Rousseau, J.-J. (1762; 1927). *The Social Contract and Discourses.* New York: E. P. Dutton.

Rowell, A. (1996). *Green Backlash: Global Subversion of the Environmental Movement.* London: Routledge.

Runte, A. (1987). *National Parks: The American Experience.* Lincoln: University of Nebraska Press.

Russell, S. A. (1994). *Kill the Cowboy: A Battle of Mythology in the New West.* Reading, Mass.: Addison-Wesley.

Sager, T. (1994). *Communicative Planning Theory.* Aldershot, Hants, England; Brookfield, Vt.: Avebury.

Sagoff, M. (1988). *The Economy of the Earth.* Cambridge: Cambridge University Press.

Sandercock, L. (1998). *Towards Cosmospolis.* Chichester: John Wiley and Sons.

Sax, J. L. (1980). *Mountains without Handrails: Reflections on the National Parks.* Ann Arbor: University of Michigan Press.

Schad, J. (1988). *California Deserts.* Helena, Mont.: Falcon Press.

Schama, S. (1995). *Landscape and Memory.* New York: Alfred A. Knopf.

Schine, E. (1996). Nuclear Waste with Nowhere to Go. *Business Week* (June 10): 44.

Schön, D., and M. Rein (1994). *Frame Reflection: Toward the Resolution of Intractable Policy Controversies.* New York: Basic Books.

Schwandt, T. (1994). Constructivist, Interpretivist Approaches to Human Inquiry. In *Handbook of Qualitative Research,* ed. N. K. Denzin and Y. S. Lincoln. Thousand Oaks, Calif.: Sage Publications: 118–37.

Seidman, I. E. (1991). *Interviewing as Qualitative Research: A Guide for Researchers in Education and the Social Sciences.* New York: Teachers College Press, Columbia University.

Soden, D. (1991). National Parks Literature of the 1980s: Varying Perspectives but Common Concerns. *Policy Studies Journal* 19(3): 570–76.

Soulé, M., and G. Lease, eds. (1995). *Reinventing Nature?: Responses to Postmodern Deconstruction.* Washington D.C.: Island Press.

Sowell, T. (1987). *A Conflict of Visions.* New York: William Morrow.

Strong, A. L. (1975). *Private Property and the Public Interest: The Brandywine Experience.* Baltimore, Md.: Johns Hopkins University Press.

Susskind, L. (1995). Resolving Disputes the Kinder, Gentler Way. *Planning* (May): 16.

Susskind, L., and J. Cruikshank (1987). *Breaking the Impasse: Consensual Approaches to Resolving Public Disputes.* New York: Basic Books.

Susskind, L., S. McKearnan, et al. (1999). *The Consensus Building Handbook: A Comprehensive Guide to Reaching Agreement.* Thousand Oaks, Calif.: Sage Publications.

Taylor, N. (1998). Mistaken Interests and the Discourse Model of Planning. *Journal of the American Planning Association* 64(1): 64–75.

Tett, A., and J. Wolfe (1991). Discourse Analysis and City Plans. *Journal of Planning Education and Research* 10: 195–200.

Thayer, R. L. (1989). The Experience of Sustainable Landscapes. *Landscape Journal* 8(2): 101–10.

——— (1994). *Gray World, Green Heart: Technology, Nature, and the Sustainable Landscape.* New York: John Wiley.

Throgmorton, J. (1996). *Planning as Persuasive Storytelling.* Chicago: University of Chicago Press.

Tonn, B. (1986). 500 Year Planning. *Journal of the American Planning Association* 52(2): 185–93.

U.S. Bureau of Land Management (1979). *Desert Planning Team Report.* Riverside, Calif.: U.S. Department of the Interior.

——— (1980). *The California Desert Conservation Area Plan.* Riverside, Calif.: U.S. Department of the Interior.

——— (1988). *East Mojave National Scenic Area Management Plan.* Needles, Calif.: U.S. Department of the Interior.

U.S. Bureau of Land Management and Division of Mineral Resources (1991). *The California Desert: Why Mining Is Important.* Sacramento: U.S. Department of the Interior.

U.S. Bureau of Mines (1990). *Minerals in the East Mojave National Scenic Area, California: An Economic Analysis.* Vols. 1 and 2. Sacramento: U.S. Department of the Interior.

U.S. Census Bureau (1992). *1992 Economic Profile: Retail, Wholesale, Services.* Washington: Bureau of Census.

——— (1993). *1990 Census of Population and Housing, Supplementary Reports, Urbanized Areas of the United States and Puerto Rico.* Washington, D.C.: U.S. Government Printing Office.

U.S. Department of the Interior (1999). *The National Parks: Index 1999–2000.* Washington, D.C.: Office of Public Affairs and the Harpers Ferry Center, Division of Publications, National Park Service.

U.S. National Park Service (1987). *Resource Assessment for the Features Proposed in the California Desert Protection Act.* Denver, Colo.: National Park Service Western Regional Office.

———. (1993a). *Economic Considerations for a Proposed Mojave Unit of the National Park System.* Denver, Colo.: National Park Service Western Regional Office.

———.(1993b). *Guiding Principles of Sustainable Design.* Denver, Colo.: Department of the Interior.

———. (2000). Mojave National Preserve Homepage, U.S. National Park Service. Available: http:www.nps.gov/moja/home.htm [3/27/02].

———. (2001). *Final General Management Plan / Abbreviated Final Environmental Impact Statement for Mojave National Preserve.* Denver, Colo.: U.S. Department of the Interior.

Van der Ryn, S., and P. Calthorpe (1986). *Sustainable Communities: A New Design Synthesis for Cities, Suburbs, and Towns.* San Francisco: Sierra Club Books.

Van Dyke, J. C. (1901; 1999). *The Desert.* Baltimore, Md.: Johns Hopkins University Press.

White, R. (1991). *It's Your Misfortune and None of My Own: A New History of the American West.* Norman: University of Oklahoma Press.

Wikle, T. (1991). Proposals, Abolishments, and Changing Standard for the U.S. National Parks. *The Historian* 54: 49–63.

Wilkinson, C. F. (1992). *Crossing the Next Meridian: Land, Water, and the Future of the West.* Washington, D.C.: Island Press.

Wilshire, H. (1992). Wasting of California's Deserts. In *Proceedings of the East Mojave Desert Symposium, ed.* C. Luke, J. Andre, and M. Herring. Los Angeles: Natural History Museum of Los Angeles: 115–19.

Worster, D. (1992). *Under Western Skies: Nature and History in the American West.* New York: Oxford University Press.

Yin, R. K. (1989). *Case Study Research: Design and Methods.* Newbury Park, Calif.: Sage Publications.

Zaslowsky, D., and The Wilderness Society (1986). *These American Lands: Parks, Wilderness, and the Public Lands.* New York: Wilderness Society.

Index